Praise for *Born on*

"A call to action for America's wealthy and a warning shot across the bows of their yachts if they fail to act, *Born on Third Base* offers a clear and compelling case for why the privileged and powerful must act to reverse widening inequality of income, wealth, and political power in America." — **Robert B. Reich,**
former US Secretary of Labor; author of *Saving Capitalism*

"This is the engaging story of a courageous rich white guy who gave it all away, journeyed to the dark heart of inequality and deprivation in America, and became a leading thinker and activist for something much better for all of us, including the rich. Collins doesn't disappoint. He is the real deal." — **James Gustave Speth,**
author of *America the Possible* and *Angels by the River*

"I have never read a story remotely like the one Chuck Collins has to tell. Born to the one percent, in circumstances few of us can imagine, he grew an outsized conscience and gave up his inherited wealth for a life of fighting the vicious inequality that is destroying our country. Somewhere along the way, he came to understand that the rich can be part of the solution instead of the problem and started organizing them to join in the struggle for a fair economy. The result is an electrifying challenge to the affluent as well as the one percent. 'Come out of your gated communities and gated hearts,' he writes, because outside lies the warmth of human solidarity." — **Barbara Ehrenreich, author of *Nickel and Dimed***

"Chuck Collins has already organized the rich against their own immediate economic interest. He and his colleagues at the Institute for Policy Studies were instrumental in blocking the Republican repeal of the federal estate tax for the wealthy. So when he writes in *Born on Third Base* about all the good that can come from the enlightened rich pressing for justice, not just charity, he speaks from experience as both an organizer and a former affluent heir. Partly autobiographical, this empowering light into a brighter future is a narrative you won't want to miss. Chuck Collins walks the talk and can motivate, if anyone is able to, the super rich to fund systemic drives for change." — **Ralph Nader,**
consumer advocate, author, lawyer

"Sobering and inspiring, Chuck Collins has written a Declaration of Interdependence. A must-read for anyone on third base who has forgotten that they're part of a team." — **Peter Buffett, copresident, NoVo Foundation;**
author of *Life is What You Make It*

"The American dream assures us that, if you work hard and play by the rules, you'll succeed. But the facts tell a different story: Everyone knows the system is rigged. In these trickle-down times, income inequality threatens to pit the 99 percent against the 1 percent in violent revolution — and, really, who can blame them? My fellow plutocrat Chuck Collins gets it. *Born on Third Base* explodes the myth of the self-made man, but it also celebrates true achievement in the classic American sense. This isn't some self-hating rich guy; Collins has thought seriously about what it means to be a citizen, and to be a patriot. He makes the case that we all do better when we all do better, and he does it with compassion and humor. This book would give Ayn Rand nightmares." — **Nick Hanauer, venture capitalist; coauthor of *The True Patriot* and *The Gardens of Democracy***

"Chuck Collins does the soul-searching, fundamental work of reminding us all that wealth inequality and injustice make everyone's life worse, including those of us who are supposedly better off. No matter what your class background, Collins's work is an insight into and inspiring call to action for why we *all* need to be two feet into the fight for a more just world — one that is based on shared prosperity and community, not individualized notions of success. People and the planet literally depend on it." — **Jessie Spector, executive director, Resource Generation**

"Collins, born to great privilege, takes a thoughtful, well-written, and carefully researched approach to solving the extreme imbalance in wealth distribution, directed toward one- and 99-percenters alike. . . . What Collins does even better than describing the challenge is, in the book's second half, outlining significant and specific solutions. . . . Wherever readers fall on the economic scale, this is a worthwhile book to read, digest, and share." — *Publishers Weekly*

"There are few tasks as urgent as a radical reorientation of the 1 percent, a radical re-engagement of 'us' with 'them' — and a radical redeployment of the wealth created over the past century in order to address the problems of the next. Chuck Collins is our personal guide." — **Woody Tasch, founder, Slow Money Institute; author of *Inquiries into the Nature of Slow Money***

"No one explains inequality better than Chuck Collins, and no one walks his talk with more integrity. All Americans — rich, poor, and in the shrinking middle — will benefit from his insights and be inspired by his example." — **Peter Barnes, cofounder, CREDO Mobile; author of *With Liberty and Dividends For All***

"Chuck Collins may have been born on third base, but he hits a grand slam with this powerful call to even the richest Americans to join their fellow citizens in challenging the obscene wealth gap that characterizes America today. He hammers all the curve balls thrown to justify inequality, writes eloquently but humbly of his experiences, and lays out a winning lineup of ways to bring Americans across class lines together for economic justice." — **John de Graaf, coauthor of *Affluenza* and *What's the Economy for, Anyway?***

BORN ON
THIRD BASE

Other Books by Chuck Collins

99 to 1:
How Wealth Inequality Is Wrecking
the World and What We Should Do About It

Wealth and Our Commonwealth:
Why America Should Tax Accumulated Fortunes
(with Bill Gates Sr.)

Moral Measure of the Economy
(with Mary Wright)

Economic Apartheid in America:
A Primer on Economic Inequality and Insecurity
(with Felice Yeskel)

Robin Hood Was Right:
A Guide to Giving Your Money for Social Change
(with Pam Rogers and Joan Garner)

BORN ON THIRD BASE

A One Percenter
Makes the Case for
Tackling Inequality,
Bringing Wealth Home,
and Committing to
the Common Good

Chuck Collins

Foreword by Morris Pearl

Chelsea Green Publishing
White River Junction, Vermont

Editor: Joni Praded
Project Manager: Angela Boyle
Copy Editor: Deborah Heimann
Proofreader: Laura Jorstad
Indexer: Peggy Holloway
Designer: Melissa Jacobson

Printed in the United States of America.
First printing September, 2016.
10 9 8 7 6 5 4 3 2 1   16 17 18 19 20

Chelsea Green Publishing is committed to preserving ancient forests and natural resources. We elected to print this title on 100-percent postconsumer recycled paper, processed chlorine-free. As a result, for this printing, we have saved:

62 Trees (40' tall and 6-8" diameter)
28 Million BTUs of Total Energy
5,314 Pounds of Greenhouse Gases
28,821 Gallons of Wastewater
1.929 Pounds of Solid Waste

Chelsea Green Publishing made this paper choice because we and our printer, Thomson-Shore, Inc., are members of the Green Press Initiative, a nonprofit program dedicated to supporting authors, publishers, and suppliers in their efforts to reduce their use of fiber obtained from endangered forests. For more information, visit: www.greenpressinitiative.org.

Environmental impact estimates were made using the Environmental Defense Paper Calculator. For more information visit: www.papercalculator.org.

Our Commitment to Green Publishing

Chelsea Green sees publishing as a tool for cultural change and ecological stewardship. We strive to align our book manufacturing practices with our editorial mission and to reduce the impact of our business enterprise in the environment. We print our books and catalogs on chlorine-free recycled paper, using vegetable-based inks whenever possible. This book may cost slightly more because it was printed on paper that contains recycled fiber, and we hope you'll agree that it's worth it. Chelsea Green is a member of the Green Press Initiative (www.greenpressinitiative.org), a nonprofit coalition of publishers, manufacturers, and authors working to protect the world's endangered forests and conserve natural resources. *Born on Third Base* was printed on paper supplied by Thomson-Shore that contains 100% postconsumer recycled fiber.

Library of Congress Cataloging-in-Publication Data
Names: Collins, Chuck, 1959- author.
Title: Born on third base : a one percenter makes the case for tackling inequality, bringing wealth home, and committing to the common good /Chuck Collins.
Description: White River Junction, Vermont : Chelsea Green Publishing, [2016] | Includes bibliographical references and index.
Identifiers: LCCN 2016022977| ISBN 9781603586832 (pbk.) | ISBN 9781603586849 (ebook)
Subjects: LCSH: Collins, Chuck, 1959- | Rich people — United States. | Philanthropists — United States. | Income distribution. | Poverty. |Wealth. | Social responsibility of business. | Humanitarianism.
Classification: LCC HC110.W4 C64 2016 | DDC 303.48/40973 — dc23
LC record available at https://lccn.loc.gov/2016022977

Chelsea Green Publishing
85 North Main Street, Suite 120
White River Junction, VT 05001
(802) 295-6300
www.chelseagreen.com

For Mary

We are here to awaken from the illusion of our separateness.

THICH NHAT HANH

Those who do not move, do not notice their chains.

ROSA LUXEMBURG

Contents

Foreword *by Morris Pearl*   ix

Preface   xiii

Introduction: Time to Come Home   1

— PART I —

BORN ON THIRD BASE

1. I Heart the 1 Percent   9
2. Proceed with Empathy   15
3. Cracking Hearts Open   28

— PART II —

SEEING OUR COMMONWEALTH

4. I Didn't Do It Alone   37
5. In the Same Boat:
   On the Road with Bill Gates   49

— PART III —

UNDERSTANDING ADVANTAGE

6. The Privilege Drug   59
7. The Greatest Subsidized Generation   63
8. Black Wealth, Brown Wealth, White Wealth   77
9. Unequal Opportunity   86

— PART IV —

UNNECESSARY SIDE TRIPS

10. Miro in the Bathroom:
    Encounters with the Charitable
    Industrial Complex   103
11. When Charity Disrupts Justice   115

— PART V —

WEALTH, COME HOME

12. The Moment We Are In   129
13. A Stake in the Common Good   141
14. Neighborhood Real Security   151
15. Community Resilience   159
16. Bringing Wealth Home   169
17. Openhearted Wealth   185

— PART VI —

THE INVITATIONS

18. Wealthy, Come Home   207
19. All Hands on Deck   220

Conclusion: I'm from Bloomfield Hills   231
Acknowledgments   237
Resources   239
Notes   243
Index   261

Foreword

I am part of the group that is supposed to learn from Chuck Collins's *Born on Third Base* — the 1 percent. I have a pretty good life; I retired from the financial services industry at the age of 54. I am now the chairperson of the Patriotic Millionaires, a group of wealthy Americans trying to make the point that the policies that create gross inequality in our society are not good for regular Americans and are also not good for the rich. I have two sons who both graduated from college, never took out loans, spent their time off on career-oriented activities and leisure, and have money left over to start businesses or to save for the next generation.

Did I work especially hard? Maybe a little, sometimes. Most of my work involved sitting in an office reading and writing emails and talking on the telephone. Did I work harder than the guy who had to connect the hoses to the fire hydrant in the snow or the woman who had to smile while schlepping pitchers of beer around all night? Not really.

Was I lucky? You could call it luck, but it wasn't like everyone bought a lottery ticket and my number happened to come up. It was more like, as Chuck puts it, I was born on third base. My father went to college on an ROTC scholarship, spent his career as the owner of clothing stores that were started by his parents' brothers, built a house with the help of a VA mortgage, and had enough wealth that he told me to ignore the financial aid forms when I was applying to college. I went to the University of Pennsylvania (which was funded by the taxpayers) without any financial need to work, so when I felt like it, I could take part-time jobs exploring work I might do after I graduated (for a bank and a tech start-up). After all that, I cannot really look at the people who had to take minimum-wage jobs to earn money all through school and to plan their careers around making loan payments and think that I am more successful (financially) because I am more deserving.

The difference between me and many other wealthy Americans is that my kids and I all know that none of us hit a triple. I kind of knew that before I read Collins's book, but I understand it a lot better now.

Many of the people who have huge advantages don't even know it. Mitt Romney (who went to the same elite high school as Collins, a decade earlier) gave a speech at Otterbein University and told the students to ". . . borrow money if you have to from your parents, start a business . . . ," like his friend Jimmy John who started his namesake restaurant chain with an investment from his father. Romney honestly did not realize that getting tens of thousands of dollars from one's parents is not an option for many young people. He really does live in a world where money is not a constraint and the only thing standing in the way of a teenager is having enough creativity and initiative to use easily obtained money to start a new business. If you come from that worldview, of course you think that spending the taxpayers' money to help people is a stupid idea. Why should those people who are perfectly able to make money, but choose not to, be allowed to take money from their more industrious neighbors?

The answer is that Mr. Romney's children, my children, and the others born on third base have some huge advantages that have nothing to do with being industrious. They graduate from top schools, never having any loan payments to make. They have introductions to anyone they want to meet — from lawyers and government officials to potential employers. The wealth that their families have built up gives them the ability to take a chance on a speculative venture, knowing that they have enough resources to do something else if it turns out to be a total failure. They have the confidence to go out into the world knowing that any problem that can be solved with money is not a problem. An unexpected bill, plane fare across the country for a funeral, or having your car break down can be a big deal to most Americans but will not make our kids bat an eye.

The real inequality that makes the world in which my family and I live totally different from the world in which most Americans live is inequality of wealth and assets. Income is a smaller issue. Wealth spans generations.

So many young professionals make their mortgage payments every month and feel like they are "living on their own" while having forgotten that their parents gave them money for a down payment. So many feel proud of themselves for managing to make sacrifices so that they can afford to spend a few hundred dollars every month or so at their children's private school fund-raisers, and they forget that the grandparents are paying the tens of thousands of dollars per year for the tuition.

One part of *Born on Third Base* explains how some of the white members of the greatest generation have been able to retire comfortably and subsidize their white baby boomer children's lifestyles in part because of government policies that subsidized the building of houses after World War II and the rise in home prices through the 1990s. This did not apply to people of African American descent. The government programs were only available for people buying homes in "stable neighborhoods," by rule, meaning those that were racially segregated, further solidifying a divided society already encouraged by intolerance.

The real estate empire that Donald Trump inherited from his father was built selling homes to white, middle-class people in Queens, who never would have been able to buy them, except that they got government-subsidized mortgages. Collins explains that some people (all white, mostly wealthier people) were able to take advantage of these types of government programs and how, even to this day, the children and grandchildren of those people are much better off than the children and grandchildren of other people.

And most often, they don't even know it. That is a key message of *Born on Third Base*: that the wealthy must understand the advantages they were born into and their commensurate responsibility to their society.

But there is a deeper message, too, and bold recommendations for changing both national policy and personal behavior. Collins shows us how everyday aspects of our lives actually perpetuate inequality — again, without our even knowing it. When does our charity actually work against those with less, or no, advantage? How far should we go to protect our children's futures, even at the expense of others? I am not Chuck. I read about the Occupy movement in Zuccotti Park in the newspaper from the comfort of my Park Avenue apartment. When I have wanted to complain about something to President Obama, I have arranged to do it face-to-face. But Chuck invites us all to step out of our bubble, back into the real America, and find ways to apply ourselves to the common good. He goes on to profile many who have done so and become happier thereby.

Born on Third Base speaks to the non-wealthy, too — showing them how, by working together, we can begin to reconstruct truly equitable communities, piece by resilient piece. Rarely do startling new insights and prescriptions for change come wrapped in such a winning trio of great storytelling, careful scholarship, and a compassionate voice, for both sides of the divide. If you think you know all there is to know about the nation's gripping inequality crisis: You don't. There are more than a few surprises in the pages ahead.

MORRIS PEARL
Chairperson, the Patriotic Millionaires
Former managing director, BlackRock, Inc.

Preface

Have you ever lived in a mobile home? Not me. Until the age of 24, I had never set foot in one. But two years later, I'd been inside hundreds. My first job out of college was to work with mobile home owners who rented their homesites in private parks around New England. The goal was to help them organize and buy their parks as resident-owned cooperatives.

On an April day in 1986, I was sitting at the kitchen table of a spacious double-wide owned by Harlan and Mary Parro in Bernardston, a small town in Western Massachusetts. We were joined by seven other leaders from their thirty-unit park.

At 26, I still had distressing acne that made me feel quite self-conscious. People regularly assumed I was 17 years old, which compounded my insecurity in situations like this one. The tenant group leaders were all looking at me — this kid with bad skin — waiting to hear my assessment about the fate of their mobile home park.

They were understandably anxious. An unknown buyer had made an offer to purchase their park from its current owner. Some buyers around the region were jacking up rents, knowing the residents were basically hostages. And with land values rising, some developers were buying up parks, kicking out the mobile homes, and building subdivisions and condominiums.

Thanks to a state tenant protection law, the Bernardston tenants had forty-five days to match the offer and buy the park themselves. The clock was ticking.

One of the first things I learned on the job is that mobile homes are not so mobile. Moving a home can risk damaging it and diminishing its value. And it presumes you have a piece of land or another park to relocate to. Across New England, local towns were passing snob zoning laws to prohibit new mobile homes.

Equally important, people in mobile home parks put down roots and build tight-knit communities. They construct additions, add carports and garages, put skirts around the base of their homes, landscape and plant trees and gardens. Harlan and Mary proudly showed me the day's vegetable harvest from their garden plot. All this would be wiped out if the park sold and closed, scattering the residents.

I was in agony, sitting at that kitchen table.

You see, I knew all their secrets. I had confidentially surveyed every member of the community about their personal finances. I knew how much each of them could pay toward rent (and a future mortgage) and how much savings they could apply toward the purchase of their share price in the cooperative. If enough residents could buy their shares outright, we would have the estimated $150,000 required for a down payment.

From my survey, I knew that a third of the residents had no savings and barely enough income to pay current rents. Most residents had low-wage jobs or were living on Social Security. Only a dozen had any savings of more than $5,000, including the retirees. These were people with very low incomes with little to fall back on.

Because I had determined that they didn't have the money to buy the park, I was distraught. In my analysis, they were about $35,000 short of what the association needed for the down payment, a sizable sum. I was going to have to break them the bad news.

I was also in agony, however, because I had a secret. I was wealthy. I was born on third base, having inherited a substantial sum a few years earlier.

I could write a check for $35,000 and make it possible for these thirty families to buy the park. And I was seriously thinking about doing just that. Contributing $35,000 would have had a negligible impact on my personal finances.

I broke the bad news to the assembled leaders. There was a quiet pall in the room. And then an extraordinary thing happened.

First, one of the residents named Reggie said he could buy his share and put another $5,000 toward the purchase. Now I happened to know, because of my confidential survey, that this was all the money that Reggie had.

Then a retired couple, Donald and Rita, pledged an additional $8,000. Ms. Dundorf would put in $7,000. Again, I knew that this was all the money they had.

Harlan and Mary said they would buy their full share and put in another $15,000. This was their entire nest egg, saved while Harlan had worked at Greenfield Tap and Die for thirty-five years. "We'd like to buy Ms. Rivas's share on the condition that she must never find out, in order to protect her dignity," Harlan said.

Before I knew it, they had come up with $30,000. Mary and Harlan's daughter, who arrived late for the meeting, pledged the last $5,000, as she worked at a bank.

The group cheered and immediately started writing out personal checks and handing them to me to take to the bank and deposit.

I was physically shaken by what I had seen. These people were *all in*. They were willing to risk everything they had to buy this park. I wiped away tears as I drove to the bank.

And they succeeded. They bought the park. On the day of the closing, all the men had cigars like proud parents. Harlan told the local newspaper, "We are hostages no more. We bought the land from Pharaoh."

Mary approached me after the closing to thank me for my work. "You're a smart young man, you could get a job on Wall Street. You don't need to hang around with a bunch of old fogies like us."

"Oh, that's not how I feel," I replied. "There is nowhere I'd rather be."

Then Mary leaned confidentially toward me and whispered, "Have you ever tried Noxzema? You know, for your skin."

The Bernardston tenants — now owners — had taught me something about solidarity, about the power of community.

I did not have to write a check that day. But sitting there had opened the door to a thinking process. Why not? What would happen if I gave the money away to meet some of the urgent needs around me? I was beginning to understand the rather remarkable privileges that had flowed my way.

At the age of 26, I had three or four times as much money as all the residents of the Bernardston mobile home park combined. There is no rationale I could find that could justify this disparity.

So I decided to give away the wealth. I wrote my parents a letter thanking them for the tremendous opportunities this wealth made possible. And I explained that while having the money was a boost in helping pay for my education, it was now a barrier to my making my own way in the world. I intended to "pass the wealth on."

My father immediately called me when he got the letter. He flew out from Michigan to Massachusetts to meet with me. We talked for a day, and during that time he lovingly asked me a dozen what-if questions. "You're young and single. But over the course of a lifetime, bad things can happen," he said. "What if you get married and your spouse becomes ill? Wouldn't this money make life easier? What if you have a child and that child has a special need, wouldn't you wish you had this money?"

I had thought about many of these scenarios and more. And my response to my father was, "Well, then I would be in the same boat as 99 percent of the people I know, and I would have to ask for help."

"Without this money, you might have to fall back on the government," my father warned. "And that's a terrible system."

"Well, then I'll have a stake in making that system better," I replied, appreciating his parental concern.

"That's pretty idealistic," said my father. But after a day of walking and talking, he was reassured that I had not been possessed by an alien cult.

A few months later I drove to the National Bank of Detroit and signed the paperwork to transfer all the funds in my name to four grant-making foundations.

My trustee at the bank was an African American woman named Glenda whom I'd had very little contact with. We talked briefly about my decision. She looked at me at one point and said, "Are you going to be all right?"

"Yeah, I think I'm going to be all right," I replied. But I didn't know for sure.

Nor did I fully understand the tall mountain of privilege I still had. I was a white college-educated male in the United States, with a debt-free education and an extended family and social network. At the time, it felt like I was taking a leap of faith. I had my father's what-if questions in my head, and an awareness of the fragility of life.

A few months later, something bad did happen. The top floor of the house I was living in burned down. No one was injured, but I lost everything I owned. What wasn't burned was destroyed by the hundreds of gallons of water that had been dumped into the house.

The next morning, the sun came out and shone down on the sooty mess that was our house. My housemate Greg was sifting through piles, recovering little fragments of photographs.

Four cars pulled up to our house. Out climbed a dozen people from the Bernardston mobile home park. They had casseroles and shovels and trash bags. They had come to help.

At that moment, I thought, "I'm going to be okay."

Time to Come Home

Inequality is shorthand for all the things that have gone to make the lives of the rich so measurably more delicious, year after year for three decades — and also for the things that have made the lives of working people so wretched and so precarious.

THOMAS FRANK

The extreme levels of inequality in our society are personally painful to behold.

As someone who was "born on third base," I watch these polarizations and know that no good will come of them. In the jostling and shrill voices, I hear the dogs of war approaching, a war between the classes.

Actually, there are two class wars, though they are not comparable. There is a top-down class war against the non-rich. As billionaire super-investor Warren Buffett quipped, "There's class warfare, all right, but it's my class, the rich class, that's making war, and we're winning." This is the war of the powerful few against the many.

But there is also a bottom-up class antagonism expressed in rhetorical attacks against the rich, some of which I take responsibility for creating. Does rich-bashing move us forward? As Gandhi said, "An eye for an eye is making the world blind."

Can we suspend the economic class hostilities long enough to consider what would move humanity forward? Is it really good for anyone that most of society's wealth is pooling at the tippy-top of America's income and wealth ladder? Do we — including the 1 percent — really want to live in an economic apartheid society? All the evidence now suggests that too much inequality is bad for everyone, even the super-rich.

There are many reasons why we need to rethink our predicament, but for a moment let's consider this one, which in many ways trumps them all: As a planet, we are experiencing an ecological crisis. Climate change and ocean acidification — along with breaches of other planetary boundaries — will alter our food and energy systems and transform our way of life.

There have been recent news accounts about US billionaires buying mountain fortresses in the Rockies and Davos billionaires buying "getaway" farms in New Zealand with airplane landing strips. But these escape fantasies are delusional thinking. The island paradises will be swamped from rising sea levels. The mountain redoubts will be choked with the smoke of burning forests. It is in no one's interest to continue operating as if a few privileged people are going to escape on a spaceship or retreat to a mountaintop enclave.

The ecological catastrophe at our door will wipe out our most treasured assets — our natural ecosystems, the foundations of all private wealth. What is wealth without clean water and healthy oceans? What is wealth on a degraded Earth? As scientist Johan Rockström writes, "We're still blind, despite all the science, to the fact that wealth in the world depends on the health of the planet."

All of humanity — billionaire hedge fund managers, suburban soccer moms, and Bangladeshi farmers — is now wound together, our fate linked to our ability to respond to a planetary challenge bigger than anything we've faced before. At the same time, we are confronting a societal challenge of unprecedented inequality. The accelerating polarization of income, wealth, and opportunity is moving us quickly to a society that no one will want to live in, including the most privileged.

But many people remain unperturbed by inequality, in part because they appreciate the freedom of a society where some can become wildly wealthy. They remain unconvinced that inequality adversely affects their lives. However, a growing interdisciplinary body of research points to myriad ways that extreme inequality matters, that it undermines shared national values of equal opportunity, social mobility, community, economic stability, and democracy.

Widespread public attention became riveted on these inequalities only recently in the United States — when the Occupy movement began stirring in 2011 and when, two years later, the work of French economist Thomas

Piketty stormed the national consciousness by exposing the inevitable outcome of our current trends.

Piketty argues that if we don't intervene in the current economic system, wealth and power will continue to concentrate in fewer and fewer hands. We are moving toward a society governed by a hereditary aristocracy of wealth.

The wealthy have already hijacked our democracy. Roughly a year before the 2016 presidential election, nearly half the money in the campaign had come from just 158 families, many of them billionaires.[1] Realities like this have led former President Jimmy Carter to describe our political system as a political oligarchy.[2]

At a fundamental level, it is wrong that so few people have so much wealth and power. Winston Churchill, in a famous speech commemorating the sacrifice of British airmen during World War II, said, "Never in the field of human conflict was so much owed by so many to so few." Many decades later, we have a different kind of imbalance. With apologies to Churchill, never in the history of human suffering and economic conflict have so few been in a position to do so much for so many. This condition in human affairs should not exist.

Younger people are feeling the brunt of this polarization, with deteriorating livelihoods, crushing debt, and stagnant wages. All these forces undermine excellence and opportunity — and the quality of life for everyone.

The debate over solutions to growing inequality is polarized and stuck in the old story of class deservedness and antagonism. This book is aimed at disrupting these narratives and proposing a way forward.

It is written for two audiences. The first is the planet's most wealthy and privileged citizens — my own people — those of us in the top 1 to 5 percent of the planet's wealth holders. It is not a plea for charity or altruism, but an appeal to our real self-interest, as these inequalities are bad for everyone. Those of us with wealth have an important role to play in the transition to the next phase of human evolution.

In the pages ahead, I invite my fellow wealthy to "come home," to make a commitment to place, to put down a stake, and to work for an economy that works for everyone. Coming home means sharing our wealth and paying our fair share of taxes. I urge us to move investment capital out of the old fossil fuel economy, offshore accounts, and speculative financial investments — and redirect it to the new relocalized economy, including regional food and energy systems and enterprises that broaden wealth ownership, such as cooperatives.

The second audience is my friends in the 99 percent, who must defend our communities against the worst aspects of predatory capitalism. Like the Bernardston mobile home park tenants, we need to stand in solidarity against the rapacious rich. But to succeed, we need allies among the reachable wealthy. We must find ways to engage and invite the 1 percent home, back to the table, to be partners in transforming the future.

Where there are opportunities to win allies, I urge us all to proceed with empathy, adopting powerful tactics of active love and nonviolent direct action to make this happen. Instead of a class war of shame, I advocate an appeal to common humanity and empathy. This shift in tactics will help open new possibilities.

There is good news. A movement of what I call "openhearted wealthy people" understand that their genuine self-interest is inextricably linked to the rest of humanity and our ability to fix the future. They want to "come home," reestablish a stake in the commonwealth, and commit their time, networks, skills, and capital to building healthy, equitable, and resilient communities. I want you to meet some of these people and visit my neighborhood of Jamaica Plain and other communities that are building alternatives.

There is a new economy emerging in the shell of the old economy. This includes people and enterprises rejecting the system of extractive and looting-based capitalism and embracing a "generative" economy that operates within the boundaries of nature and promotes equality rather than division.

Our current modes of thinking about wealth, class, and racial differences are preventing the transformation required of us. We need to rewire ourselves as a species and change the economic system that is destroying nature and producing escalating inequalities.

We all have a daily vote as to which system will prevail. Will you vote with your time, energy, and capital for a dead end? Or will you throw your lot in with the rest of humankind, and vote for a system that gives humanity the possibility of flourishing?

This book explores the interaction between individual action and system change — and how, in order to transform our economic system, we must change power relations, policies, and our stories about the world.

In part I, Born on Third Base, I share my own experience as an activist and campaigner on wealth inequality and climate change issues, and as someone born into privileged circumstances. Over time, I realize the limits of fomenting "class antagonism" and learn that the rich are no different from the rest of humanity.

There is an empathetic barrier to change. Those of us in the top 1 percent are steeped in a mythology of deservedness, confusion, shame, and fear for the future. Cracking hearts open is one of the steps along our path to healing and transformation.

If we don't see the "commonwealth," or commons, that is the primary source of wealth and well-being, then we succumb to the myth that wealth is entirely the result of individual actions. The myth of deservedness says, *My economic status is solely a reflection of my effort, intelligence, and creativity.* The myth of disconnection says, *An injury to you doesn't really matter to me.* The myth of superiority implies, *I know better*, and blinds us to the resourcefulness, skills, and wisdom of less-privileged people.

Unlearning these stories is key to both building a healthy society and fixing some of our deepest problems. We need a more accurate narrative about wealth, opportunity, and success. Part II, Seeing Our Commonwealth, tells a number of stories that address the mythology of wealth and deservedness, including traveling with Bill Gates Sr. to defend the estate tax.

Part III, Understanding Advantage, explores the ways that privilege clouds our understanding of why some people have wealth and others don't. Privilege has a narcotic effect, boosting our comfort and sense of importance, but ultimately disconnecting us from our neighbors and our own better nature.

One huge barrier to change is that privileged people don't always see the countless ways that the deck is stacked in our favor. In four chapters, I look at how advantages *accelerate* for the wealthy few and how disadvantages *compound* for the majority. This includes the generational advantages of being born into the greatest subsidized generation, the one that came of age during World War II and benefited from what amounted to white affirmative action programs. I include a reflection on attending an international reparations summit and on the demands for reparations for slavery.

Race and class privilege dampen our empathy so that we are unable to see how these accelerating advantages accrue to us and our progeny. In one chapter, I dissect the new politics of inherited advantage — the myriad ways that privileged families give their children a head start in school, work, and life.

Part IV, Unnecessary Side Trips, examines whether charity is the cure. Many believe that the responsibility of the wealthy begins and ends with "giving back" through traditional philanthropic institutions. But what philanthropist Peter Buffett calls the charitable industrial complex is sometimes worse than the cure. I illustrate how some philanthropy exacerbates existing inequalities and then make the case for major philanthropic reform. Funding real social change through charity is an important component of bringing wealth home, but it is a massive distraction from the full work required. Charity is not a substitute for public investment and taxation.

Part V, Wealth, Come Home, begins with a closer examination of our current economic and ecological realities and what it means, quite personally, to move to a deeper systems approach. I introduce you to people who are struggling with what it means to ground capital in local new economy enterprises, rather than global speculative capitalism and offshore tax dodges.

The final section, part VI, The Invitations, concludes with two invitations. The first is to my fellow wealthy people, to be bold in the coming years and in coming home. The second is a call to the broader 99 percent to protect our communities and bring compassionate pressure on the wealthy.

Thank you for engaging with the ideas and stories of this book. Each of us holds a piece of the puzzle to our common human destiny. Here's my piece. I look forward to joining with you.

PART I

BORN ON THIRD BASE

Some people are born on third base and go through life thinking they hit a triple.

BARRY SWITZER

I Heart the 1 Percent

It's mind-boggling how many different worlds people live in on this one planet.

RICHELLE E. GOODRICH

I am the great-grandson of the Chicago meatpacker Oscar Mayer. I won the lottery at birth.

For the last five decades, I have been traversing the race and class divides in our society. I can attest: The relationship status between US people and our super-wealthy is complicated. At one talk I gave, I asked the audience: "How many of you feel rage toward the wealthiest 1 percent?"

Almost everyone in a room of 350 people raised a hand. There was nervous laughter.

"How many of you have admiration for some of the things wealthy people have done to make our society better?"

About two-thirds of the people in the room raised their hands.

"How many of you wish you were in the wealthiest 1 percent?"

Again almost everyone raised a hand, laughing.

"So you feel enraged, admiring, and wish to be the object of your own anger?" I observed. See, I told you it was complicated.

On the one hand, our society expresses a fawning exultation of the wealthy that conflates great riches with virtue. We are a culture that worships wealth and the celebrity of those with great fortunes. On the other hand, we possess a deep resentment toward America's most endowed. The rich — according to this worldview — are greedy, selfish destroyers who are fundamentally different from other people, an alien race apart from the rest of humanity.

For the rich-bashers, all acts of apparent generosity by a wealthy person are suspect. Acts of giving that used to be celebrated are now scrutinized, as Mark Zuckerberg discovered when he announced he was giving away 99 percent of his Facebook stock over his lifetime.[1] A munificent gesture by a 1 percenter can only be explained as a venal attempt at calculated public relations, pride, or an extension of ego.

Born on Third Base

I grew up in a wealthy and advantaged family with all the benefits that proffers: country club tennis lessons, international travel, elite private schools, access to quality health care and healthy environments, a debt-free college education, a trust fund. I was clueless as to how advantaged I was.

Every couple of years I squeeze into my leather lederhosen shorts and eat bratwurst with my extended Oscar Mayer clan at our family reunion's German Night.

I love these people.

With few exceptions, my extended family are the people you want on your team to solve any major civic or personal problem. They are generous, compassionate, and civically engaged. And, four generations after the founding of a successful family enterprise, many are comfortably in the top 1 percent of household wealth.

I'm not letting my family affections confuse my understanding of current realities. I'm painfully attuned to the grotesque inequalities of wealth, power, privilege, and opportunity that bombard my sensibilities. I'm simply reporting the facts as I see them. The 1 percent is by no means monolithic and may not be the root cause of our problems, as some suppose — as we'll explore later. But for now, back to life as I've known it.

Raised in the leafy suburbs of Detroit, Michigan, I attended Cranbrook School, a boys' prep school modeled after Cranbrook School in Kent, England. Cranbrook had odd British aristocratic pretentions in its formalities and language, especially sitting in the midwestern United States. We had "masters," "prefects," and "forms" instead of teachers, advisors, and grade levels.

One of my classmates, who was an upperclassman in multiple meanings, was Mitt Romney. Our Cranbrook School motto was "Aim High." To this day, the motto is depicted by an archer shooting an arrow straight up into the air, which, if you think about it, is a really reckless thing to do. Nevertheless, Mitt and I have heeded our school motto, though obviously Mitt has aimed considerably higher!

When I was 16, my father told me I would inherit enough wealth to pay for college and beyond. The sum was significant enough that I wouldn't have to work, but my father encouraged me to pursue a career as if the money wasn't there. He himself had worked his whole life.

I was the only member of my graduating senior class at Cranbrook School not to go straight to college. I was hungry to experience the wider world. At age 17, I was beginning to understand the contours of the privilege bubble I had grown up in, and I wanted to venture out.

Undercover Trust Fund Kid

At age 17, I moved from Bloomfield Hills, Michigan, to Worcester, Massachusetts, a working-class city that was down on its luck during the economic recession of the late 1970s.

In Worcester (or "woo-stahhh" as it is called by locals) I worked for two years at a collection of jobs, including as a teacher in a day care center, a tenant organizer in Worcester public housing, and a volunteer at a Catholic Worker soup kitchen. I made friends with people from dramatically different circumstances — from homeless Vietnam vets, radical Catholic nuns, and working-class teachers to neighborhood business owners and black and Latino youth my age who lived in public housing.

But I was completely "undercover" in terms of my privileged class upbringing. Some of my friends probably figured it out. But I certainly didn't volunteer my full story. I was listening and soaking up a radically different education about the world from my Bloomfield Hills and Cranbrook School childhood.

Between the ages of 20 and 25, I attended college, studied history and economics, and traveled to Mexico and Central America for international service projects, including working with an earthquake relief effort and in a refugee camp. I thought a lot about class and racial identity and what to do with my life.

During these years, I also watched the value of the wealth in my name literally double, even though I was making withdrawals to pay my college tuition. I had a front-row seat to wealth creating more wealth. Meanwhile, I was surrounded by people who worked long hours and were unable to save.

A trusted older friend of mine helped me put my wealth in perspective. "How long would you have to work," she asked, "before you could save $250,000, a portion of what you have, above and beyond your expenses?" This put this wealth into dramatic relief for me. At the rate I was going, about a hundred years.

The good news is I wasn't alone in winning the lottery at birth. I found a community of people who were trying to navigate the tension between having substantial inherited wealth and facing the poverty and inequity around us. When I was 18, I met George Pillsbury, the heir to the flour fortune. He had already been depicted in news accounts as the "dough boy." George had plowed some ground for people like me by cofounding the Haymarket People's Fund to support "change, not charity" organizations.

"Guilt gets a bum rap," George explained to me when we I first met him in Boston. "There are two kinds of guilt. One thing we label as guilt is a normal and healthy emotional reaction to feeling the disparities of wealth, suffering, and opportunity. If you don't feel something about that, then you're not human."

The other emotion that we call guilt, George explained, is self-hating and paralyzing. "It keeps you from taking action." George counseled me to avoid paralyzing guilt and embrace empathetic guilt as a motivation to change the system.

It is hard to explain to my friends who've grown up in poverty how disorienting it is to be given something that others aspire their whole lifetimes to have. And to reject it must look as odd as a baseball player running the wrong way around the base path, from third base to first base.

I met other wealthy people, some racked by paralyzing guilt, immobilized by their wealth, and struggling to make their way in the world. I came to appreciate, as Andrew Carnegie wrote, that sometimes giving a child an inheritance is a curse. While feeling grateful to my parents for the head start they provided to me, I saw how inherited wealth interfered with finding my own way in work and life.

We Gave Away a Fortune

At the age of 26, I made the first real adult decision of my life. I gave away the half-a-million-dollar trust fund that my parents had set up for me. If I'd held on to the wealth and kept it invested, I'd have over $7 million today, according to a journalist who later interviewed me.[2]

I also got help from three friends who met regularly to discuss what to do with our wealth. We interviewed over twenty-five people who had given away substantial assets, resulting in a book, *We Gave Away a Fortune: Stories of People Who Have Devoted Themselves and Their Wealth to Peace, Justice and the Environment*.[3] One member of the group, Edorah Frazer, shared my conviction to give away all our assets. We decided to take the leap on the same day.

On the day I went to the National Bank of Detroit and signed the paperwork to transfer my assets, Edorah did the same thing in Portsmouth, New Hampshire. We called each other from pay phones to share the news.

I felt buoyant and unshackled. Instead of being cramped up by the ambivalence of holding money I didn't earn, I shared it effectively to boost economic fairness.

I would make my own way. At the time, I could not fully comprehend how the financial wealth was just one part of the substantial inheritance of advantages that flowed to me. I gave away the money, but a lot of my privilege was hardwired.

Thirty years later, I have no regrets. If anything, I feel liberated. My decision enabled me to live my life more aligned to my values. It opened up a source of energy.

I'm not advocating this path for others, nor judging those who choose to hold on to wealth. I was 26 years old, unmarried with no children or responsibilities. I know we live in a deeply insecure society, where people experience accidents or job losses — and there is little safety net in the United States compared with other countries. But for me, it was the right path.

Being stuck in a role where wealth automatically flowed to me, thanks to the rigged rules of the current system, undermined my personal and spiritual sense of well-being. Witnessing poverty and injustice, both in the United States and globally, deepened my understanding of these structures.

Passing the wealth along has allowed me to look unflinchingly and nondefensively at the workings of the "inequality system" and the suffering it causes. I don't hate the 1 percent. But I deeply hate the ways extreme inequality wounds people's lives, fuels racial divisions, rips our communities apart, and destroys our ecological home.

To change this situation, we need a movement, led by those hurt and excluded by the system. But we also need the beneficiaries of the rigged game, those of us in the top 1 percent, to play our part.

CHAPTER 2

Proceed with Empathy

It is not learning we need at all. Individuals need learning but the culture needs something else, the pulse of light on the sea, the warm urge of huddling together to keep out the cold. We need empathy, we need the eyes that still can weep.

LYDIA MILLET, *OH PURE AND RADIANT HEART*

"We need to make the world safe for class war," said Felice Yeskel. "As inequality grows, people go in two directions — either very regressive or progressive."

It was 1999, and Yeskel and I were leading a program about "The Growing Divide" for a group of ironworkers in South Boston. Sixty men and a handful of women sat on metal chairs in a drafty union hall.

"Regressive populism is when people feel anxious and insecure and look for scapegoats," Yeskel continued. "Unscrupulous politicians deflect people's concern and anger toward whoever is the easiest target — new immigrants, women of color on welfare, religious minorities.

"Progressive populism is when people understand that the rules have been rigged by a powerful group of wealthy people and multinational corporations. Our job is to get people to look up the economic ladder, to target their populist wrath at the richest 1 percent."

Four years earlier, I had teamed up with Yeskel, who grew up in a working-class family on New York's Lower East Side. We were instant collaborators, sparked by our differences. She was working-class, female, lesbian, and Jewish — and I was none of those things.

Together we cofounded Share the Wealth, later changing our organization's name to the less incendiary United for a Fair Economy. We agreed that our mission was to make the world safe for class war. And we wrote a popular book, *Economic Apartheid in America: A Primer on Economic Inequality and Insecurity*.

Our theory was that social change movements were fueled by anger and needed targets. We studied how the political right wing built its power by deflecting a cesspool of white resentments toward people of color, new immigrants, poor people, and folks with diverse sexual orientations.

I thought about that theory of change as I looked out at the members of Ironworkers Local 7, working-class people who were taking two hours out of their weekend to talk about the roots of economic insecurity. They seemed fully engaged in the conversation.

A few days earlier, I had heard a Boston area comedian, Steven Wright, say, "I was in Davis Square the other day. I went by Mike's Deli, Dave's Cookies, Steve's Ice Cream. Okay, what happened to the days when men made steel?" Well, here they were: the men and women who bend steel, build the bridges and office tower buildings, and put highways underground. They were still here.

As my part of the presentation I talked about the policies that would reduce inequality: raise the minimum wage, tax the wealthy, make it easier for people to join a union. I mentioned in passing the Responsible Wealth network, formed to amplify the voices of business leaders and wealthy individuals to speak out for tax fairness.

"Wait a second," said a man named Steve, a tall fellow with a full beard and New England Patriots jacket. "Are you telling me there are rich people who give a shit about working-class people in this country?"

"Yes," I said. "They believe the rules have been rigged in their favor. And they are speaking out."

I watched Steve shake his head, take this in, and, for an instant, I swore I saw him tear up. "Why would they do that?"

"One of our wealthy members, Charles Demere, says he doesn't want his children and grandchildren to grow up in an apartheid society. He's lobbying Congress to raise his taxes. He's not doing this out of charity. He believes it is in his selfish interest to live in a more equal society."

"Wow," said Steve and others murmured in agreement. "I'd like to meet that guy and buy him a beer." Everyone laughed.

Misguided Class Warrior

My various jobs have enabled me to see a wide diversity of places, people, and perspectives. I've talked about the dangers of growing inequality in union halls, church basements in the rural South, and swanky Manhattan corporate boardrooms, including atop the World Trade Center in 2000. I've worked with mobile home park tenants, rural black sharecroppers, billionaire philanthropists, and everyone in between.

Prior to cofounding United for a Fair Economy, I coordinated a coalition of 650 groups in Massachusetts concerned about affordable housing, homelessness, and adequate social welfare. We politically got our butts kicked by people whose anger was focused at the poorest and most vulnerable in our state. In 1994, the Massachusetts legislature was more interested in punitive welfare reform than progressive taxes. One of our leaders, Marion Dowe, a strong-voiced woman from the Caribbean island of Dominica, used to say, "Without us poor folks to blame, people would have to wake up and notice who was really picking their pockets."

Between 1999 and 2004, I worked on a campaign to defend the federal estate tax from repeal. I helped organize over a thousand multimillionaires and billionaires in this effort and teamed up with Bill Gates Sr., father of the founder of Microsoft, to write *Wealth and Our Commonwealth: Why America Should Tax Accumulated Fortunes.* I've lobbied to raise the minimum wage, close corporate tax loopholes, and restore fair tax policies.

On a personal level, I got married, bought a house, raised a remarkable daughter, and put down roots in the urban Boston neighborhood of Jamaica Plain. But as I turned 50, I hit a rough patch. I lost my little brother to his struggles with mental illness. I got divorced after twenty years of marriage, and I buried my mother. And in January 2011, I lost Felice Yeskel, my closest collaborator, after her long battle with cancer. Eventually, I found new love, picked up two bonus sons, and built a cabin in Vermont, while remaining rooted in Jamaica Plain. For a decade, I've been working with an amazing team of colleagues at the Institute for Policy Studies, doing organizing and coediting Inequality.org, a portal for commentary, analysis, and data. I wrote a book, inspired by the Occupy movement, called *99 to 1: How Wealth Inequality Is Wrecking the World and What We Can Do About It.*

When it comes to fomenting class resentment, I plead guilty. The words coming out of my mouth for the last couple of decades have been no different from those coming from the leaders of major labor unions: "the reckless rich," "plutocracy," "endless greed," and so on.

Wealth is concentrating at a dizzying pace, and it is hard to imagine anything changing soon. But I also see a promising tectonic realignment happening at the base of US society. Bernie Sanders's campaign for president has tapped into this desire for change. We are waking up to these inequalities, understanding how the rules have been rigged.

For readers who come from the 99 percent, I do understand the frustration and rage you may be feeling. If I hear another story of an arrogant hedge fund manager buying a prescription drug and jacking up the price 5,000 percent, I'll be leading the pitchfork brigade.

If I had read the beginning of this book a couple of years ago, I would have shaken my head with doubt. And I'd have had a lot of questions: Are you saying not to be angry at the wealthy? Aren't some rich unreachable? How big is this group of "openhearted wealthy," compared with the closed-hearted greedy, which seem to be the majority? When are you going to talk about wealth redistribution?

My labor activist friend, Les Leopold, wrote in his book *Runaway Inequality*, "Economic elites will only give up power and wealth when they're forced to do so by a powerful social movement."[1] This echoes the famous speech by black abolitionist Frederick Douglass, "Power concedes nothing without a demand. It never did and it never will." Less than a decade ago, I would have agreed. I still believe a mighty struggle will be required, that movements of workers and the excluded will be the driving force in change. But I believe these movements will make swifter progress if they open up another set of tactics, based on our growing knowledge of empathy. This will require us to have a deeper understanding of who these power elites are — and where alliances can be forged.

I'm changing my tune because we are missing an opportunity to build a more powerful movement. To make my case, I'll have to tell you a few stories.

Most of us can relate to being on the privileged end of the equation in at least a few relationships and systems. But my experience with economic class is that people want to constantly deflect the resentment onto someone with more income and wealth.

For instance, wealthy Latin Americans point to the wealthy Americans. People in the top 5 percent in the United States will point to the top 1 percent. People in the top 1 percent will point to the super-wealthy — and they in turn, will point to the tippy-top, the wealthiest 100. It's like there's a collective powerlessness to change the system. What's missing here is an understanding that all of these people, who are in the global 5 percent, have a tremendous capacity and opportunity to make change.

If you live in the United States, you are probably in the top 5 or 10 percent *globally*. If you earn more than the US median income of $55,000, then you are in the top 2 percent globally.[2] You also have considerable leverage over the kind of future we will have — and I invite you to engage with the world's wealthy to do the right thing.

Road Map to Richistan:
What Do I Mean by Wealthy?

One barrier to building effective social movements is that most of us don't entirely understand who the wealthy are and where opportunities for alliances might be built. We operate largely on caricatures and stereotypes that the wealthy look like Monopoly Men, chubby little plutocrats wearing top hats. It is strategically important to understand the different segments within the "wealthy."

Journalist Robert Frank offered a helpful geographic overview of the wealthy in his 2007 book, *Richistan: A Journey Through the American Wealth Boom and the Lives of the New Rich.*[3] To explain the distinctions among different subdivisions, Frank divided the wealthy into several village tiers, what he calls Lower Richistan, Middle Richistan, Upper Richistan — and Billionaireville.

I've modified and expanded Frank's concept, adding an additional community called Affluentville. I've also updated his original information and added some of my own sociological markers. What people own, in terms of wealth and assets, remains more important than factors such as income, because they tell us more about status and power differences. There are, of course, serious limits to this type of topography. The experience of first-generation wealth holders is radically different from "old wealth." And the source of one's wealth may create a cultural difference in attitude as divergent as age, region, race, and religion. Disclaimers aside, here's a road atlas of Richistan.

Affluentville is home to the top 10 percent of wealth holders whose wealth ranges from $680,000 to $3 million. This includes about 11 million households.[4] They fly commercial, but likely own a luxury car that they replace every couple of years. They are concentrated on the East and West Coasts and are clustered into about one hundred zip codes.

By most indicators, the residents of Affluentville are "wealthy." But they may not actually think of themselves as wealthy if they compare themselves with the rest of Richistan. They are very concerned that subsequent generations don't lose economic status. As a result, they invest substantially in opening doors and opportunities to their children, as I describe more fully in chapter 9. For these reasons, there are challenges in forming alliances with them around policies that reduce inequality.

Lower Richistan includes approximately three million households with wealth between $3 million and $10 million. They are in the top 3 percent of wealth holders.[5] Their wealth comes from businesses, salaries, stock investments, and inheritance.

This diverse group shares many of the same affluent zip codes and suburbs with inhabitants of Affluentville. But they are increasingly moving back into city centers, driving up the cost of urban real estate. They populate upscale restaurants, country clubs, and luxury vacation destinations. They likely have second homes. They still fly on commercial airlines, but sometimes sit in first class.

This group also includes an older generation of "millionaire next door" households, folks whose wealth grew steadily in the decades after World War II, thanks to small-business ownership and long-term investments. These next-door millionaires are the opposite of flashy wealth, often living in their first homes and leading relatively thrifty lives.[6]

Building alliances with people in Lower Richistan is more promising. They are more economically cushioned and secure than residents of Affluentville. They are less anxious about their children, yet are not as deeply disconnected from the rest of society as residents of Upper Richistan.

Middle Richistan is inhabited by roughly 1.6 million households that are all in the top 1 percent of wealth holders. With assets between $10 million and $100 million, this group also includes the top 0.1 percent of households, recipients of over 90 percent of the income and wealth gains since the 2008 economic meltdown.[7] Their wealth comes from business ownership, investments, and some earned income. The range of property and assets is enormous between the top and bottom of Middle Richistan, influencing how many properties they may own. At the upper end of Middle Richistan, residents fly on private jets or own fractional interests through businesses like Netjet.

While the residents of Middle Richistan are starting to grow more distant from the rest of humanity, their children are not as they spread their wings and venture out. This connects Middle Richistan to cities, colleges, community institutions, nonprofit organizations, and concerns about inequality.

Upper Richistan is home to roughly sixteen thousand households with wealth over $100 million, the top 0.01 percent. These are the folks that Credit Suisse would characterize as the top end of "Ultra High Net Worth Individuals."[8] Their ranks include heirs to multigenerational wealth dynasties, alongside first-generation entrepreneurs, hedge fund managers, and CEOs. They own and fly in private jets.

Managing wealth and property is a major activity of Upper Richistanis. Each of their properties and residences has caretakers and trained house staff and servants. Many extended families set up family offices or enlist private law firms and advisors to help administer investments, trusts, and philanthropic foundations.

This group thinks generationally about wealth and assets. As Frank writes, "When you live in Upper Richistan, your entire philosophy of money changes. You realize that you can't possibly spend all of your fortune, or even part of it, in your lifetime and that your money will probably grow over the years even if you spend lavishly. So Upper Richistanis plan their finances for the next hundred years. They don't buy mutual funds; they buy timber land, oil rigs and office towers."[9]

Upper Richistan and Billionaireville are pretty disconnected from the plight and concerns of ordinary working people, unless they choose otherwise. They may elect to take in news from the world and allow it to move their hearts and money. Or they choose to live in a parallel universe of privilege. They do, however, have foundations that sometimes serve as proxies for their concerns — which in turn put them in contact with the most planet's most needy. Some are eloquent allies for larger public policies connected to inequality, such as fair taxation.

Billionaireville is the enclave for at least 540 households in the United States, some of whom are on the *Forbes* 400 list.[10] Many conceal their wealth in complicated trusts and offshore bank accounts, making an accurate estimation of their number impossible. Like those in Upper Richistan, the Billionaires take a longer view about most financial and life endeavors.

They own multiple properties and move, on a cyclical basis, from compound to compound, with personnel flying ahead to prepare for dinner parties and seasonal activities. From New York City and Los Angeles to Sundance and Sun Valley, from Palm Springs to Palm Beach, the migrations of the very wealthy are tied to social events, sunshine, and high culture.

The income of Billionaireville comes almost entirely from interest on their assets and capital gains, not in the form of a weekly paycheck. Ironically, many of these Billionaires wear unassuming T-shirts every day, a far cry from the tuxedo-clad elites of generations past.

Some are still actively making money, especially in new media, technology, and finance. There are founders of hedge funds as well as technology companies like Google, Amazon, and Facebook. Others are part of American wealth dynasties, such as the Waltons, the Kochs, and the Mars candy empire. The concentration of wealth in Billionaireville is on track to see its first Trillionaire within two decades.

At this level, families focus on multigenerational legacies, landholdings, and philanthropic institutions. Left unhindered, our society will become a hereditary aristocracy, governed by the sons and daughters of Billionaireville.

Reconsidering the Virtues of Class Antagonism

I remember my first inklings that I should rethink my "class war" theory of change. It was back at that union hall in 1999.

"Aren't some wealthy people just plain evil?" asked Steve, the ironworker. "I mean, aren't they different from you and I, no offense?"

Yeskel looked at me to answer this question, the resident expert on the sentiments of all wealthy people. I felt flushed with anxiety, trying to decide how to respond to this question. I didn't have a map to Richistan yet. Do I tell them my story? It seemed like several minutes passed, but only in my anxious imagination.

"Well, first I should tell you, I grew up in the 1 percent," I said. "I'm the great-grandson of the meatpacker Oscar Mayer." I paused as people laughed in disbelief. "My father used to say, 'Bringing home the bacon had a different meaning in my family.'" More generous laughter. Phew, I got through that.

At most of the union meetings I attend, people begin their speeches by establishing their labor credentials. At that Boston meeting, one union officer recounted how his grandfather was in the carpenters union and his mother was a member of the textile workers union. I'm very thin in the labor credentials department.

"Look, there are badass sociopathic wealthy people who use their wealth and power to rig the rules to get more wealth and power," I continued. "We need to organize to protect ourselves and our livelihoods from this segment of the 1 percent, these rule riggers and game fixers."

I didn't verbalize it, but in my experience some of these "rule riggers" actually believe they are acting for the common good. They genuinely think that cutting taxes for the already wealthy and weakening government oversight will create a freer economy that will lift up the poor. They live according to cultural "we know better" stories of racial supremacy and class privilege. But if that narrative is disrupted and shifts — based on experience with real human beings — so does their point of view.

Only a small pathological segment of the rule-rigging 1 percent are cynically thinking, "Damn all others — I just want more for me." And wealthy sociopaths are no more plentiful than sociopaths across the entire society. They just happen to be highly visible and have more levers of power at their disposal and can do more damage.

The vast majority of the top 1 percent is coasting along, happily benefiting from a system that disproportionately rewards them. They are, like the society as a whole, busy, distracted, addicted, or focused on caring for children and elders.

I carried on with my spoken thoughts. "The reason we are organizing wealthy people is because we think, in order to build a powerful countervailing movement to the rule riggers, we need wealthy allies in our camp. Some rich people will be unreachable," I acknowledged. "And some people will be incredibly thin-skinned and feel personally attacked if we simply talk about the percent of wealth owned by the 1 percent."

"The big difference I see," said Steve, "is those people have an entire police-military-industrial-complex at the ready to defend their property rights."

"But the human reality is we are *all* thin-skinned," I replied. "When we are poked, we bleed. No one likes to be stereotyped or feel as if they are targeted as a group for wrath. Think how you feel when someone makes a sweeping statement about unions."

Steve nodded. He and his colleagues were still with me. There was a lot more to say here, but I didn't want to distract the discussion too much. It felt like we were getting closer to the heart of the matter, both the power issues that hold inequality in place and the possibility of enlisting wealthy allies into movements for justice.

Can the Super-Rich Save Us?

In 2009, consumer advocate Ralph Nader wrote his first and only work of fiction, a novel called *Only the Super-Rich Can Save Us!*, weighing in at 733 pages. I hosted Nader for a forum about the book and read it twice, finding it loaded with insights.

"When you've lost enough battles, you have the fodder for a utopian novel," Nader told me. "You imagine what it would have taken to win and there is my utopia. In this case, I imagined the billionaires providing the resources to win deep reforms around clean elections, strengthening democracy, environmental protection, and reining in corporate power." Indeed, the novel is something of a playbook for political transformation.

Only the Super-Rich Can Save Us! is an imaginary tale of seventeen real-life billionaires and multimillionaires, including Warren Buffett, Ted Turner, and Bill Gates Sr., who decide to use their wealth and savvy to equalize the odds on behalf of working people, like the ironworkers in South Boston. As I read the novel, I found the super-wealthy weren't the only real-life characters. Nader included the names of dozens of other organizers and activists in roles as campaigners for change.

The title of the novel comes from the opening scene. A fictional Warren Buffett is watching the horrors of Hurricane Katrina unfold on television in September 2005. He sees the helicopter footage of thousands of stranded citizens, waving desperately from rooftops. After four days of continuous watching, he is disgusted by the paralysis and incompetence of local, state, and federal authorities to undertake basic rescue and provisioning operations. "How could this be happening in the world's wealthiest country?" he fumes.

The fictional Buffett organizes a convoy of supplies and trucks and personally drives with a team from Omaha to New Orleans, arriving twenty-six hours later at roadsides crowded with thousands of hungry and thirsty refugees from a great American city. Word spreads that the planet's second-wealthiest man, dressed in jeans and rolled-up sleeves, is approaching an encampment of a dozen adults and children huddled around a crude campfire. Buffett holds their hands and hugs the trembling children, looking them in the eye.

The old-timers notice that there are no reporters, no photographers, no television crews. A composed elderly grandmother cups his hands in hers and cries out, "Only the super-rich can save us!"[11]

Nader, of course, doesn't believe that the rich are superheroes; nor will the private charity of billionaires serve as a substitute for a functioning and adequately funded government. But his point is that, given the incredible concentration of wealth and power, the very wealthy, if inclined, could radically transform our political and economic system for the better.

A System Built on Fear

We now have the potential to build a powerful movement to reverse these inequalities. But in order to succeed, we need to enlist allies among the 1 percent. And many are waiting to be called.

For this reason, the class antagonism strategy will not get us to where we want to go. There are limits to the kind of change we can build from anger and stoking resentment. In the United States, we're more likely to get Donald Trump regressive populism than Bernie Sanders's progressive populism.

To fix the system, we need to alter the rigged rules. To change the rules, we need to build a powerful social movement. To build a movement, we need to win hearts and minds to the shortsightedness of an economic system that funnels most income and wealth to the few. Ultimately, we need to change the story of wealth, how it is created, where it comes from, and why it is distributed the way it is.

One access point is engaging wealthy people about their commitment to a particular community, inviting them home to bring wealth, energy, and a stake into making localities more equitable and fair. While national debates on inequality are polarized, the more state and local we go, the less ideological the solutions become. There is some room to move, as we shall discuss later.

Here's the dirty secret: The current system is built on fear. Fear and insecurity ripple through the households of the American working class, the impoverished, and the precarious middle class in a nation where one job loss, illness, or other misfortune could leave one destitute. And at the very top of the economic class pyramid, the wealthy are afraid, too. They are afraid that they and their children will fall from economic comfort and status. They are fearful of pitchforks and race riots. And they are wounded by verbal attacks as well.

Fear is very powerful. If people feel attacked, they respond from fear. If they are shamed, they respond from anger. If ridiculed, they withdraw. But if they are respectfully engaged, people show up.

Think about the last time you fundamentally changed your behavior or view about something. What were the ingredients of your shift or transformation?

Adults change through a combination of respect, affirmation, challenge, inspiration, and accountability. People don't change when they feel shamed, hated, targeted, and disrespected.

In a quote attributed to F. Scott Fitzgerald, he said, "The rich are different than you or I."[12] But my life experience observation is that *the rich are no different* than the rest of humanity. There are structural, cultural, and class identity reasons why we disconnect and stay in our own lanes. But we are no different.

People don't become a different breed when they accumulate wealth. But they do unplug and disconnect from large swaths of humanity. And there is a weakening of empathy.

The comforts of privilege are frankly narcotic. Privilege dulls our sensibilities and emotions. It shuts down empathy, allowing those of us with advantages to disconnect from our humanity and place in the natural order. Privilege enables us to distance ourselves from huge parts of the human experience, both the suffering and the joyful aliveness.

So what is to be done? The alternative to class war is empathy and love.

How do we teach empathy to someone? We treat them with empathy. Here's my suggestion: Proceed with empathy. Consider us your long-lost cousins who have been taken from you. Find a way to welcome us back to the full human fold.

Given that most approaches haven't changed the picture, it might be worth a try.

CHAPTER 3

Cracking Hearts Open

I have tried both ways: I have gone back to sleep in order to resist the forces of change. And I have stayed awake and been broken open. Both ways are difficult, but one way brings with it the gift of a lifetime. If we can stay awake when our lives are changing, secrets will be revealed to us — secrets about ourselves, about the nature of life, and about the eternal source of happiness and peace that is always available, always renewable, already within us.

ELIZABETH LESSER, *BROKEN OPEN*

"Last year, the Boeing Corporation paid no federal taxes," I say to an attentive audience of 150 people at a suburban Los Angeles church.

"We taxpayers gave Boeing over $20 billion in contracts, 4.4 percent of all federal contracts. They reported $5.9 billion in profits. For years, Boeing has paid their CEO more than they pay in annual taxes."[1]

I've been invited to give a speech about wealth inequality — and I'm talking about corporate loopholes and the need to close down offshore tax havens that enable transnational corporations like Apple and General Electric to aggressively avoid taxes.

After the program, I'm approached by a tall silver-haired man who introduces himself as Hank, a retired high-ranking executive at the Boeing Corporation.

"Uh-oh," I think. I just called him a tax dodger. But he isn't perturbed.

"I'm embarrassed," Hank says, gently touching my shoulder. "I'm embarrassed that my company takes so much from taxpayers and pays so little to support our nation's infrastructure and education systems. It's wrong."

This is not what I was expecting.

Hank is a foot taller than me, and maybe two decades older. He has enormous hands that he waves around as he explains that he has an "important question" for me. First, though, by way of background, he tells me a story.

"I was part of a delegation of engineers helping to build water systems in rural Kenya," Hank explains. "You see, I was an engineer before I was an executive — so it was a kick for me to participate in some very hands-on rural development projects.

"I was visiting a very remote village, standing by an irrigation project, when I noticed six children watching quietly from under a tree. Slowly they inched closer and closer to get a better look at us. I guess we were the best entertainment in town." He smiles at the memory.

"Each day these children came to watch. They had beautiful eyes and faces and a lively curiosity. The girls wore colorful dresses. They were quick to smile and laugh. I told them my name was Hank, and I learned their names. One day, I asked them where they lived. They led me to an aged wooden building that I discovered, to my surprise, was an orphanage. I met the adults in charge and they introduced me to the twenty-five children for whom that orphanage was home. The building was tidy and simple, but in very tired shape — with weathered, sagging beams and porch boards.

"As I walked back to our van — that was going to shuttle us to our first-world hotel an hour away — I was overcome with emotion. I am not much of a crier, but I started to weep. That night I could not sleep. I lay awake all night thinking about those children.

"The next day, the children were waiting at the construction site again — and they waved and smiled brightly when they saw me. 'Uncle Hank,' they called me, a term of respect and endearment. They sat in the shade of a tree, watching our every move."

Toward the end of his trip, Hank went back to the orphanage and talked to the director about how he could help. "He humbly said they would welcome any financial help — including building a new facility," said Hank. "There were many more children in the community without homes."

Hank's eyes sparkle and glisten as he tells the story, explaining that this was four years ago, after his 70th birthday. "I came back to Los Angeles, but all I could think about were those kids. I threw myself into raising money and leading construction brigades to Kenya."

"My heart was cracked open," Hank says, his voice itself cracking. "My life was transformed. I thought I was going to Kenya to work on an engineering project and then these children wormed their way into my heart. I was defenseless."

Hank tells me about the multiple buildings and the hundreds of children that are now better housed. For Hank, this isn't about charity. "I feel like my life was saved, that I was the walking dead before. My wife noticed that I was alive. She said to me, 'You remind me now of the sweet guy I married forty-eight years ago.' My children said I was more present, connected with them and generous." He pauses, tears now streaming down his cheeks. I wonder if the man who never cried before he was 70 is moved to tears every day.

"So my question is — " He is quiet and turns inward for a second. I was so enraptured by his story that I had forgotten he had a question. I too have begun to cry.

"My question is, is it too late . . . for me?" He returns from his inward glance and looks at me with more certainty. "Is it too late for me to change? To . . . make changes?"

I am thrown off balance by the question.

"No," I reply without thinking at all. "It's not too late. You're so alive."

He nods. "I'm so thankful. I feel like I was living inside a corporation for decades, responding to a different universe of signals, incentives, and messages about what was important. They are good people, my Boeing colleagues. But we were focused on a different set of goals, a sort of logic of its own. In three decades, I can't remember anyone talking about alleviating poverty.

"Now I feel like the curtain has been lifted — and I'm making connections between everything around me — nature, people, kids in Africa, kids in LA, poverty, inequality, food and diet. It's all coming together in my mind."

"No, it's not too late at all." I smile. "You have a lot of gifts for the world."

"Thanks." He smiles back. "But we don't have a lot of time to turn things around, right?" He references comments I made about climate change and extreme inequality.

"Yes, so how can we reach more people?" I ask him. "We need more Hanks."

"I'm working on it," Hank grins. "First, I take them to Kenya. There is something about meeting children far away that is disarming. We can't pretend they deserve to be poor or justify their situation by blaming their parents or government ineptitude. We just have to contemplate the basic unfairness of a world where some children are born with so much and others with so little.

"The first step is cracking open people's hearts," Hank says with confidence.

Our Attitudes Toward the Rich

I've thought a lot about Hank's story since we met. And I've met other people whose stories offer important clues about how we might change things related to the 1 percent.

This is what coming home looks like. But some people have to travel halfway around the world to outwit the powerful stories that justify poverty and inequality.

Certainly part of the journey is to feel one's heart cracked open. Another is to reflect on the ways that we live inside powerful narratives and myths that explain the world, but also distance us from one another and nature. Another ingredient of change is to understand the deep systems that are driving us toward climate catastrophe and economic polarization.

New brain science reveals that we are hardwired for connection, empathy, and mutuality. When afraid, we shift to a protective stance — of fight or flight. But when we feel loved, respected, and fully seen by others — we have another set of reactions.

Buddhist master Thich Nhat Hanh writes, "We are here to awaken from the illusion of our separateness." Indeed, we seem to sparkle when we activate this connection-oriented part of our nature.

So the path toward change — and engaging the 1 percent that hold so much of the power in our society — starts with connection, empathy, respect, and love. Only then can we connect through inspiration, accountability, and challenge.

Some of my friends are rolling their eyes. I would ask them to consider three things. First, honestly, how do *you* change? How do other people change? What do we know to be true about human transformation?

Second, how does the 1 percent live inside of you? Are you really better than these other people? Do you really think you would behave differently if you had the same fearful conditioning and daily dose of meritocracy and privilege mythology coming at you?

Third, how is that rage and class war thing working for you? Is it leading to any real social change? And how is it affecting you personally?

People fundamentally shift because of love, respect, inspiration, accountability, and challenge. If I want to continue to be righteous but largely ineffective, I can hold on to my rage and resentments. You have the same choice. You can target me and others for our blind spots. Or you can get about the process of transforming yourself and one another.

Story of Deservedness

For two decades I've walked around with my graphs and charts documenting the growth of income and wealth inequality. For some, this alarming data is shocking and motivating. But for others, it doesn't make a dent.

We know from opinion research that Americans have a rather high tolerance for inequality and concentrated wealth. We don't really care how rich the rich are as long as the rules of the system are fair and anyone can have the opportunity to get rich.

Most people look at the story of inequality through the lens of deservedness: People get what they deserve. Inequality exists, according to this narrative, because of unequal effort, intelligence, and creativity. The implication is that people are poor because they don't try as hard, have made mistakes, or lack wit and wisdom. And people are rich because they work harder, smarter, or more creatively.

There are, of course, differences in effort, creativity, and pluck. Myths are powerful because they build on kernels of truth. We all have personal experiences of people who are both slackers and drivers.

There is a segment of first-generation ultra-high-net-worth individuals that is working and operating at an intense pace. They are taking private jets from New York to Hong Kong to Dubai to put together another deal, with all the physical strain and disconnection from family that entails. They live the meritocratic life, and believe that because of the sacrifice and stress, any compensation is justified. They don't see the social context of their wealth — nor do they see the fact that others work equally hard with no comparable rewards. They are wound up in their own story, replete with their own wounds.

Differences in output might justify some differential in compensation and rewards, such as one person being paid ten times more than another. But one thousand times more? Ten thousand times more? The personal stories that justify these megadisparities fail to factor in the deep historical differences in opportunity that propel some and restrict others. In the misunderstood physics of inequality, advantages accelerate for the privileged while disadvantages compound for many unprivileged people.

Our present inequalities can only be explained by historical systems of racial and class advantage and huge economic and political distortions in the economy. Yet the story of deservedness is hard to dislodge.

To unpack the deservedness narrative requires honesty in public storytelling that presently doesn't exist. Why do we have a deep and persistent racial wealth gap between whites and blacks and Latinos? How do wealthy people accumulate and preserve wealth over generations? How is wealth created — and what is the role of individuals and what is the role of societal institutions and investment?

When I started to work on preserving the federal estate tax, I was thrust into the debate over wealth and deservedness. It started with a call from Bill Gates Sr. and a talk radio show.

PART II

SEEING OUR COMMONWEALTH

Transformed realities require transformed imaginations.

WALTER BRUEGGEMANN

— CHAPTER 4 —

I Didn't Do It Alone

Self-made men, indeed! Why don't you tell me of the self-laid egg?

Francis Lieber[1]

"We've got Charlie from Hillsborough," announces the host, Danny Bliss, in a deep melodious radio school voice. "Hello, Charlie, what's your question for Mr. Collins?"

"It is parasites like Collins that make me crazy," starts Charlie.

It is 11:20 p.m., well past my bedtime. I am sitting at my desk at home, wearing cutoff shorts on a hot summer night. Everyone in my household has gone to sleep, but I've stayed up to be the bleary-eyed guest on a conservative talk radio show beaming across New England. The subject: America's estate tax, our nation's only levy on inherited wealth.

At the beginning of the program, the host tees up the discussion by saying that his guest (me) supports retaining the "death tax" — the "curse upon hardworking Americans that enables bloodsucking politicians to pillage small businesses, family farms, and innocent livelihoods. Call our number and give him a piece of your mind."

This has put callers in a certain frame of mind. I've already been called a "communist" and "antibusiness," but "parasite" is a first.

"Hi, Danny. Good show," says Charlie from Hillsborough. "Your guest Collins is like a typical government leech. Let me tell you something: I started my metal stamp business almost thirty years ago, and *no one* helped me. And I can tell you, I *worked very hard*, sometimes seven days a week . . ."

I have just published a book with Bill Gates Sr. making the case for preserving the estate tax. So I am doing several interviews a day and several public speaking appearances a week. I am listening to a number of callers with a remarkably similar narrative line.

Charlie from Hillsborough continues, "So why should I pay a friggin' death tax on wealth that I built by *myself*, with no government help. I made huge sacrifices to get this business going. Sometimes after all my employees are gone for the day, I am still at the office. I miss my kid's theater and sporting events . . ."

I close my eyes and try to visualize Charlie in Hillsborough.

"I pay my property taxes and income taxes, and I have created eighteen jobs here in central New Hampshire."

I'm not sure what compelled me to say yes to being a guest on this nocturnal edition of "whack the liberal." But I'm intrigued by stories I hear that embody an individual success ethos in our country. I'm getting a good dose tonight.

"Tell me, Mr. Collins, if you keep punishing the people who do the real work and grow the enterprises of America . . . What happens when we all throw up our hands and say, 'I'd rather go fish at the lake today'?"

There is truth and power in Charlie's story and similar testimonials of individual wealth and success. I've heard hundreds of them, each with their unique flourishes. Some are original inventors, small real estate developers, or multigenerational owners of family enterprises. Some are super dealmakers, jetting around the planet. They are unquestionably hardworking. Many have made heroic sacrifices, especially the first-generation immigrants and business owners.

The basic narrative goes like this: "I was born with little or nothing, worked hard all my years, and earned a comfortable life. I didn't get any help along the way. I didn't get any handouts. I worked as the sun rose, while others were sleeping. Now, at the end of my life, the government has no damn right to take my money."

This narrative, celebrated among the prosperous, is "the great man theory of success." It is told by small-business owners like Charlie and billionaire entrepreneurs like casino mogul Sheldon Adelson or Google founders Larry Page and Sergey Brin. I frequently encounter this story while working to prevent Congress from abolishing the estate tax, a levy on accumulated wealth paid exclusively by multimillionaires and billionaires — otherwise known, thanks to a well-financed campaign by antitax advocates, as the "death tax."

If I only heard these great man stories of individual success, I might have become a true believer. But I've also been fortunate to listen to hundreds of stories from wealthy individuals and business leaders that include descriptions of the help they have received. These add another dimension to the narrative of wealth creation.

I Got Help Along the Way

In June 2000, Congress voted to abolish the estate tax. President Bill Clinton pledged to veto the bill, arguing we should reform but not repeal the tax. The White House asked my organization for help recruiting business leaders to stand with the president at the veto press conference.

We enlisted Martin Rothenberg, the owner of several technology companies. Speaking at a press conference in the West Wing of the White House, Rothenberg explained, "My wealth is not only a product of my own hard work. It also resulted from a strong economy and lots of public investment in others and me."

The son of first-generation immigrants, Rothenberg grew up in Brooklyn. "My parents didn't have any money. But I went to great public schools, with excellent teachers. Someone else paid for my education.

"There was a great local public library — open on weekends and evenings," he continued. "When I was about 12 or 13, I got very interested in electricity and radio. When I came into the library, the librarian would say, 'Martin, I have a book for you.' Someone else paid to keep that library open and pay that librarian's wages."

Rothenberg attended college for free on the GI Bill. His graduate school education was also free because he participated in a fellowship program that forgave his loans after several years of teaching. "Someone else paid for my college and university studies," he noted.

After school, he went into the emerging high-tech field, a sector built with huge public investments in research and technological infrastructure. Then he started his own private company, founded on a platform of publicly funded research. "So that's in large part where my wealth came from.

"When I started my company, where did I find qualified employees?" he asked, waving his hands. "I hired them from the university, where they were trained with government scholarships! Someone else paid to train my employees."

Rothenberg sold his company for $30 million. But like many entrepreneurs he started another company and continues to be engaged in a number of enterprises.

"All along the way, other people paid for my early education, graduate studies," Rothenberg concluded. "The entire field of Internet technology I work in was built with public investment. I didn't do it alone.

"So should I pay an estate tax?" He paused and looked at President Clinton and the crowd of reporters. "Of course I should!" he cried passionately. "Don't I have an *obligation* to pay back to the society that has made *everything* possible for me? Don't I have an obligation — a duty — to ensure that other kids, who grow up poor like I did, should have the same opportunities for education and employment?

"I have no problem paying an estate tax. I've never once heard my children complain that part of their inheritance will go toward an estate tax. I was able to provide well for my family, and, upon my death, I hope taxes on my estate will help fund the kind of programs that benefited me and others from humble backgrounds — a good education, money for research, and targeted investments in poor communities — to help bring opportunity to all Americans."

President Clinton approached the rostrum and shook Rothenberg's hand. He was visibly moved and momentarily speechless before leaning into the microphone, shaking his head and saying, "This is the best of America."

Ayn Rand Has a Point: Individuals Matter

Martin Rothenberg's "I didn't do it alone" is a striking contrast with the "No one helped me — so leave me alone" stories that I often hear.

Thinking about Charlie from Hillsborough and then listening to Martin's story makes me realize that we need a more nuanced narrative of success, one that appropriately celebrates the gifts of individuals — but also chronicles the complex constellation of other forces at work.

Is there an alternative to the *Great Man Theory of Wealth Creation*? Is there a more balanced narrative that recognizes the role of the individual while fixing a more accurate lens on other factors?

Individual effort *does* matter, and we should celebrate it. Some people accumulate great wealth because of their hard work, extra effort, intelligence, creativity, faithfulness, and sacrifice. And leadership does make a difference, especially when presiding over large complex organizations — as do some of those CEOs we love to hate because of their oversized pay packages and short-term profit grabbing.

Our society needs these individuals with leadership abilities and would be impoverished without their skills in the world. They should be appreciated for their efforts with social recognition and rewarded with reasonable material rewards.

Most people rightly consider Ayn Rand as an apostle of extreme individualism and libertarian views about government. The philosophy she infused into her writings is yet another object of debate in our contemporary political-culture wars. But I have read *The Fountainhead* and *Atlas Shrugged*, and the thing I like about Ayn Rand is that her individuals are heroic. They buck the trend and take the road less traveled. They work hard and with precision. They take pride in their work and make the railroads run, the steel mill hum, and the buildings soar. They are doers.

I appreciate characters who don't go along with the herd, who value freedom and individual conscience.

But what Ayn Rand missed was the role of society, and the importance of public infrastructure and investment in creating the conditions for wealth creation and preservation. Her now-famous characters and their achievements seem to float outside any societal or ecological commons that makes their existence and activities possible. Those characters may be admirable, but the story told about them is incomplete.

After listening to hundreds of real-world "I did it alone" stories, what I've come to appreciate is the wounded voice of the people who tell them. Behind the heroics are sacrifices and losses. To work hard is to miss out on life's other delights. It means missing one's family and loved ones and sacrificing one's health and life balance.

In her book *Plutocrats*, Chrystia Freeland tells the story of one hard-charging executive who took his daughter on a trek to climb Mount

Kilimanjaro as a college graduation gift. It was the most time they had ever spent together. If I worked so hard that I missed my daughter's childhood, I also might believe I should be well compensated for the sacrifice.

It is from such wounds that people construct a self-narrative of deservedness, the belief that "I can never be paid too much" or "I have a claim on all this wealth." It may be hard to empathetically listen to these stories. They sound too much like privileged whining. But hearing and acknowledging these wounds is the first step to opening up a real dialogue about how society has also contributed to one's wealth.

In a cultural sense, we need to lay a wreath at the altar of individual achievement — to acknowledge the truth of people's sacrifices on both sides of the wealth and income divide. If we ignore the role of the individual — the small and large acts of heroism that people undertake — we cannot have a conversation about societal factors in wealth and success.

How are these sacrifices any different, you might ask, from those of the minimum-wage worker who misses important moments in her children's lives by working two jobs to simply pay the rent and feed the family? Such is the story of many low-wage workers, and they have little wealth and security to show for their heroic acts. There are also many gifted people who contribute to the world in vital ways that do not lead to great wealth. What about teachers, coaches, and music instructors who choose to serve the next generation rather than command higher salaries in other occupations? Or those working in nonprofits to protect our environment or improve the lives of others? These people feel compensated in part by the inherent meaningfulness of what they are doing, but they are often undervalued and sometimes paid less than a livable wage.

For people like me who were born on third base, it is easy to see how I didn't do it alone. It is more complicated with the first-generation entrepreneurs I know. How do we unpack the various threads of individual temperament, social privilege, and luck in any of our lives? We can't deny that there are some individuals who seem to stick out for various reasons — some personal qualities, creativity, a spark. But weighing those qualities against other factors such as historical timing, social investments, or economic environments can prove daunting.

One of the best aspects of Malcolm Gladwell's book *Outliers: The Story of Success* is how he untangles the many factors that contribute to wealth and societally celebrate achievement. Gladwell writes, "We cling to the idea that success is a simple function of individual merit and that the world in which we all grow up and the rules we choose to write as a society don't matter at all." His stories and case studies point to hard work, but also the good fortune of timing. "To build a better world," he concludes, "we need to replace the patchwork of lucky breaks and arbitrary advantages today that determine success — the fortunate birth dates and the happy accidents of history — with a society that provides opportunities for all."[2]

US culture appears to have nailed the "individual" part of the equation. We see almost everything in terms of individual action, not society. Our business magazines, talk show interviews, and folklore are chock-full of modern-day Horatio Alger testimonials that start with the word *I*.

Perhaps this individual tilt is in the nature of the questions we ask: *Tell us, Mr. Welch, how did you lead General Electric from a $14 billion company to a diversified conglomerate with market capitalization of $410 billion? What were you thinking, Mr. Zuckerberg, when you launched Facebook? What personal qualities and character traits do you have that made this possible?*

It is no wonder that many wealthy people think they are so special and smart, given the way their stories are told. Imagine being surrounded by fawning exultation and people clinging to your every utterance, encouraging you to believe that it is all about you. This culture creates a dangerous threat to maintaining one's humility.

Seeing Commonwealth

It is difficult to tell a human-interest story about the invisible systems that make wealth creation possible, such as property laws or a regulated capital market system. It's hard to find the personal angle on the socially created and managed institutions that are responsible for mountains of individual private wealth. Or the pithy quotes to dramatize the impact of technological investments. What does common wealth look like?

When I talk to businesspeople like Charlie from Hillsborough, I try to strike this balance of celebrating the individual and honoring the sacrifices but also inviting people to see the remarkable common wealth around us.

"Congratulations, Charlie," I say. "Kudos to you for your hard work and dedication — and the successful enterprise you have built. I believe what you said about your sacrifices and long hours of work. And congrats that you have accumulated wealth over $5 million and that you even have to think about the estate tax.

"But Charlie, you didn't do it alone. You do business in a society that has fostered a remarkable fertile soil for wealth creation. This doesn't detract from what you said about hard work, but you are riding a wave – a wave of economic growth since World War II that the US government largely made possible through careful public investment. For over seven decades, our government has invested billions of dollars in research, infrastructure, technology that boost every business in this country. Together our tax dollars created a remarkable fertile ground for business development and wealth creation.

"So what you've done, Charlie, is certainly impressive and inspiring and should be celebrated and financially rewarded. But you wouldn't have anywhere near your current wealth without massive *public* investments in the economy.

"The estate tax is one of the fairest ways we pay for that. The people who have gotten the most benefit from it and made millions of dollars are asked to give back a percentage so that the next generation has a chance, not just those who inherit their parents' money."

But explaining how public investments in the economy boost private wealth like Charlie's doesn't always go over well in the partisan sound-bite culture of our current media. When President Obama talked about the role of public investments in creating a foundation for private enterprise during his 2012 campaign, his opposition isolated one quote, taken out of context, and featured it in an ad campaign depicting Obama as antibusiness.[3]

Inherited Wealth Meritocrats

There are a lot of people who were born on third base, like myself, but have recast themselves as meritocratic success stories. I fully understand the desire to obfuscate one's advantaged origins. Most of us don't want to go through life confessing we got a free ride or a massive head start. But people go through some unusual contortions to recast themselves as hardworking and deserving, especially if they want to get elected to office.[4]

Former President George W. Bush was born with a silver foot in his mouth, as Texas governor Ann Richards once so colorfully explained. In his campaigns for political office, he cast himself as a "successful businessman." Bush told reporters that his family name and connections may have opened up opportunities for him, but his business success was the consequence of "results and performance." Bush tapped family networks of wealthy investors to start an oil business. But his biggest wealth boost came from the taxpayers of Arlington, Texas, who paid for a baseball park for the Texas Rangers baseball team. Bush was lifted up by the other team owners to be the visible and principal owner of the team, because of the Bush family name. The city of Arlington donated land, offered tax breaks, and levied a property tax increase to pay for the stadium, a totally subsidy of $200 million. Bush invested $600,000 of his own money, eventually selling his stake in the team for $14.9 million. Bush prospered less by his own bootstraps than with help from wealthy family friends and taxpayer subsidies.[5]

Mitt Romney was the son of the CEO of American Motors and governor of Michigan. I used to see his dad, George Romney, jogging on the golf course near our family home. His family paid private school tuitions at Cranbrook School and Brigham Young University. In 2012, Romney told attendees at a high-donor event in Boca Raton, Florida, that he had "inherited nothing." "Everything that Ann and I have we earned the old-fashioned way, and that's by hard work," he said to applause.[6] But in reality, Romney was the beneficiary of inherited wealth. As Ann Romney explained to the *Boston Globe*, during one stretch in their family life together, "neither one of us had a job, because Mitt had enough of an investment from stock that we could sell off a little at a time." Ann Romney elaborated, "The stock came from Mitt's father."[7]

Romney did give due to our national commonwealth. He told the Boca Raton campaign audience that "frankly, I was born with a silver spoon, which is the greatest gift you could have, which is to get born in America. . . . 95 percent of life is set up for you if you're born in this country."

Donald Trump frequently tells his business success story, but he often omits the glide path to gold embodied in his life. His father, Fred Trump, was a successful and well-connected real estate developer in New York City. The elder Trump made a lot of his money building Federal Housing Administration (FHA)–financed new homes in Brooklyn. During World War II, he got the contract to build FHA housing for US naval personnel near major shipyards along the East Coast. Donald Trump not only inherited a real estate empire valued between $40 million and $200 million, but he also received family training, social networks, and financial connections.[8]

No one can alter the circumstances of their birth or the family they are born into. No one should judge another for something out of their control, whether they were born in a mansion or a public-housing tenement. But to selectively omit a privileged start or inherited wealth from one's personal biography is problematic, in part because it requires you to change other people's stories, too.

As author Gwendolyn Parker writes, "I wouldn't think less of Governor Bush, if he just admitted that he'd been lucky, certainly very lucky, and left it at that. But I worry about a Presidential candidate who feels compelled to reform luck and privilege into primarily the sweat of his own brow. I worry particularly about how many American lives he'll need to misinterpret so that he can continue to tell the story he likes to tell about himself."[9]

There are hundreds of people from wealthy families that gravitate toward business networks such as the Social Venture Network and Investors' Circle. It is often at their meetings that wealthy people meet business owners and provide investment capital to socially beneficial enterprises. Describing oneself as an entrepreneur has a mountain of social cachet compared with "I was born rich." In a quick maneuver I can shift from being "inheritor" to "venture capitalist."

There is, no doubt, individual effort involved in each individual circumstance, which is what validates and puts a spin cycle on one's narrative. But as Edgar Bronfman, heir to Seagram Company Ltd., the Canadian liquor giant, said, "To turn $100 into $110 is work. To turn $100 million into $110 million is inevitable."

Makers and Takers

One powerful example of this myth of deservedness in action is the "makers" versus "takers" narrative. In this explanation for US inequality, the virtuous "makers" are the hardworking job creators, the engines of the train, who also pay most of the taxes. And the "takers" are freeloaders, getting government handouts and not contributing.

My high school classmate Mitt Romney lost the 2012 Presidential election in part because he was caught by secret camera parroting this worldview at a

$50,000-a-plate donor event in Boca Raton, Florida.[10] "There are 47 percent of the people who will vote for the president [meaning Obama] no matter what," complained Romney. "They are victims, who believe the government has a responsibility to care for them . . . these are people who pay no income tax. . . . My job is not to worry about these people. I'll never convince them they should take personal responsibility and care for their lives."

Shortly after the videotape incident, Romney's 2012 running mate Paul Ryan told a conservative audience, "We're coming close to a tipping point in America where we might have a net majority of takers versus makers in society."[11]

There are loads of factual inaccuracies in these stories, including the tired canard that almost half of Americans pay no taxes.[12] But the important point here is the power of this narrative that smugly portrays the wealthy as virtuous makers, subsidizing the slothful takers. In the more caustic words of Ayn Rand, society is divided between the righteous "prime movers" against the "parasites" and freeloaders. The white racist mind casts these "takers" as brown and black people and freeloading immigrants.

One clue to shifting this dynamic comes from Paul Ryan's own change of heart and subsequent rejection of the "maker–taker" language. Ryan was home in his Janesville, Wisconsin, district, attending the Rock County 4-H Fair. He was chatting with people, shaking hands, when a man approached him with a question.

"Who, exactly, are the takers?" the man asked, as Ryan recounted in an article in the *Wall Street Journal*.[13]

"Excuse me?" Ryan replied.

"The makers and the takers," the man said. "I know who the makers are, but who are takers? Is it the person who lost a job and is on unemployment benefits? Is it the veteran who served in Iraq and gets medical care through the VA? When you talk about the takers, who exactly do you mean?"

Ryan had adopted the "makers and takers" language after reading a study by the Tax Foundation comparing the amount of government benefits people received compared with what they paid in taxes. The Tax Foundation labels the 60 percent of Americans who receive more benefits than they pay as "receivers." The other 40 percent are considered "givers."

Ryan confessed that the man's question at the fair was the first time he really heard how the phrase sounded. "Who was a taker?" Ryan wrote. "My mom, who is on Medicare? Me at 18 years old, using the Social Security survivors benefits we got after my father's death to go to college? My buddy who had been unemployed and used job-training benefits to get back on his feet? The phrase gave insult where none was intended."

Ryan is still an advocate of greatly reducing government spending and privatizing Social Security and Medicare. But he recognizes that splitting the world into "makers" and "takers" is bad politics and personally insensitive. Once real human stories enter the picture, the story falls apart. But the "makers" and "takers" labels live on, in the chatter on talk radio and in bar-stool debates. Part of their power is an abstract sense of "us" and "them," and a listener can fill in whoever they like in the "them" category.

This catchy narrative has punishing implications. It attaches a stigma of shame to those who need help, including the most vulnerable segments of our society — the young, the old, those with mental illness and disabilities. It stigmatizes people who ask for help or confess their real needs. And it discourages those celebrated as successful from confessing to help they get along the way.

The alternative is a "we did it together" story. Over our lifetimes, we all have needs and gifts to share. We are all dependent and interdependent. There is a fluidity of giving and receiving that cannot be reduced to a dehumanizing binary set of labels that flow from crude economic measurements.

— CHAPTER 5 —

In the Same Boat:
On the Road with Bill Gates

*No one accumulates a fortune without the help of our society's invest-
ments. How much wealth would exist without America's unique property rights protections, public infrastructure, and academic institutions? We should celebrate the estate tax as an "economic opportunity
recycling" program, where previous generations made investments for
us and now it's our turn to pass on the gift. Strengthening the estate
tax is important to our democracy.*

BILL GATES SR.

"**B**ill," I say. "You really should wear a hat."

"No thanks," he says, looking out the side window of our rented
Blazer at three-foot snowdrifts. It is a frigid January morning in Portland,
Maine. There is an inch of fresh snow and more on the way. Bill Gates Sr.
and I are driving to a breakfast program.

"It's like 15 degrees below zero with the windchill," I needle. "Let's stop
and get you a nice wool cap?" After being on the road for several weeks, I
still feel responsible if the big guy gets sick.

"No thanks," he says stubbornly. "It's not *that* cold."

We pull up to a hotel where 250 small-business owners crowd into a
sold-out morning breakfast discussion of the estate tax. Bill and I are the
featured speakers.

"Oh boy," Bill says as he bounds out of the car onto a sheet of ice. "This
is gonna be fun."

Defending the Estate Tax

During the first two months of 2003, I traveled with Bill Gates Sr., promoting our book, *Wealth and Our Commonwealth: Why America Should Tax Accumulated Fortunes*. With George W. Bush in the White House and Congress in GOP hands, there was another push to abolish the estate tax. Gates and I did press conferences, interviews, talk shows, and lectures in major cities, attracting audiences of six hundred and seven hundred people on some evenings. We recruited thousands of people for our campaign to preserve the estate tax.

Our first stop was Washington, DC, where several senators cohosted a private luncheon for George Soros, Bill, and me with fifteen US senators in the Capitol. After we made our case for preserving the estate tax, Senator Ted Kennedy's hand was the first to shoot up with a comment.

"Well, I agree," said the senator from Massachusetts. "I agree with all these points you make. That it would be fiscally irresponsible to cut the tax. And it would be a terrible blow to charitable giving. But I don't really understand your last point." The senator beamed impishly. "What do you mean about the *dangers of hereditary wealth and power*?" All the senators roared with laughter.

Bill — a retired attorney whose son frequently tops the list of the world's wealthiest — is great with people. All along our tour, he listened patiently to all kinds of questions — and graciously fended off two dozen grant requests a night. "I am not here on foundation business," this co-chair of the Bill and Melinda Gates Foundation would carefully explain. He gave out stacks of his business card, with his own personal email.

One night, after an estate tax program at the historic Society for Ethical Culture in New York City, I noticed Bill was absent from the reception. I found him alone in the cavernous lecture hall engaged in a conversation with a woman. Most of the lights had been extinguished except a single spotlight, aimed at the stage, that framed them in brilliant light.

The woman was wearing a long black coat and a green wool cap, her tangled long gray-black hair flowing from under it. She was wide-eyed and her arms fluttered up and down like a bird flying in slow motion. "Oh no," I thought to myself. "She's not stable, alone with Bill." His Seattle staff had asked me politely to protect him from potentially dangerous people — and later, after several death threats, an undercover security person began attending some of our events.

Bill hunched toward her, straining to hear her words. His hands were pressed down on the stage, his long legs dangling over the edge.

"Which one do you want?" the woman asked, her unblinking gaze fixed on Bill. In her gyrating hands she held snapshots: photographs of a cornice of an office building, a fragment of a doorway, a broken park bench. Every picture was out of focus. "You can have whichever one you want as a gift."

"Excuse me, ma'am," I said firmly. "Mr. Gates has to leave now."

"Which do you like?" she asked, ignoring me. "How about this one?" She thrust a photo of a gray concrete wall into Bill's hands. He gazed at it quizzically, tipping his head from one side to another.

"Okay, Bill, time to go." I gently tugged at his arm, and he slowly slid off the stage, standing up to his full six and a half feet.

"Okay," he said. He leaned toward the woman. "I'll take this one." He held up his selection, a wavy snapshot of the corner of a building against the sky. "Thank you very much."

We turned and walked to the exit. I looked back to see her laying out her pictures on the stage, as if setting up for an exhibition.

"She wanted to give me a gift," Bill said, his face breaking into a smile. "How could I refuse?"

Pleading Clemency for the Death Tax

In Portland, Maine, I give the warm-up talk at our business breakfast. In the previous three weeks, I have given this talk twenty times, explaining the myths surrounding the estate tax and the costs and political context of it. My role is to enlist people who come to our events to join our campaign. But this morning is different. Many of the people in the audience are business owners with GOP lapel pins, and they would probably have been happy to see the estate tax get axed.

When it is Bill's turn to talk, he starts with a story. "A name like mine can get you into trouble," Bill says, squinting at the audience. "My daughter Libby went into a ski store to buy a set of skis for herself and her two children. When she went to pay with a credit card, the guy in the store saw her middle name was Gates. 'Are you related to *him*?' the ski salesman asked.

Libby was in no mood to discuss her famous brother. 'No,' she said. 'I didn't think so,' said the salesman. 'You'd have bought better skis.'"

The room bursts into guffaws, and Bill chuckles with them. Then he looks down at his notes, shakes his head, and looks up at them with a grimly serious face.

"Many of you probably want to get rid of the estate tax — or what you might call the death tax," he says, and the room is silent. A few people shift in their seats and put down their coffee cups. "But before we lead it to the gallows, I'd like to make one more case for clemency."

I have a prime seat next to Bill, and I study the audience and the expressions on people's faces. The listeners are evenly split between men and women, most dressed in business suits and dresses. Their eyes are riveted on the father of Microsoft's founder.

"Why should someone who has $10 million, $50 million, or $50 billion pay an estate tax?" he asks and then smiles broadly. "Actually, I know only one person with $50 billion." The audience titters again, with this reference to his successful son.

"If you have accumulated tens of millions, hundreds of millions, or billions, you did *not* do it alone. You got help.

"Of course, this is not to take away anything from that person. Those of you in business know what it takes. These are probably hardworking and creative people who have made sacrifices. They deserve some reward for their leadership or entrepreneurship. But they didn't get there alone.

"Where would they be without this fantastic economic system that we have built together? Where would they be without public investments in infrastructure? Roads? Communication? Our system of property rights — and the legal system to enforce them? How much wealth would they have without the public investment in new technology? These advances have made us all more prosperous, whether we are software designers, restaurant owners, or neighborhood real estate agents.

"Who is the greatest venture capitalist in the world today?" Bill stops and repeats his question. He rocks back on his shoes and looks at the audience over the rim of his glasses. They are rapt.

"No, he's not one of those angel investors who live on Sand Hill Road down from Stanford University. The greatest venture capitalist is Uncle Sam." He repeats: "Uncle Sam.

"Has your business become more productive thanks to these public investments? You bet it has." Bill describes the early government investments in technology that led to the creation of the Internet and World Wide Web. He talks about jet engines, publicly funded university research, and the human genome.

"Where would we be without the fertile ground we have plowed together? Would we be as wealthy and successful if we had to toil in different soil?" Outside the window, the sky is darkening, and the snowfall is intensifying, but no one is slipping away to avoid driving at the height of the storm.

"I recently was in Nigeria. Jimmy Carter and I met with African leaders seeking an end to the AIDS crisis." He describes his recent trip. Most people in attendance have probably seen the widely published newspaper photographs of Bill cradling an infant with AIDS in his large arms.

"I was deeply impressed by the spirit and resourcefulness of the people I met. But the infrastructure and conditions for business are quite different in Abuja than here in Portland, Maine. Take your sweat and talents and try and grow a business in Abuja or Kinshasa. Many years later, you will still be toiling with little to show.

"Most of us benefit from society's investments. And those who have accumulated $10 million or $10 billion have *disproportionately* benefited from them. I believe it is fair to have an estate tax that captures a third of that wealth when it transfers to the next generation. It is a reasonable levy for the privilege of growing such wealth in our society."

I have heard Bill speak some of these words before, but today he seems to be drawing on a deeper well. His hand trembles slightly as he takes a drink of water.

"The estate tax is an appropriate mechanism for a wealthy person to pay back society, a means of expressing gratitude for the amazing opportunities that we have. *Gratitude* — there's a word largely absent from our business publications. We live in a marvelous system with abundant commonwealth, yet we don't see it around us. We inherit some of it from those who came before us."

I look across the audience. People's faces have softened. Several women are silently weeping, and a few men dab tears from their eyes. What is going on here?

"A woman came up to me after a talk in California." Bill shifts his voice into a conversational tone. "She said, 'Mr. Gates, what I hear you saying is that we are all in the same boat.'

"Yes, we are all in the same boat. We won't get very far if we leave people behind. No one achieves wealth alone. If you meet someone who tells you they are self-made, invite them to try and grow wealth while living on an island. Our wealth is only as good as the commonwealth and societal investments around us.

"I'd like to close with a parable. I hope no one is offended by this image of our maker. Imagine that God is sitting in *her* office."

Everyone laughs, and several of the women applaud and cheer.

"She is agitated, fretting really. It appears that the treasury of heaven has been depleted. It was probably overly invested in technology stocks." More laughter.

"Suddenly she realizes a solution. She summons before her the next two beings about to be born on Earth. She explains to these two spirits that one of them will be born in the United States and the other will be born in an impoverished nation in the global south. Her scheme for raising revenue is to auction off the privilege of being born in the United States."

People have eager smiles on their faces. Still, no one is concerned about the steady snowstorm that is burying their cars in the parking lot. They are Mainers, after all, confident in their municipal snowplows.

"Of course, God is not a nationalist, nor a believer in cultural superiority. But she recognizes that the United States has an advanced infrastructure of public health, stability, education, and market mechanisms that enhance opportunity. She understands that some humans might consider it a privilege or advantage to be born in such a society. The spirits are instructed to write the percentage of their net worth they pledge to God's treasury on the day they die. Whoever offers the highest percentage will have the good fortune to be born in the United States."

Bill looks calmly at the audience. "Okay, I want you to write on a piece of paper the percentage of *your* net worth that you will yield on the day you die. What is it worth to *you* to do business in the United States?" He pauses to give people a moment to jot down a number.

"We'll do a poll. How many of you wrote 25 percent?" He looks around, beaming with delight. "No one.

"How about 50 percent?" Again, no hands in the air. "That's more than an estate tax, which has an effective rate of 30 percent.

"How about 75 percent?" Three hands shoot up. "Okay, we have a few takers.

"And how about 100 percent!" Every remaining hand in the room goes up, with several bolted straight up like the confident kids in the class. More people wipe tears from their eyes and blow their noses.

"One hundred percent. What is it worth to you to do business is in this remarkable society? What is it worth to be an American?"

Bill sits down. There is a brief shocked pause, then people bolt up from their chairs with applause. Several listeners lunge forward to shake Bill's hand or touch his arm.

I marvel at the emotional temperature in the room. What did Bill say that moved these people? Was it the spiritual truth of "we are all one body," or "we are nothing without each other?" Was it a refreshing alternative to the "great achieving men of business" story that they usually hear? Was it Bill as the messenger?

Whatever it was, Bill had touched something in these people, some universal truth of our interconnectedness. He had tapped into a basic sense of goodness and fair play. Perhaps for the first time, they had recognized the help that all of us receive.

——◇——

"Bill, I had about twenty people come up to me and say they were Republicans and agree with us now." We are back in the car, driving to a radio station. I have collected about fifty business cards — along with pledges to call the two senators from Maine, two swing votes in our campaign to preserve the estate tax.

"Yeah, we got some converts," says Bill.

"Bill, your comments about 'No one does it alone' — I would keep doing that. All your examples about society's investments were great." If people could understand that concept, then you could have a sober conversation with them about taxes.

"That seemed to strike a chord," he agrees. He looks straight ahead, grinning and jingling the coins in his pant pocket. "Golly, this is the most fun I've had in years."

PART III

UNDERSTANDING ADVANTAGE

You're not under attack when others gain rights and privileges you've always had.

DR. DaShanne Stokes

— CHAPTER 6 —

The Privilege Drug

Privilege is driving a smooth road and not even knowing it.

AMPERSAND[1]

It is a bright sunny June morning and I am in bliss. I'm on a solo bicycle ride on the Cape Cod Rail Trail, a paved path that runs down the center of the Cape's grassy sand dunes and around freshwater kettle ponds.

As I pass the 10-mile marker, I feel great. I am pleased with my speed and how physically strong I feel. "I'm in better shape than I thought," I think to myself.

I decide to press on farther than I originally planned. I'm clipping along at over 25 mph. The mile markers shoot by, and I pedal on for another 10 miles. After the 20-mile mark, I stop for a granola bar and look at my phone for the time. It's time to head back to the campground. I turn around and start my return journey.

Suddenly, I'm hit with a headwind.

After 2 miles riding north, I feel depleted. I stop for a drink of water and look at my map. Eighteen miles to go. Damn this headwind! When did it start?

I realize that the subtle wind has probably been constant, but that I hadn't noticed it before. On the first part of my ride, the wind was at my back and I was oblivious. Now that it's in my face I can't ignore it. After another 2 miles riding into the wind, I'm exhausted. I've been riding about 10 mph. I dial my cell phone to see if anyone in my group might be willing to pick me up in a car.

Lying in the grass, waiting for a ride, I laugh at myself, and at this apt metaphor for privilege. Privilege is like a wind at my back, propelling me forward. Of course, I'm pedaling so I can claim some credit for my forward motion. But the wind makes an enormous difference. And here I thought it was all about me!

The Wind at My Back

Even after explaining how we together as a society build a fertile ground for wealth creation, some people still come back and ask, "Hey, anyone could have done what I did. So how come they didn't?" In other words, doesn't everyone have equal access to the same societal investments? Isn't it only a few motivated people who actually do something with them?

Once again, there is a reason to celebrate individual initiative. But often this question is clouded by confusion over privilege. Not everyone has the same access to the societal resources that make wealth creation possible. Nor do we all share the same sense of agency in relation to making things happen.

People who are privileged in our society, for a variety of reasons, don't see the wind at their own back, nor do they see the headwinds that other people encounter.

If you're like me, judgments toward others run through your head all the time. Why don't you work harder? Why don't you exercise? Why don't you eat better food? In these hasty judgments, I often forget all the significant privileges that have come my way. From healthy food and suburban open space to enrichment experiences, I had a mammoth boost long before kindergarten. But like most people in my circumstances I sometimes forget I was born on third base. It is easy to think I got here on my own.

Sociologists talk about the "intergenerational transmission of advantage," the ways that affluent parents give their children a head start in school readiness, college admission, and professional work opportunities. I was fortunate to have been given both substantive privileges — small classrooms in school, private tutors, summer recreation classes, quality health and dental care, on and on. There are thousands of ways that race and class privilege have shown up in my early life, providing an invisible wind at my back.

Works Project Administration for Affluent Kids

In my affluent hometown of Bloomfield Hills, Michigan, there were a lot of unskilled work opportunities for young men and plenty of money to pay us. It was a veritable "Teenage Works Project Administration" of mowing grass, clipping hedges, sweeping tennis courts, painting sheds, planting flowers, moving stuff, cleaning pools, walking dogs, pulling weeds, clearing brush, shoveling walks, raking leaves, hauling give-away junk. There were retired adults with huge properties and seemingly nothing to do but organize projects for young workers. Girls had ample babysitting jobs and took kids to the country club, slathering them with suntan lotion, and making sure they didn't drown.

Because these were neighbors hiring neighbors' kids, the adults often offered friendly coaching to one another's teenagers in their first work experiences. One summer, my father hired the daughter of a close family friend to work in his front office. And my dad's friend reciprocated by hiring me to do a series of summer odd jobs including painting a barn, landscaping, and helping him train a hunting dog. For an hour every day, I'd take a break from other projects and stand out in a field throwing live birds, their wings clipped, into the air. The dogs were trained to retrieve them. Both of us teenagers learned basic jobs skills: punctuality, clear communication about tasks, working steadily without interruption, and negotiating money.

My supervisors were friendly, caring adults who knew my family. But they also created a different accountability dynamic than working for one's parents. This gave me a tremendous head start when I got a job as a golf caddy or started my own landscaping business and starting mowing lawns, and applied for other jobs. These neighborhood opportunities, all before the age of 16, paved the path to adulthood and the world of work.

By contrast, in my neighborhood in urban Boston, there are far fewer opportunities for younger men and women. Most adults are Do It Yourself, saving money by doing their own chores and snow shoveling. And most jobs in restaurants, fast food, and retail appear to be occupied by older adults. There is a youth summer jobs program, but it only employs a fraction of the teenagers eligible for work. Nationwide, as the labor market tightened over the last decade, young people were the biggest losers. Teenagers between the ages of 16 and 19 experienced the largest plummet in employment rates, which declined from 45 percent in 2000 to 26 percent in 2011, the lowest teen employment rate since the post–World War II era.[2] And the opportunities for urban youth of color are even more diminished.

In addition to work skills preparation, I was also coached to have a sense of agency, a belief that I could make a difference, whether it was organizing a fair or passing out homemade leaflets on Earth Day. In elementary school I had a committed science teacher who instilled in me an early environmental sensibility. She exhorted us to be engaged, to be doers.

These advantages for privileged teens seem to accelerate. Whereas the disadvantages for other youth seem to compound, especially when we mix in unequal encounters with the criminal justice system. For many privileged people, these hidden advantages are ascribed to growing up in communities with so-called better values. This sows the notion that "if only these other people were more like us" they, too, would prosper. We don't see the wind at our back.

Seeing privilege is hard, and it is by no means just a challenge for the very wealthy. Class and race privilege is a disconnection drug; it anesthetizes people and allows us to disconnect from one another. It numbs us to other people's suffering. It buffers and bubble-wraps us and emotionally distances us from the cries of those around us. It causes amnesia when it comes to seeing the gifts we've received. Something in US culture makes it embarrassing to admit advantage, a head start, or event direct government subsidies.

— CHAPTER 7 —

The Greatest
Subsidized Generation

*My glorification of independence and individualism made me an
easy target for the myth of meritocracy, and overshadowed in my
heart what I knew to be true; the deep interconnectedness I longed for
with family, friends, colleagues, and even strangers is core to human
survival. Interdependence is our lifeblood.*

DEBBY IRVING

"Good morning, gentlemen," I say, greeting a table of six men at the
VFW hall in Norwood, Massachusetts, a suburb of Boston.

The room is buzzing with 150 or so men talking and sipping coffee at
round folding tables. I don't know a soul.

An acquaintance has asked me to talk to the Norwood Retired Men's
Club about my work on wealth inequality and taxing the wealthy. I enjoy
doing these programs and hearing what people from all walks of life have to
say. But my usual circuit is unions, churches, and progressive-minded civic
groups. I am nervous about speaking to a group of suburban white men
over 65. I have my notes in hand, but I am prepared to ad lib if necessary.

"You must be our speaker this morning," says a man with dark-brown
eyes and tufts of gray hair sticking out from under a cap that reads *U.S.S.
Washington*, a World War II battleship. I am easily 25 years younger than any
of the men present, so he must have surmised I wasn't a prospective member.

"I'm Phillip," he says, patting the seat next to him. "Set yourself down."
Phillip looks like a slimmer version of a handsome Sean Connery with a

cane. All of the men introduce themselves, and Phillip pours me a cup of coal-black coffee from a carafe on the table.

"So you're gonna talk about rich and poor?" He grins.

"Yes, sir," I say cautiously.

"See Lonny there." Phillip points a thin long finger to a balding man with a bow tie and hearing aid who sits across the table. "He's the super-rich guy here. He owns half of Norwood. He's the one to blame!" Everyone at the table laughs, especially Lonny.

"You know that movie with Jimmy Stewart, *It's a Wonderful Life*?" Phillip continues.

"Of course," I reply.

"He's Mr. Potter," quips Phillip. "He wants this to be Pottersville. He's squeezing us all by the balls!"

"Yikes," I say, smiling at Lonny. "Who's George Bailey?"

"All the rest of us," says another man, and everyone nods good-naturedly.

The chairman calls the meeting to order. Hats came off and everyone stands for the Pledge of Allegiance except the disabled men, some in wheelchairs. The treasurer reports $254 in the bank and, before I know it, I am being introduced as the author of *99 to 1: How Wealth Inequality Is Wrecking the World and What We Can Do About It*.

As I look over the room, I'm reminded of how my father periodically took me to the 10 a.m. *kaffeeklatsch* at the firehouse when I visited him in the small Northern Michigan town of Leland. I enjoyed the banter, complaints, cornball humor, and easy friendliness — but I always knew better than to talk about politics.

"J. Paul Getty, the oil company founder, once said it's not that hard to become rich," I begin. "You just have to do three things. First, get up early every day." I look out at audience. "How many of you got up early this morning?"

All the men raise their hands.

"Only 'cause it was trash day," says one fellow.

"Second thing, according to Getty, you have to work hard all day. I know you guys work hard, even in retirement, right?"

Most of the men raise their hands.

"Mostly under the table," quipped one of the class clowns.

"The third key to great wealth, according to J. Paul Getty, is to FIND OIL."

The group hoots.

For the next half hour, I talk about the growing polarization of wealth and income and its significance for their children's and grandchildren's generations. With stagnant or falling wages, many families and individuals have to work longer hours, take on additional debt, and spend less time with family. Add to this job insecurity, and the middle-class standard of living is imploding.

"I have some personal questions for you," I say, suddenly inspired to query the group. "How many of you bought a house after World War II, thanks to a low-interest mortgage program?" I ask. "Like a mortgage subsidy or insurance from the Federal Housing Administration, Veterans Administration, or Farmers Home Administration?"

About three-fourths of the men in the room raise their hands.

"I'd still be renting without that," says one fellow in a wheelchair.

"How many of you graduated from college without any debt, thanks to the GI Bill or another federal education grant program?"

Three-fourths of the men raise their hands.

"How many of you gentlemen," I continue, "received public support to help your business — a Small Business Administration grant or loan, a block grant for a building, government funds to train employees, or for something else?"

More than one-fourth indicate they got such help.

"So how many of you think those government programs were a waste of taxpayer money?"

A few chuckles but no hands go up. "A *helluva* good investment," shouts one guy from the back of the room.

"It was the Marshall Plan for America," says another guy, referring to the aid program that rebuilt war-ravaged Europe after World War II.

"Saved my life," says another man wearing a green vest with a veteran's insignia.

"It was a *great* investment," I say passionately. In the decades after World War II, our country made an unprecedented outlay to expand our middle classes, enabling millions of families to achieve the American Dream.

The Magic Carpet to the Middle Class

The GI Bill of Rights of 1944 gave returning World War II servicemen and -women scholarships for education and training; loan guarantees for homes, farms, or businesses; unemployment pay for a year; and job training assistance. The United States has aspired to take care of its veterans, especially disabled soldiers and widows. But we continue to fall short generation after generation. The post–World War II benefit package exceeded anything before or since in generosity.

Congressional advocates of the GI Bill, many of whom were World War I veterans, were well aware of the societal and family upheaval caused when soldiers returned to massive unemployment, economic hardship, and inadequate pensions. In 1932, an estimated seventeen thousand World War I veterans protested their impoverishment in the streets of Washington in the "Bonus Marches."[1]

Demobilized, unemployed, and destitute soldiers have been a restless force in history, from post–World War I Germany to contemporary Iraq with the US government's disastrous decision to disband the Iraqi military after 2004, sowing the seeds of the Islamic State.[2] Farsighted planners think ahead to the years after war. The GI Bill's education benefits both boosted the skills of millions of World War II veterans and staggered their absorption into the workforce after the war.

But the GI Bill almost didn't pass. Conservatives in Congress argued it was too costly and would promote sloth among veterans. Elite colleges and universities warned it would lower standards in education. Harvard president James Conant said the bill would encourage "the least capable among the war generation, instead of the most capable, flooding the facilities for advanced education in the United States."[3] University of Chicago president Robert Hutchins feared that "colleges and universities will find themselves converted into educational hobo jungles."[4] Final passage of the bill narrowly squeaked through Congress and was signed by Franklin Roosevelt in June 1944, thanks largely to a well-organized campaign led by the American Legion.

"Do people talk about the programs after World War II?" I ask the men in Norwood. "Are your children aware of the impact the GI Bill and other education and housing benefits had for them back when they were growing up, and even now?"

"No," says the chairman of the meeting. "No one seems to know."

"The GI Bill was a remarkable program," I say, glancing at my notes for some numbers. "Between 1945 and 1955, more than 7.8 million returning veterans received debt-free college or vocational educations.[5] During the same period, 4.3 million veterans purchased homes. By the end of the 1950s, eleven million new homes were financed with Veterans Administration loans. Veterans received millions for small-business ventures. And veterans facing unemployment could get $20 a week for up to a year."

"We called that the 20/52 unemployment plan," shouts one youthful-looking retiree. Others laugh and murmur recollection. "That was a lot of money back then to me."

"How many of you served in the military?" I ask.

Two-thirds raise their hands.

"The rest of you got help that wasn't tied to military service." Government-subsidized mortgages provided over thirty-five million Americans with tickets on the wealth-building train after the war, whether they were veterans or not.[6]

"Between 1940 and 1960, the percentage of Americans owning their homes rose from 44 percent to 62 percent.[7] Fully one-fifth of the population moved from tenancy to ownership — a seismic demographic shift in one generation. That's incredible."

These programs were no waste of taxpayer money. World War II historian Stephen Ambrose, writing in the 1990s, called it the "best piece of legislation ever passed by the US Congress."[8] Instead of diminishing educational standards, returning veterans were "hogging the honor rolls," according to one 1947 account in the *New York Times*.[9] A 1986 government study showed that every $1 invested in the GI Bill yielded $5 to $12 in tax revenues.[10] Some famous recipients included Harry Belafonte, David Brinkley, Art Buchwald, William Rehnquist, Johnny Carson, Paul Newman, Joseph Heller, and Bill Gates Sr.

Even so, the GI Bill and mortgage-assistance programs were not the only publicly funded efforts laying the foundation for postwar prosperity. In 1947 an unprecedented infrastructure project, constructing 37,000 miles of highways, got under way. In 1956, the Interstate Highway Act funded the construction of an additional 42,500 miles. These initiatives created millions of jobs and opened up rural land for suburban residential construction. Public works spending in 1950 at all levels of government accounted for nearly 20 percent of total expenditures — a tremendous shot in the arm for economic expansion.[11]

Other social supports came through the problematic but profitable military-industrial doorway. Billions of taxpayer dollars were invested in research, thanks in part to Cold War "Sputnik" anxieties that the Soviet Union was going to surpass the United States technologically. The National Defense Education Act reworked scientific education, providing subsidies to US industry and higher education. According to one account of the period, "more than $50 billion of government-funded wartime inventions and production processes were turned over to private companies after the war, creating whole new fields of employment."[12]

But in this room of veterans, I didn't even need to elaborate on these extras.

Intergenerational Help

"How many of you are helping your children purchase a home or start a business through what I call the Parental Down Payment Assistance Program — you know, money for the kids?"

"That's all I do," shouts one man.

"I'm the grandpa ATM," says another.

Almost every hand goes up. The room buzzes with side conversations. They are all helping their kids and grandchildren.

Here is living proof that our country's commitment to wealth building for a sizable group within one generation — World War II veterans and their peers — had immeasurable benefits over multiple generations.

"So," I ask above the conversations, "How many of your children and grandchildren think of themselves as second-generation beneficiaries of government subsidies?" I know this will be controversial. "I mean, you're all helping your kids, right?"

"It's the only way they could stay in Norwood," says one man in a veteran's beret.

"This form of help, those *subsidies*, were expensive," I say. The first GI Bill — characterized as "the magic carpet to the middle class" — cost $14.5 billion at a time when $500 could pay a year of tuition at Harvard. But the magic was paid for by a very progressive federal tax system. In 1953, under the presidency of Republican Dwight Eisenhower, the top income tax rate on the wealthy was 92 percent on income over $400,000, roughly $3.5 million in today's dollars.[13] Today, the top tax rate is 39.6 percent. In 1953, the corporate income tax rate was 52 percent, compared with a 35 percent rate today (and, for *Fortune* 500 companies, an average effective rate under 20 percent, thanks to loopholes).[14]

The post–World War II tax system put a brake on the buildup of concentrated wealth and power — but also raised revenue to pay for an unprecedented wealth expansion program. The only comparable event in US history is the Homestead Act of 1862, which allocated over 10 percent of the country's land to over a million new residents.

I reach the point I am most nervous about — the racial dimensions of this issue. It is one thing to talk about the plight of the middle class; it's another matter altogether to discuss the racial dimensions of inequality. I anticipate some defensiveness to my point that not all the advantages we white people have enjoyed have been the result of merit.

I take a breath and plow ahead. "Part of the story we don't talk about is that these government wealth-building programs went overwhelmingly to white men. African American and Latino war veterans returned after World War II to Jim Crow laws and segregated education systems in most parts of the United States. They couldn't take advantage of the housing programs some of you did because mortgage lending practices and local attitudes still discriminated against people of color."[15]

"Aw come on," says one man, half rising from his chair. "Let's not do the white guilt thing."

"Shut up and let the man talk," replies a firm voice from the back of the room. Others murmur in assent.

"To me it is not about guilt. I have no doubt that the veterans who received government support deserved it. What I want to talk to you about is recognizing our obligation, in turn, to help those who were excluded from the magic carpet ride."

I explain that the current homeownership rate for whites is 72 percent, for African Americans 43 percent, and for Latinos 45 percent. "If people were barred from getting on the wealth-building train a generation ago, it has an impact on the next generation's prospects."

If there were ever a barometer of middle-class well-being, it would be the homeownership rate. The national homeownership rate peaked in 2005 at 69.1 and since then has been in steady decline. By the end of 2014, it had fallen to 64.4.[16]

I can't tell if this makes an impression on the veterans or whether politeness has won out. When it comes to discussions of race, the mythology of deservedness takes some twists and turns. This is probably not the place to spell out a program of reparations for slavery, I think to myself, and my commentary retreats to the safe ground of a universal solution for reducing wealth disparities.

I conclude the program by talking about another big idea, a campaign to expand the estate tax and bring back programs that broaden wealth rather than consolidate it for a tiny percentage of people.

"There is no reason we can't do it again," I say and stop.

Subsidy Is a Dirty Word

"Sit down here again, young man," says Phillip. He is sitting with a cane between his legs. I pull up a folding chair. The meeting is over, and most of the men are filing toward the exit doors.

"I liked your presentation," he says. "This rich–poor gap is terrible. I was in the South Pacific in the navy, and I got the GI Bill you were talking about. I went to Worcester Polytechnic after the war — and bought a house with a VA mortgage right here in Norwood." Phillip described his several decades of work at Raytheon Company as an optical engineer. He is one of the "greatest generation" that Tom Brokaw wrote about in several books — men and women who grew up knowing hunger and want during the Depression, fought World War II, and built the modern nation. I wonder if Phillip had experienced such hardships.

"I have one objection to what you said," Phillip says cautiously as he taps his cane on the floor. "You used the word *subsidy* to describe those benefits."

"When I say subsidy," I explain to Phillip, "I just mean 'help' — people and society helping each other."

"*Subsidy* is kind of a dirty word," says Phillip softly.

"Why?" I ask with genuine curiosity.

"It sounds like you don't deserve it, like a handout."

"I meant no disrespect by it," I say, wondering how many other listeners in the room had also bristled at the word. "I think it's great that veterans got those benefits. It was the least our society could do to pay back veterans."

"No," says Phillip gently. "You don't understand. I didn't expect any more than my combat pay. I was just doing my duty, my service to my country.

The VA mortgage, the scholarship to Polytechnic, it was an amazing bonus. And it made *all* the difference."

Phillip pauses, looks around the empty room, and says in a slightly embarrassed voice, "I don't mean to keep you."

"No, not at all," I say, leaning back in the chair. I know from talking to World War II and Korean War veterans that they have a deep sense of sacrifice and duty. I feel spoiled and embarrassed when I'm around them. The only sacrifices my country has asked of me are to pay my taxes and do jury duty every three years. There really is a generation gap — not just between me and Phillip, but even between Phillip and the countless men and women who've served the country in more recent times. Without a military draft, those who do military service are a smaller segment of society, disproportionately brown and black and rural and poor. And the social supports that exist for them have seemingly diminished.

The America that this greatest generation grew up with has disappeared, in many ways. There are still plenty of people who make sacrifices. Conspicuously AWOL are the affluent.

"You know what's funny?" Phillip says. "When you asked who got a free education, government housing help, business loans, there were guys here in the room that got all three of those but didn't raise their hands."

"Why do you think that was?"

"I don't know. Privacy maybe. Hell, guys our age like to think we did it all alone. We're ashamed to admit we got any help."

Did it alone. There's that myth of individual achievement again.

"There is no shame in getting help," I say. "No one does it alone."

"Yep," says Phillip. "That's the *dirty* little secret."

None of us like to think of ourselves as subsidized. For Phillip and his cohort it was a bonus. For their children, it was a family gift. Yet few in my generation make the link to the government programs that made it all happen.

Telling True Stories

This is what I propose: A GI Bill for the next generation is the best way to honor the families that serve their country, in the military or in other ways. This time it should be a universal benefit, providing a debt-free college education and first-time home-buying assistance for the next generation of teachers and nurses, firefighters and scientists, as well as veterans — without racial or other kinds of discrimination. Young people who complete military or national service should have access to education and wealth-building opportunities, and we can pay for those opportunities by retaining the federal estate tax and dedicating its revenue to programs that provide them.

It will never happen, however, without a better rearview understanding of how we got here, particularly from the beneficiaries themselves. And it requires an admission that good fortune is never all one's own doing, that government help of some kind is almost always a factor in the equation.

GI Bill recipients need to step forward and testify to the boost they got. Where is the GI Bill Alumni Association, lobbying for educational opportunity for today's veterans and their generation?

The children and grandchildren of GI Bill recipients must also acknowledge the benefits their families received, thanks to the education, housing, and small-business investment benefiting their parents and communities.

The first step in repairing the racial wealth divide is to understand the impact of excluding people from programs like the GI Bill. The historian Ira Katznelson notes in *When Affirmative Action Was White* how the racially discriminatory ways these benefits were applied worsened the racial wealth divide. Many black veterans returned to communities divided by Jim Crow laws or culture, with "separate and unequal" or nonexistent higher education opportunities. And federally subsidized mortgage programs were notoriously discriminatory.

Like a lot of people, I grew up with a wind at my back, a bundle of advantages. Many of us who were not in the military also benefited from direct and indirect government subsidies, such as programs to help first-time home buyers, debt-free college educations, small-business loans, and more. These subsidies propelled millions of household into the middle and even upper classes.

It is fascinating to me how people won't even see the most obvious subsidies, such as direct government grants and low-interest loans.

Phillip is right. The dirty little secret is we are a nation of subsidy recipients. But we don't admit it. Worse, we take our subsidies, forget about or deny them, and too often ignore or even turn against others who need the same kind of help we got.

We look at *our* subsidy as deserved. But the other person's subsidy is "welfare" or "wasteful" or a "handout." My own middle-class subsidy, the home mortgage interest deduction, is hardwired into the tax code. But year after year congressional budget committees scrutinize and cut poor people's rental assistance housing subsidies, investigating and shaming the recipients.

As a result, we have some rather odd scenes in the United States. We have corporate chieftains who deduct their corporate perks and pocket our corporate tax subsidies, with no strings attached, all the while downsizing their payroll, and then pointing their fingers at the unemployed or single parents for being "on the dole."

Farmers and ranchers whose businesses are floated with $20 billion in annual taxpayer subsidies lean on their tractors and lecture others about the virtues of hard work and small government.[17]

We have states such as Indiana, North Dakota, and Louisiana, where residents get back twice as much in spending and government subsidies per capita as they send in federal tax dollars (South Carolina gets back almost eight times what they send). Yet they send politicians to Washington to shrink the federal government and shift responsibility to the states. Other states, such as New York, Minnesota, and Illinois, get back considerably less of what they pay in federal taxes yet routinely elect congressional members that support strong federal spending and shared responsibility across states.[18]

A Nation of Subsidy Recipients

During my work to preserve the estate tax, I would sometimes be pitted against farmers who were being used as poster people for the campaign to eliminate the "death tax." Since the estate tax is only paid by households with wealth over $10.8 million, very few farmers are actually subject to the tax. It is mostly paid by wealthy people with appreciated financial wealth. If someone's primary wealth is tied up in productive farm assets, there are pages of special provisions to protect them and minimize or delay the tax. But that doesn't stop anti-estate-tax lobbyists from trotting out farmers, some of whom ironically are huge recipients of government subsidies.

In 2014, conservative election groups ran $1.8 million in advertising in defense of incumbent Senator Mitch McConnell. The ad features farmer John Mahan of Bourbon, Kentucky, saying "Mitch McConnell has been fighting to end the death tax to help us keep our Kentucky family farms. For our family farms to survive, we've got to get in this fight." What the ad fails to disclose is that Mahan is the sixteenth biggest recipient of farm subsidies in his part of Kentucky, cashing $138,310 in checks between 1995 and 2012. If you get generations of farm subsidies — and you've got over $10 million in wealth upon your death — do you owe anything back to the government?

We have workers whose employers accept "tax incentives" — essentially bribes to keep their jobs in their communities — but then bellyache about pork barrel spending.

At our worst, we engage in collective dishonesty. We moan about our tax burden and government waste without admitting that most of what government spends money on is *us*: our roads, public safety, schools, health care and medicine for our elders, retirement security, military defense, fire protections, stock market oversight, transit systems, and national parks. A large part of our federal budget goes to pay massive interest payments on the federal debt, since we aren't willing to pay as we go.

I see this in my own family. For over a decade, my brother required mental health services in Michigan — counseling, medication, and residential hospitalization on a couple of occasions. At one point, my father joined me for a meeting with Rita, my brother's overworked social worker in Flint, Michigan. He was genuinely moved by her skill and commitment. A few hours later, we were having a political conversation about his support for an antitax initiative in Michigan.

"Dad, who do you think pays Rita's salary?" I asked. "All those budget cuts have already doubled her workload."

He sat quietly for a couple of moments and then said, "I hadn't really thought about that." And my father is a thoughtful and compassionate person.

We say we want government to "leave us alone," but we expect it to bail us out when we get into trouble. We want to "starve the beast," but if a disaster hits our country, we want our government to rapidly come to the rescue.

We don't bother to learn how our tax dollars are actually used. We would rather point to any simplistic example of waste and government tomfoolery to justify our opposition to paying taxes. We don't admit that our federal government is largely a social insurance company with a sideline in military defense, and that all other spending is minuscule.

A national confession is in order:

I am subsidized. I have been subsidized my entire life. If I'm white, my family has probably gotten more subsidies than the families of people of color. There is no shame in getting help. That's what decent families and societies do for one another. It is what makes us a WE. We create opportunities for all. We help those in greatest need. We provide a ladder of opportunity to people not born with wealth. We provide for the aged, the disabled, widows and orphans, and others who need help because all of us encounter misfortune at some point in our lives, and someday we will all be disabled and aged. There is NO SHAME in this. We are in the same boat.

$\diamond$

The meeting hall is empty except for a custodian sweeping around the front door. I am listening to Phillip talk about his South Pacific experiences.

"Yep, we were part of a massive gunship battle at Guadalcanal," Phillip says. "Just about shit in my pants.

"But back to this subsidy thing," he says. "You got me thinking about my kids. I have two sons and a daughter. All three are married with kids. Their lives are . . ." He pauses to look for the right word. "Their lives are loony. They work so damn hard. I worked hard when I was their age. But now both parents are working, and they're racing around taking their kids to soccer and gymnastic and tutors."

Phillip's eyes are ablaze now and watering slightly. There is an edge of anger in his voice I hadn't heard before.

"I try to help them out, take my grandkids places. My oldest son comes home from work at 8 p.m., and he's got a briefcase full of papers. And they have so much debt, Jesus Christ, the credit cards and the second mortgages and the 'save for college' funds — and their health costs are so damn high.

"And they have to read the fine print on everything — and make all these calls to credit card companies and fight the cable company for overbilling. Everyone is trying to nickel-and-dime them or tack on a fee they have to fight. Who has time for this?

"God." He shakes his head. "I was home for dinner every night at 6 p.m., and my wife didn't have to work. We had the VA mortgage on the house but no other debt. I mean, our lives were so different.

"These kids could use some help," Phillip says, appealing to me. "I mean I'm helping them with college funds and summer camp fees and stuff. But just to know they didn't have to save $40,000 a kid for them to get a decent education."

"I think it's more like $100,000 or $130,000," I interject quietly.[19]

"People call our generation the 'greatest generation.' Hell, I guess we were the greatest *subsidized* generation."

"There you go again, using that dirty word *subsidy*," I tease. "Swearing like a sailor."

Phillip laughs and smiles. "Too much excitement for me," he says, tapping his cane as he stands up. "Time for a nap."

CHAPTER 8

Black Wealth, Brown Wealth, White Wealth

It is time for all of us to tell each other the truth about who and what have brought the Negro to the condition of deprivation against which he struggles today. In human relations the truth is hard to come by, because most groups are deceived about themselves.

DR. MARTIN LUTHER KING JR.,
WHERE DO WE GO FROM HERE? CHAOS OR COMMUNITY

Kathy is not a racial bigot.

She voted twice for Barack Obama for president and twice for Massachusetts's first black governor, Deval Patrick. And like a lot of white people who have wrestled with some aspect of their racial privilege, she knows she has a lot to learn. But Kathy bristles at the suggestion that she has a lot of advantages over people of color. As a woman approaching 60, she's been around the block. She knows, in her words, "the good, the bad, and the ugly" of race relations. She grew up in the South in a white working-class family and has played and worked alongside people of color her entire life.

The Black Lives Matter movement that rose up in 2014 in response to the shootings of unarmed black men in Ferguson and Staten Island has triggered heated feelings for Kathy.

"I know our society has a long way to go to undo the legacy of racism," Kathy said to me on a long car ride. "But this is not Jim Crow America. When do we move on from the accusations of racism at every turn?"

It is not uncommon to hear my white friends speak from a sense of "race fatigue," after having been part of thousands of conversations. Or to adopt a "postracial" view focused on how much progress we've made. "This isn't Selma anymore. George Wallace couldn't be elected today," Kathy points out (this is before Trump ran in 2016). "We should be talking more about class."

Having grown up in Detroit, I see the mash-up of race and class in people's lives. It is impossible to untangle the complex interaction between class and race privilege — to suggest that one trumps the other. So what do we know to be true?

The State of the Dream

We know that legal segregation is over and overt discrimination has diminished. But what is the state of the dream that Dr. Martin Luther King Jr. spoke about, particularly as it relates to economic opportunity?

Racial inequality in earnings remains persistent. African American workers under the age of 35 earn only 75 cents on the dollar compared with their white contemporaries. Young Latinos earn only 68 cents.[1]

Examining income alone, however, is like trying to understand the tectonic shifts of Earth by studying the weather. Wealth and net worth — what people own minus what they owe — gives us a window into multigenerational trends.

Not surprisingly, according to researchers, there's a high correlation between wealth and economic security. Wealth in the form of savings, investments, and homes provides a cushion to fall back on in the face of hardship. Homeownership in particular is a foundational asset, something to pass on to one's children.

According to the Pew Research Center, the median wealth of white households in 2013 was a stunning thirteen times greater than the median wealth of black households — up from eight times greater in 2010. White households had ten times more wealth than Latino households.[2]

The racial wealth gap widened after the Great Recession of 2007–2009, as the median wealth tumbled downward for people of color while ticking slightly upward for whites.

Median wealth for black households in 2013 was $11,000, down from $16,600 in 2010, a staggering decline of 33.7 percent. For white households, the median wealth in 2013 was $141,900, up from $138,600 in 2010, an increase of 2.4 percent. Between 2010 and 2013, the median wealth of Hispanic households declined 14.3 percent, from $16,000 to $13,700.[3]

While people of all races saw their net worth implode during the 2008 recession, recovery has come much more quickly to whites than to people of color. This is partially because whites tend to own more financial assets, such as stocks and bonds, which have rebounded since 2009. Home values — which represent the largest share of assets for households of color — haven't recovered at the same rate.

Behind these statistics are stories of lives under stress, of people losing homes, jobs, savings, and stability. The collapse of middle-class wealth has touched people of all races, but has been most severe in communities of color.

Such dramatic shifts in racial wealth disparities can't be explained simply in terms of the latest recession. The story goes back, tracing through parents, grandparents, and elders. Today's racial wealth gap is an economic archaeological marker, embedded within the multigenerational story of plunder and discrimination.

White Affirmative Action

"It is time for all of us to tell each other the truth," Dr. King wrote in 1967, "about who and what have brought the Negro to the condition of deprivation against which he struggles today."[4] The truth is that some of us have benefited at the expense of others.

Black wealth matters. Until we tell each other the truth about the racial wealth divide, King's dream will remain deferred. But telling the truth is not always that easy. As Dr. King wrote, "In human relations the truth is hard to come by, because most groups are deceived about themselves."

For whites to understand the racial wealth divide requires some demythologizing of our own narrative of wealth creation. For me, it also means fixing my eyes on the full horror of dispossession. I've tried to learn about the history of the plunder that has created present inequalities. *The Atlantic* summed it up succinctly when introducing "The Case for Reparations" by Ta-Nehisi Coates: "Two hundred fifty years of slavery. Ninety years of Jim Crow. Sixty years of separate but equal. Thirty-five years of racist housing policy. Until we reckon with our compounding moral debts, America will never be whole."[5]

A century after the formal end of slavery, in 1965, African Americans were largely excluded from programs that helped build middle-class wealth. In the decade following World War II, our nation made unprecedented public investments, described in the previous chapter, to subsidize debt-free college education and low-cost mortgages. These wealth-building measures benefited millions of mostly white households.

People of color, facing overt discrimination in mortgage lending and separate-and-unequal school systems throughout the United States, generally didn't share these benefits. Many federal mortgage programs were implemented with enormous racial bias, both in lending rules and home-sale practices. When eligible blacks and Latinos did obtain mortgages, they were often steered away from neighborhoods with appreciating property values and amenities. In terms of debt-free education, there were a handful of people of color who got GI Bill education benefits. But many veterans returning to Jim Crow South education systems did not share in these opportunities. They were left standing at the railway station as the express train for the white middle class departed.

White homeownership rates eventually rose to as high as 75 percent, while black rates peaked at 46 percent, a 30-point gap that remains today. That means generations of white families have enjoyed access to wealth that has long eluded their black counterparts.

Since 2004, the homeownership rate has declined steadily for everyone, from 69 percent to 64.4 percent in the third quarter of 2014. For blacks, the homeownership rate fell from 45.6 percent in 2010 to 42.9 percent in the third quarter of 2014. For Latinos, homeownership declined over the same years from 48.5 to 45.6 percent. For whites, it dropped from 74.5 percent to 72.6 percent.[6]

As someone born in the top 1 percent, I've tried to place my multigenerational story of family wealth alongside the history of black wealth dispossession. No one was looting our family wealth. No angry mobs destroyed German businesses along Sedgwick Street in Chicago in 1921, as they did in Tulsa, Oklahoma, when rioting whites destroyed that city's "Black Wall Street" by burning down most of its 191 businesses and more than twelve hundred homes, not to mention a school, a hospital, churches, and other staples of the black community. By June of the following year, Tulsans had filed riot-related claims for more than $1.8 million, or nearly $26 million in today's dollars.[7]

Once again, my history is a story of multigenerational advantage building on itself alongside the compounding disadvantage of people of color and working-class whites.

Understanding Racial Wealth Disparities

I ask Kathy why she thinks the racial wealth gap has grown since 2009. "Probably multigenerational hits," she replies. "Discrimination, lower annual incomes, lack of job opportunities." But then she drifts into cultural explanations. "There is a persistent culture of poverty, lack of education, inability to delay gratification and save money, absence of working men, single mothers."

"People always default to personal narrative explanations," says Tom Shapiro, one of my neighbors in Jamaica Plain who happens to be a national expert on racial wealth disparities. "No one disputes the data about the racial wealth divide. But everyone has their own explanation. It's sort of a racial Rorschach test."

I meet Shapiro at the Ula Café for coffee. I've known him since 1995 when he and another sociologist, Mel Oliver, wrote a groundbreaking book, *Black Wealth, White Wealth*. He has a dozen conversations a day with media and individuals about the causes of racial wealth inequality. "Most of the explanations are narratives of individual responsibility and deservedness. I've learned when I talk about these issues to leave no fact unexplained. Otherwise someone will fill it in with their own story."

Like Kathy's, their explanations include people failing to save money, failing to delay gratification, and having children outside marriage. Shapiro spends a good amount of time unpacking these various narratives. "For example, let's take the assumption that the racial wealth gap is the result of unmarried black women and absent husbands. So let's give every single black woman a black husband with the black median net worth. Each one would need four or five husbands, ideally doctors, to close the racial wealth divide."

I told Shapiro about my visit to the Norwood Retired Men's Club and my informal poll there about government assistance. "People turn deservedness on its head," he observed. "It is easier to raise your hand to say that you got help from a government program. But to admit that the ways families share wealth with children is a form of privilege is a leap."

Shapiro tells me a story about an interview that was part of a study he conducted with a white family about their journey to homeownership. The family told Shapiro that they "aspired to move to a better neighborhood." They had garage sales every Sunday and worked hard to save money, including not going out for meals. Over dinner with one of their mothers, however, they mentioned their struggle and quest to relocate. The mother pulled out a checkbook and wrote them a check for $30,000.

Later in the interview, Shapiro asked this couple to recap the key factors that enabled them to buy their house. They repeated their story of personal sacrifice and Sunday yard sales, omitting the crucial detail of the family money. Shapiro asked gently, what about the family assistance? The couple was adamant: It was not a significant factor. They worked hard for their house.

This reminded me of my conversation with Charlie from Hillsborough, New Hampshire, and how we remember the hardship and sacrifice but not the help. As a culture we seem deeply attached to stories of our individual efforts, but amnesia sets in when it comes to family or government help.

Repair and Reparations

"Reparations is not an issue of the distant past," said Dr. Ron Daniels, standing in the rostrum of Harlem's historic Mother AME Zion Church. "The Japanese American community demanded — and got — reparations in the late 1980s for how they were treated by the American government — their own government — during World War II!

"And the parliaments of Russia and Greece are voting to demand Germany pay them for the damage inflicted on them by the Nazis," Daniels added. "So this issue is not going away, and should not, particularly where African-descended people are concerned."

It is a cool April evening and I'm feeling a rush of history move through me. I'm sitting in a well-worn pew in the oldest African American church in the United States, founded in 1796.

"If you listen between the beats of your heart, you might sense the presence of runaway slaves," invokes senior minister Dr. Richard Chapple, during an opening prayer. "This church was a stop along the underground railway. Sojourner Truth was a member and Paul Robeson sang here."

I am attending the opening plenary of the International Reparations Summit, a gathering of intellectuals and activists from the Caribbean and the United States. I'm one of a handful of white people, soaking up the historical sensibilities of those who have pondered what Randall Robinson calls "the debt": what we owe people of African heritage for the crime of slavery.

In 1988, President Ronald Reagan formally apologized for the US government's internment of Japanese Americans and, under the provisions of the Civil Liberties Act, paid each victim $20,000 in reparations. But there have been no reparations for slavery, even though the crime is uncontested and we are surrounded by wealth created by enslaved labor, in our buildings, institutions, and bank accounts.

Here at the Reparations Summit, I learn the full story of the restitution paid to the victims of a 1923 pogrom in Rosewood, Florida. That attack, as Rosewood descendant Lizzie Jenkins has described it, was "one of the bloodiest acts of terrorism in the state, resulting in seven recorded deaths, injuries, shattered dreams, derailed lives, burglarized homes and the burning down of the town."[8] After decades of silence, the descendants documented the rioting and destruction of the black sections of Rosewood, making a case for violated property rights. In 1994, the Florida legislature signed a $2.1 million compensation bill that paid funds to nine survivors and established state university scholarships for Rosewood descendants.

As I consider reparations and repair, I hear many voices in my head. The material facts of a racial wealth divide are undeniable. It is the result of, in the words of President Lyndon Johnson, "ancient brutality, past injustice, and present prejudice." There is a debt, but, like many white people, I get stuck on the mechanism of repayment. Should we just write checks to people? Which people? Won't low-income whites be enraged? Where will the money come from?

I recall a previous conversation with Kathy, where I raised the issue of reparations. "Hey, I never owned slaves and neither did my ancestors," she quipped, representing the conventional wisdom of many working-class whites with little in the bank to show for their white skin advantage. "When will the statute of limitations be over?"

Her reaction reminded me of questions I'd heard before from first- or second-generation Americans whose ancestors fled their own hardships to arrive here: They feel miles apart from slavery but seldom consider the way their lives would have evolved had their fathers, mothers, or grandparents not arrived on these shores white. It also made me recall a quote by Rabbi Abraham Heschel: "Few are guilty, but all are responsible."

My ancestors were not involved in the slave trade and most didn't show up until after the Civil War and Emancipation. It is easy to deflect any feeling of guilt onto descendants of slave owners, or overt racists, allowing me to avoid taking a deeper look at my own culpability and indifference. As a northerner, I took smug assurance that I wasn't like those southern white racists, fighting for the Confederacy, waving the Dixie flag, or wearing white sheets. That was until I learned the history of the transatlantic slave trade, which was largely driven by northern industrialists and shipowners. All around New England there are visible symbols of wealth from the slave trade, from Brown University to the stately homes of the cotton mill owners.

My friend Dedrick Muhammad once framed it creatively. Imagine that after playing poker for an hour, we discover that we've been playing with a rigged deck — and that for each hand dealt, a couple of us have gotten extra cards. Naturally, the beneficiaries of the stacked deck have accumulated big winnings. We all heartily agree to a clean start with a new deck and fair rules. But as the dealer begins shuffling the new deck, one of the players raises an awkward question: "What do we do about that huge pile of chips that a few of you have accumulated?"

Throughout the three-day conference, I allow these complex feelings to flow through me. I learn at presentations how reparations can take many forms, including funding for individuals and cultural institutions, scholarship funds, and targeted subsidies for wealth building. My conviction deepens that the United States must recognize the unpaid claim held by those of African heritage.

Without reparations, there will be no repair or reconciliation. Without fully exposing the history and deep costs of the slave trade, we will continue to perpetuate the cruel hoax of meritocracy and "equal starting gates." I agree with Ta-Nehisi Coates, that reparations "is the price we must pay to see ourselves squarely" as he wrote in his celebrated *Atlantic* article: "Reparations beckons us to reject the intoxication of hubris and see America as it is — the work of fallible humans."

"An America that looks away," he wrote, "is ignoring not just the sins of the past but the sins of the present and the certain sins of the future. More important than any single check cut to any African American, the payment of reparations would represent America's maturation out of the childhood myth of its innocence into a wisdom worthy of its founders."[9]

One of the honorees at the Reparations Summit is Congressman John Conyers, who since 1989 has filed legislation, HR 40, to create a national commission to study the impact of slavery and explore reparations. The number 40 in HR 40 alludes to the unfulfilled promise to formerly enslaved Africans of "40 acres and a mule." Since 1989, the legislation has languished without a vote.

I've worked with Chairman Conyers over the years on different legislative campaigns. Once we spent a day together riding a bus across rural Georgia as part of an "Economic Human Rights" tour, with actor Danny Glover, singer Harry Belafonte, and various elected officials.

"Good grief," I thought, as I joined the tribute to Conyers. Passing HR 40 and creating a commission is the least we should do. Why wouldn't we create a national study commission, formerly sanctioned by the US government? We don't have to figure out all the particulars. That's what the commission would do. A commission could give us, in Coates's words, "a national reckoning that would lead to spiritual renewal."

In the story of individual wealth, our ancestors are present. To ignore the legacy of slavery and discrimination requires a debilitating denial on the part of whites — even those whose ancestors arrived from other lands in more recent times, and especially for those of us at the top of the wealth pyramid.

— CHAPTER 9 —

Unequal Opportunity

> *It is those who are successful . . . who are most likely to be given the kinds of special opportunities that lead to further success. It's the rich who get the biggest tax breaks. It's the best students who get the best teaching and most attention. And it's the biggest nine- and ten-year-olds who get the most coaching and practice. Success is the result of what sociologists like to call "accumulative advantage."*

> MALCOLM GLADWELL,
> *OUTLIERS: THE STORY OF SUCCESS*

In my neighborhood, the Ula Café is a great gathering spot. Housed in the old Haffenreffer Brewery complex in Jamaica Plain, Ula is like my *Cheers* bar, "where everybody knows your name." I run into people, have business meetings, or sometimes hide out, sitting at a back table, a baseball cap pulled over my eyes, trying to concentrate.[1]

One morning, around Thanksgiving, I order a cup of tea from the barista Tony, whose father I've known for over twenty years. Tony boasts about winning a barista contest and tells me about his second job working as a carpenter's apprentice.

I wave to Cordelia, a young woman who was in a neighborhood theater performance with my daughter Nora and who often sat at our dinner table when she was a teenager. Her dad Jerry and I coached youth soccer together. She is working in the Ula Café kitchen.

As I sit down, I see two other children of family friends, Marcus and Miranda, both home for Thanksgiving break from the college they attend in northern New England. They were classmates with Nora at Boston Latin School, the first public school in the United States.

I like to dazzle my midwestern friends and family by asking them to guess the year that Boston Latin School was founded.

"Hmm . . . Boston, must be really old," they inevitably reply. "Maybe 1830?"

They are off by two centuries. Boston Latin School was founded in 1635. Harvard College was founded in 1636 so the scholarly graduates of Boston Latin would have somewhere to go.

I know quite a bit about these four young adults. They all graduated from Boston public high schools and are strong students. They are all white, in their early twenties, and live in my neighborhood of Jamaica Plain.

I also know something about their individual family economic class circumstances. I catch myself envisioning their individual future scenarios, in part because I'm steeped in sociological research about class and opportunity. And unfortunately, the inequalities of the last thirty years have changed the physics of social mobility.

Though each is young, with full lives ahead, I dare speculate that their work futures and life trajectories are radically divergent — and largely determined at this point. This seems perversely un-American, to use the word "determined." But the social mobility arteries in the United States are hardening.

One of these four youth will likely propel into the top income brackets, while the other three will struggle in the precarious middle and working class. The explanation for their divergence is the growing role of inherited advantage, as affluent families make investments that give their children a leg up, a dynamic that undermines relative opportunity for offspring without family wealth. Combined with the 2008–2009 economic meltdown and budget cuts in public investments that foster opportunity, we are witnessing accelerating advantages for the wealthy and compounding disadvantages for everyone else.

I know, for example, that Miranda will graduate from her private four-year college without any student-loan debt. She will have completed three summers of unpaid internships at businesses that will advance her career path. Her parents will help her, as they did her older sister, by subsidizing the purchase of a car and her housing with a security deposit and cosigned apartment lease. As affluent professionals, Miranda's parents have provided her with a list of family and professional contacts for her to network with.

While she waits to land a job with benefits, she will remain on her parents' health insurance.

I don't have a precise crystal ball, but I would confidently wager that in a decade, Miranda will have a high-paying job, be partnered with another professional, and will buy a home or condo in a neighborhood with other college-educated professionals, a property that will steadily appreciate over time because of its location in a largely white, stable neighborhood. Her parents will subsidize the purchase with assistance from their Parental Down Payment Assistance Program, enabling her to get a good fixed mortgage rate. In other words, Miranda will be fully launched into a life in the privileged top 10 percent of income earners, which is exactly what her parents hope and expect of her. If she has any setbacks, there is a huge family safety net to help her maintain her projected class status.

Sitting at Ula Café with Miranda is the other college student, Marcus. I was his soccer coach when he was in elementary school. When I see him now, I do a double take, since he's about a foot taller than me. Marcus tells me that he will graduate in a few months with over $85,000 in college debt, a maxed-out credit card, and an extensive resume of part-time food service jobs that he has taken to pay for school. Unlike Miranda, who can focus entirely on her studies and professional development, Marcus hustles and works both during summers and while in school, reducing the hours he is able to study. Though he will obtain a degree, he will graduate with almost no work experience in his field of study.

Marcus does not have the family safety net that Miranda does. After he graduates, he will find subsidized health insurance, and continue to work two part-time jobs to pay back his student loans and rent a shared apartment. A decade from now Marcus will probably still be working in low-paying jobs and renting an apartment. His student debt will narrow his options and block his ability to buy a home. He will likely feel occupationally stuck and frustrated in his attempts to network in the area of his professional degree. He will take on additional debt — to deal with various health and financial problems — and watch his hope of buying a home slip away, in large part because of a credit history damaged during his early twenties.

Tony, the barista, has the benefit of not taking on huge student loans from college. He will eventually take some classes at a local public university. But his income and employment opportunities will be constrained by not having a college degree. He will make several attempts to learn a building trade and start his own business, eventually landing a job with a steady but low income.

The good news for Tony is that his parents, while not college-educated or wealthy, are stable middle-class people with modest retirement pensions. They own a debt-free house, acquired by Tony's grandfather with a low-interest Veterans Administration mortgage over fifty years ago. Tony's parents provide a free bedroom to their son, enabling him to save money. This home will prove to be a significant factor in Tony's future economic stability, as he will eventually inherit it.

Cordelia, working in the kitchen, has even less opportunity than Tony for mobility and advancement. Neither of her parents went to college nor has significant assets, as they rent their apartment. Though she was academically in the top of her class at English High School, she did not consider applying to a selective college. The costs seemed daunting and none of her friends or siblings were college-bound. There were few close adults or guidance professionals to help her explore other options, including financial aid available at private colleges, some of which would have paid her full tuition and expenses to attend.[2] Instead, she takes courses at the local community college where she sees many familiar faces.

Cordelia will struggle with health issues, as her lack of adequate health care, in the days before the Affordable Care Act, meant that she delayed treatment of several health problems, allowing them to compound as she enters adulthood. Over time, she will have a steady and low-wage job, but she will also begin to take more responsibility for supporting members of her family who are less fortunate.

The Born on Third Base Factor

These four coming-of-age adults in no way represent the entire spectrum of young adult experience, which also includes youth of color, ex-offenders, people with disabilities, and students who are not academically strong. Young adults in rural communities and small towns, for example, face their own challenges, such as limited employment options. They will disproportionately populate our volunteer military, fill the growing ranks of disability pension recipients, or migrate to communities where they have few social supports.[3]

This unequal opportunity story doesn't include the even greater gap that opens up when affluent parents send their children to elite private schools, as mine did. These private schools — while sometimes instilling liberal sensibilities — are consciously preparing their students for privilege, power, and elite social networks. One sociological study of private schools is called "Prepped for Power."

A key determinant of the futures most likely faced by Miranda, Marcus, Tony, and Cordelia is the role of family wealth, a factor that plays an oversized role in sorting today's coming-of-age generation onto different opportunity trajectories.

The initial sort begins at a much earlier age. A growing mountain of research chronicles "intergenerational transmission of advantage," including the countless mechanisms by which affluent families boost their children's prospects starting at birth.[4] These go well beyond the fact that educated parents are more likely to read to their kids or talk engagingly with them at an early age. The mechanisms include financial investments in their children's enrichment, school readiness, formal schooling, college access, and aiding the transition to work. Meanwhile, the children in families unable to make these investments fall further behind.

Imagine a 10-mile race with some odd rules, where contestants have different starting lines based on parental education, income, and wealth. The economically privileged athletes start several hundred yards ahead of the disadvantaged runners. Each contestant begins with ten 1-pound leg weights. The race begins and the advantaged competitors pull ahead quickly. At each half-mile mark, according to the rules, the first twenty runners shed 2 pounds of weights while the last half of the field take on 2 additional pounds. After several miles, lead racers have no weights, while the slower runners carry 20 additional pounds. By mid-race, an alarming gap has opened up in the field. At the finish line, the last half of the field finishes over 2 miles behind the winners.

This race of accelerating advantages and compounding disadvantages is a disturbingly accurate metaphor for inherited privilege. As in real life, there are well-publicized stories of exceptional runners starting far back in the pack and breaking to the front of the field, therefore able to shed weights and remain competitive. And there are frontrunners who perform poorly, squandering their initial advantages and falling back. But the overall picture is one of steadily growing class-based inequality. Consistent with emerging sociological research about children and opportunity, once inequalities open up, they rarely decrease over time.[5]

A healthy democratic society that values equal opportunity could rise to this challenge, resolving to make robust public investments in time-tested interventions that level the playing field. Indeed, as demonstrated in our earlier story of "America's greatest subsidized generation," we have made such societal investments to broaden our white middle class before.

In our increasingly plutocratic political system, however, the very wealthy have less stake in societal opportunity-building mechanisms, as their own children and grandchildren advance through privatized systems. These same affluent and wealthy families maintain disproportionate influence in shaping our national priorities, such as whether to cut taxes on the wealthy or maintain investments in public education. According to surveys, the 1 percent is more politically engaged as donors and advocates than the rest of the population, use their leverage with elected officials, and support deregulation, market-based magical solutions, and private philanthropy over government investment.[6] Combined with Supreme Court rulings like *Citizens United v. FEC*, the influence of wealthy and "dark money" donors has warped our national priorities.[7] We are snagged in a cycle of declining opportunity driven by the new politics of inherited advantage.

A Growing Private Family Welfare State and a Shrinking Public One

Budget cuts at all levels of government have dismantled post–World War II public investments that had begun to level the playing field for economically and racially disadvantaged families. Higher education has taken one of the biggest hits. State cuts in higher education since 2008 have reduced spending on average by 20 percent per student, a problem as state and local revenue cover 53 percent of college costs. This has led to cuts that jeopardize the quality of education and to tuition and fee hikes averaging 29 percent, with California and Arizona raising tuition over 70 percent.[8] Over the last twenty years, the College Board reports that the cost of four-year college has accelerated faster than median income, even after factoring in federal financial aid and tax subsidies. Since 1994, median income rose about 2 percent while public college costs increased 45 percent, faster than private college costs, which increased almost 38 percent.[9]

The United States prides itself in being a socially mobile society where what you do is more important than the racial and class circumstances of your birth. Indeed, in the three decades after World War II, between 1947 and 1977, social mobility increased, particularly for the white working class. Like the members of the Norwood Retired Men's Club, the "greatest subsidized generation" has a radically different experience of mobility. This imprinted a national self-identity as a mobile and meritocratic society, especially juxtaposed with the old "caste societies" of Europe, with their static class systems and relatively calcified social mobility.

That story of European versus US social mobility has now been turned on its head. European nations and Canada, with their social safety nets and investments in early childhood education, are experiencing greater social mobility. Canada now has three times the social mobility of the United States.[10]

The American Dream has long been defined as the ability to save, take a vacation, buy a home, retire before you die, and pass something on to your children. If you want to live the American Dream, and you're not born into a wealthy family, you are better off being born in Canada.

The idea that people's futures might be economically determined deeply offends US sensibilities. We want to believe that individual moxie matters, that a person's creativity, effort, and intelligence will lead to economic success. Stories of exceptional strivers, heroically overcoming a stacked deck of obstacles, divert our attention from the data. But the large megatrends are now indisputable.

Parental Investments from Birth

When I think about Miranda, Marcus, Tony, and Cordelia, I consider the impact of their different family financial circumstances. Long before any of them considered attending college, they were on divergent glide paths. Debt-free Miranda was the beneficiary of parental investments that prepared her for school and high achievement. She grew up in a book-filled and conversation-rich home environment with college-educated parents who had more leisure and vacation time to spend with her. She spent summers in

Maine and on Cape Cod, enjoying more time in ecologically pristine environments. She had more access to recreation, health care, and healthy food. Her parents, knowledgeable about brain development, talked to her from her first months of life, using vastly more vocabulary words than parents of other economic classes. When she was away from her parents, they paid for comparably stimulating child care settings.[11]

Researcher Meredith Phillips found that by age 6 wealthier children spent as many as thirteen hundred more hours a year than poor children on child enrichment activities such as travel, music lessons, visits to museums, and summer camp. All this results in much higher math and reading skills, and other attainments later in life. These children have a school-readiness edge that they never lose.[12]

The relative advantage of wealthy families, in terms of social capital and civic engagement, has accelerated over the last thirty years.[13] For example, success-bound Miranda also had more opportunities than her nonwealthy peers to develop the important social capital that results from more time with parents and time spent in social institutions such as religious congregations, civic organizations, and extracurricular activities. As political scientist Robert Putnam, author of *Bowling Alone*, and his team of researchers write,

> *The very factors (civic and social engagement, social trust, time spent with parents, and academic achievement) in which the youth class divergence is greatest strongly predict life success. Upper/ middle class youth have always had advantage, but their relative advantage has increased significantly over the last 30 years. Family background is now more predictive of social capital and civic engagement than before.[14]*

Working-class youth, with parents working multiple jobs to make up for several decades of stagnant wages, are more socially disconnected. As a result, they develop fewer "soft skills" useful in job networking and workplaces.

When our foursome entered K–12 school, once considered the great avenue to equal opportunity, the disparities widened. Today, the early literacy and reading support conferred by more advantaged families leads their children to pull away from all other students, not just those with very low incomes.[15] Class-based disparities are translating to disparities in cognitive skills. The widening gap between reading and math test scores of advantaged and other children has grown significantly since the 1970s, mirroring the national income and wealth gap. According to researcher Sean Reardon, the academic achievement gap between children from high- and low-income families is roughly 30 to 40 percent larger among children born in 2001 than among those born in 1976.[16]

Among "high achievers," the top 4 percent of students nationwide, 34 percent come from the top quartile, households with incomes over $120,776. Only 17 percent come from the bottom quartile, with incomes under $41,472.[17] Income now plays a bigger role than race in the academic achievement gap, a reverse from fifty years earlier. The main explanation is that high-income parents of all races are investing more in children's cognitive development.[18]

Even so, the same investment in childhood cognitive development does not yield the same earnings for young workers across the board. As described in the previous chapter, African American workers under 35 will earn only 75 cents on the dollar of their white contemporaries; Latinos will earn only 68 cents.[19] And for all young workers, there is a significant "wage premium" for obtaining a degree. Over the last four decades, a person with a bachelor's degree earned 56 percent more than a high school graduate.[20]

College-Bound

Miranda, Tony, Cordelia, and Marcus all graduated from their Boston high schools in the top fifth of their classes. But their high school experience varied, depending on whether they got into one of Boston's so-called exam schools, elite public high schools that select students based on entrance exam scores.

Research indicates that the key decisions in whether to attend college and where are largely driven by disparities in income and wealth that influence parental investment, K–12 education systems, and college preparatory supports.

In the seventy years since World War II, college attendance has played a significant role in employment opportunity and lifetime earnings. Over these seventy years, college entry increased by over 50 percent, and the rate of college completion by age 25 quadrupled. But since 1980, an income-based gap has grown up in terms of college completion.[21]

Low-income students born around 1980 only increased their college graduation rates by 4 percent — whereas higher-income cohorts saw their graduation rates go up by 18 percent. The greatest inequality is among women, driven by increases in college completion by the daughters of higher income households — and the lack of opportunities for nonwealthy women.[22]

Marcus's family, like Miranda's, placed a strong emphasis on attending college and college preparation. Marcus and Miranda both attended Boston Latin School, a public exam school. Boston Latin provided college-bound students with Advanced Placement classes, college counseling, and seminars for parents. While Marcus's family is not as wealthy as Miranda's family, both families paid for the services of the burgeoning college preparation industry to boost their children's SAT scores. But in terms of family wealth, Marcus was on his own after high school, venturing into higher education and work without family resources or a financial safety net.

Wealthy Miranda and barista Tony share an important parental boost that college student Marcus didn't have: Their parents passed on financial preparation and money literacy skills. Both children learned about money from parents who gave them allowances to manage and encouraged them to open bank accounts and save money. Initial research suggests that financial literacy may be a more important factor than schooling in lifetime wealth accumulation and retirement savings.[23] Tony learned thrift and debt avoidance. These skills are much more important in the current environment, with unregulated predatory lenders and twenty-five brands of college loan financing to choose from.

Tony benefits from modest family wealth transfers, thanks to a previous generation of social investments, especially his grandfather's government-subsidized home mortgage. Tony will tap into what Sally Koslow, in her book *Slouching Toward Adulthood*, calls the "middle class trust fund": free room and board, cable, and internet access.[24] Tony's parents don't consider their support for him as a legacy advantage. They understand that the deck is stacked against their son, who will likely never be rich without a winning lottery ticket or marrying into money. Their temporary housing and modest gifts — the purchase of a truck and money to get a trade license — are hedges against his downward mobility or destitution.

Cordelia's parents did what they could to better her prospects, ensuring she was in a good elementary school and steered toward engaging teachers. They found her affordable summer day camps and other enrichment experiences. But when it came time for her to consider college, Cordelia was flying solo. This wasn't because of parental neglect or disinterest. But having not attended college, Cordelia's parents were not familiar with the college search and admission process, including junior-year college visits, SAT preparation, applications, and scholarship options. They presumed private select schools were out of reach, even for their academically strong daughter, and didn't know how to coach and support Cordelia's college oddessy. Only 34 percent of high-achieving high school seniors in the bottom fourth of income distribution attend any one of the country's 238 most selective colleges. Among top students in the highest income quartile, that figure is 78 percent.[25] And like the majority of low-income college students, Cordelia did not complete college.[26] A key missing ingredient for her was effective college guidance, within her school and at home.

How young people finance college has its own disparities. Low-income and minority students that get proper guidance can often get significant scholarships at private colleges and graduate with less debt than students attending public universities.[27] Miranda's parents paid full freight for her college. Marcus, navigating the college-financing jungle on his own, got little financial aid and signed up for a loan package that will cost him twice as much over time as the cheapest available plan, due to higher interest payments. If Marcus were attending college forty years earlier, he probably would have graduated debt-free as a result of lower tuition and public financial aid programs.[28]

There are now forty million Americans who hold student debt totaling $1.2 trillion, a number expected to increase to $2 trillion by 2022.[29] College debt now touches one in five US households and exceeds total credit card indebtedness.[30]

The student debt debacle has huge implications for the future. The average college graduate now has almost $35,000 in debt, with some holding notes over $100,000.[31] Research indicates that student debt delays household formation, homeownership, and entrepreneurial risk taking. It undermines savings, wealth creation, and economic well-being.[32]

While Miranda received family support to take unpaid internships, other college students like Marcus used every nonschool hour to earn money in jobs outside his career area. Among the huge breakaway wealth advantages are unpaid internships in one's career area, an essential leg up in the transition from school to work. Entry-level workers are now expected to show up with work experience.[33] Research shows that half of college graduate hires occur at the firms where the students previously interned.[34]

Family wealth also serves as a form of adversity insurance, as young adults face potential setbacks ranging from prolonged unemployment, bad credit, health or addiction problems, criminal arrests, car breakdowns or accidents, or early parenthood. Young adults may make poor decisions or face unforeseen circumstances, but in almost every case family wealth will help keep young people on track, whether it is legal assistance, treatment, or regular cash infusions.[35]

Closing the Advantage Gap

What, if anything, can be done to offset the torrent of perks and advantages that wealthy parents confer to their progeny as they compete for slots in schools in educational institutions, internships in their field of interest, entry-level jobs, affordable housing, and other resources?

The first step is to acknowledge the depth of the declining mobility and opportunity problem, a story that is just beginning to be understood after three decades of extreme inequality. The image of post–World War II mobility is still reverberating and dominates our national mythology, especially for whites over the age of 50. But the present inequalities of wealth, and the exponential impacts of race, have fundamentally altered the possibilities for equal opportunity for the next two generations.

Conservative Reihan Salam acknowledges the "incumbent-protection strategy" of wealthy families, observing that "it is possible that non-black families in the top three-fifths of the income distribution are giving their children advantages that protect them from scrappy upstarts in ways that might damage our growth prospects."[36] Conservatives often reject policies they consider as "antigrowth" because they redistribute wealth and power through taxation and regulation. Instead, they favor programs that foster opportunity and encourage those with grit and talent to rise through a more meritocratic system of rewards. But few honestly acknowledge, as Salam does, the ways that advantaged families undermine the meritocracy they espouse for others. Through the many mechanisms we've identified in this chapter, affluent families undermine equal opportunity by shoveling advantages to their kids.

As inequality grows and social mobility declines, the pressure increases on those in Miranda's parents' situation to do everything they can to provide a sort of safety net against downward mobility for their children.

Sustained public investments in opportunity are critical to level a playing field that is constantly being upended by wealth advantage. But there are also private-sector and personal interventions that could reduce runaway unequal opportunity.

Other industrialized countries have demonstrated that public investments in health, education, and family well-being can offset the private advantages of wealth and improve social mobility — not just to promote fairness, but also to keep economies healthy and resilient. Initiatives like the "Baby College" of the Harlem Children's Zone, Head Start, the UK's Nurse-Family Partnership Program, and universal preschool programs, such as those in France and Denmark, partially close the gaps in school achievement and subsequent wages.[37]

High-quality pre-kindergarten education, access to health care and nutrition, good K–12 public education, and early diagnosis of learning disabilities and special needs are key interventions that help level the playing field. In many European countries, there is greater investment in public recreation facilities that help build strong bodies and a culture of community sports and activity.

The fact that inequalities of opportunity now accelerate as schooling begins is testament to the need to defend and expand funding for public education at all levels. Over three-fourths of undergraduate college students attend public universities and colleges, which are facing the worst state cuts.[38]

Charitable foundations can partner with the private-sector and cultural institutions to ensure public and private funding for youth enrichment, arts and sports programs, summer camps, and stimulating after-school programs. This must include resources for outreach to the most socially disconnected families to ensure their children have access to these opportunities. But philanthropy in this area is not a substitute for adequate taxation and public investment in these enrichment opportunities.

The US Department of Labor should police the unpaid and underpaid internship marketplace, cracking down on companies that replace paid positions with unpaid. Certain sectors that disproportionately offer unpaid internships as a stepping-stone to career networks — journalism, politics, and entertainment — should do deep soul searching about the implications for the widespread exclusion of working- and middle-class youth.[39] Private-sector and government agencies that offer internships should proactively create stipend and compensation pools to ensure that nonwealthy young people have an equal shot at internships.

Some will argue that little can be done about the seemingly biological tendency of privileged families to funnel money and social capital to their children. Helping children is what parents do when they can. Miranda's parents are helping her get a head start as their parents did for them. A certain amount of adversity develops resourcefulness and capacity in a person. My daughter's circumstances are more like Miranda's than any of her other peers'. While she won't receive an inheritance, she has benefitted from social capital and early enrichment experiences. But she was not given unlimited options. She worked at after-school jobs since she was in ninth grade — and saved money for several trips and a "gap year," when she worked and traveled. She applied to one college, early decision, and got in with a strong financial aid package. She has all kinds of advantages, but the reality is, she will have to work and hustle a bit, depending on her desired standard of living.

It may, however, be hardwired to want to open doors for one's children and help them avoid the suffering that accompanies the journey to adulthood. Therefore, the most important intervention to address unequal inherited advantage is to be fully engaged in ensuring there are adequate investments in education and opportunity and supporting progressive taxes to pay for it. Restoring greater progressivity to the tax system would ensure wealthy families still contribute to the public system. One elegant solution would be to tax wealth to broaden opportunity. Revenue from a steeply progressive estate or inheritance tax could capitalize an "education opportunity trust fund" to provide debt-free college educations for first-generation college students.[40]

Another intervention would be to eliminate or cap the tax deductibility of charitable contributions to private schools and colleges, except if they are directly used for scholarships for disadvantaged youth. That would mean charity to private education wouldn't keep money out of public coffers, a phenomenon we'll visit in the coming chapters.

Wealthy families concerned about declining social mobility should use their special privileges to stop the advantage arms race. Allowing these extreme inequalities to fester and increase undermines fairness and excellence for everyone, including those at the economic top. Do we really want the next generation growing up in a rigid caste or apartheid-like society? We can't expect others to have a stake in an equitable education system if the very wealthy continue to opt out and play "winner take all." One principle of "coming home" is to ensure that all children in a wider community have the same opportunity as one's own children. They should match any family subsidies with tax dollars and donations to organizations that level the playing field.

Donors should fund internship positions at nonprofit organizations they care about, expanding the pool of young people that can intern there.

Without such interventions the United States will further drift toward being a caste society, where opportunity, occupation, and social status are based on inherited advantage, fractured along race and class lines.

PART IV

UNNECESSARY SIDE TRIPS

The gift is to the giver, and it comes back most to him — it cannot fail.

WALT WHITMAN

— CHAPTER 10 —

Miro in the Bathroom: Encounters with the Charitable Industrial Complex

The purpose of private foundations is not to live forever, but to live a life with meaning.

RAY MADOFF

"When I was growing up," Felice Yeskel whispers to me, "my family's whole apartment could fit into this foyer." We step off the elevator onto the fifth floor of a Renaissance apartment building on New York City's Upper East Side, home to the trustee of a grant foundation.

The elevator's latticed metal gate clanks and closes behind us, and we find ourselves alone in a spacious hall decorated with paintings, floor-to-ceiling mirrors, and a large Grecian urn.

"Check it out," Yeskel whispers, pointing with her head at the artwork. "We're not even inside the apartment yet!"

As I mentioned earlier, Yeskel is one of my best friends, and together we founded a national organization devoted to reducing inequality. She is Jewish, lesbian, and grew up in a working-class neighborhood on New York City's Lower East Side — kind of the mirror opposite to my Christian, straight, and privileged youth in a wealthy Detroit suburb.

Yeskel has regaled me with stories of visiting the Park Avenue homes of wealthier classmates when she attended Hunter College Elementary

School. During her entire elementary school years, she never invited a friend home because she was embarrassed by her family's humble apartment. I can imagine the disparity she felt.

"If this is the hallway, I can't wait to see the living room," I say.

Yeskel and I have come to New York City to meet with two people, a staff member and board member of a charitable foundation that is considering a $60,000 grant to our project. We are new to the world of foundations and have worn our best clothes for the occasion. Yeskel has on a blue vest and matching pants and is carrying a leather bag instead of her usual daypack. I wear a suit jacket and tie and have gotten a haircut for the occasion.

We have spent the previous hour sitting on the steps of the Metropolitan Museum of Art, cramming for our meeting and trying not to scruff up our clothes.

Yeskel double-checks her watch — we are punctual on the hour — and pushes the doorbell. A clanging series of chimes vibrates on the other side. I feel the urge to run back toward the elevator. An unsmiling woman in a frilly maid's apron answers the door and ushers us into the apartment, which occupies the entire floor of the building. After being led from one end to the other, I guess the apartment is a sprawling 6,000 square feet. Room after room, separated by large velvet curtains, is packed with paintings, sculptures, and antique furniture.

The sole occupant of this dwelling, the foundation's trustee, sits at her dining room table in front of a stack of files. She is a slight woman in her 60s, her long gray hair in a neat braid. Beside her sits her foundation's administrator, a man named Carl, whom we have met at a preliminary meeting. He is a sociable chain-smoker, with tobacco-stained fingers and a salt-and-pepper beard. Both are casually dressed, Carl in a sweater vest. The maid, averting her eyes, brings us tea and coffee.

"I have one bone to pick," starts the trustee abruptly. "You didn't follow our instructions."

Yeskel and I glance at each other, dismayed. We have traveled all the way from Boston to make our case. Are we already disqualified?

"We asked that you submit your proposal on back-to-back paper to reduce waste," she continues. "I am a big recycler."

"Sorry about that," I stammer. "We don't like to waste paper either."

The scolding out of the way, the discussion shifts toward our project work and public attitudes about inequality. We have a substantive conversation about our efforts to educate the wider public about the ways that concentrated wealth is undermining our democracy. At one point, Yeskel says something about the importance of face-to-face educational experiences compared with the limits of electronic online organizing that is becoming more in vogue.

"See, Carl," the trustee says, turning to Carl, the fund administrator. "This is exactly what I was telling you." Her excitement seems less about Yeskel's insightfulness and more about the fact that Carl is wrong.

"Right you are," defers Carl.

At the end of our meeting, I excuse myself to the bathroom. En route I peek into several other rooms and can't help wondering how much energy the recycling trustee uses to heat and cool her private museum. In the bathroom an original Miro painting hangs above the toilet.

On our way out of the building, I ask Yeskel, "Did you see the Miro in the bathroom?"

"The Mirror-O?" she asks, puzzled. We are safely in the elevator.

"Yeah, the Miro painting, above the toilet."

"No."

Yeskel and I often talk about how upper-class kids use elite cultural codes to signal their class status to others. You can sort the world into those who know George Eliot wrote *Middlemarch* and Picasso painted *Guernica* from those who don't. Perhaps Yeskel didn't know Miro's work. "Miro was a Spanish abstract experimental artist. She has an original in her loo." Had I done it again? "Maybe it's a class thing," I offer.

"I know who Miro is, silly. But I think it's more a gender thing." Now I am puzzled. "You know," Yeskel says, smiling, "standing up, sitting down?"

"Good point," I say, finally comprehending. "Maybe she's trying to impress the men."

"I don't think so. Did you see the Picasso?"

"No. Really? Where?"

"In the bathroom, on the wall opposite the toilet."

"Jeepers."

"You had to be sitting to really appreciate it."

The Charitable Industrial Complex

Discussion of great wealth inevitably flows to a discussion of charity, of sharing a portion of one's private largesse with society.

The charitable impulse is a positive thing and must be celebrated. Our society needs to unlock our generous impulses and rejoice over the power of gifts. This does not, however, need to happen only through the "charitable industrial complex." Indeed most giving – and the most important elements of the gift economy – happen outside the incentive framework of a government-created tax system.

By gift economy, I refer to the unmeasured contributions of time and money that people make through sharing, volunteering, coaching, mentoring, and mutual aid – the everyday generosity that is the difference between living in a cold atomized society and a flourishing civic life.

Consider all the people who volunteer to coach sports and mentor youth. No one is claiming a tax deduction for these offerings. Most lower-income people give to charities and neighbors in need without any consideration of the tax code – and don't itemize and claim deductions. Walk into any locally owned convenience store in a small town in America, and there is a donation jar, stuffed with bills and coins, for someone in need or a local organization.

But among the wealthy, formalized charity has exploded, reflecting not just a charitable impulse but also a successful tax avoidance strategy. Between 1993 and 2012, the percentage of annual income flowing to the top 1 percent has increased from 14 percent to 22 percent.[1] During these same years, there has been a parallel explosion of charitable foundations. In 1993, there were 43,956 private foundations with total assets of $192 billion (or $305 billion in 2012 dollars), with charitable disbursements of $20.5 billion (in 2012 dollars). By 2012, the number of foundations had grown to 86,192 with total assets of $715 billion and charitable disbursements of $52 billion.[2]

Total overall giving (including individuals and corporations) to charitable organizations in 2014 was $358.38 billion. Of this total, individual donors gave $258.51 billion, foundations gave $53.97 billion, and corporations gave $17.77 billion. Bequests accounted for the remaining $28.13 billion.[3]

Where is the $358 billion actually going? About one-third of total giving goes to religious congregations and organizations. The rest looks like this: education (15 percent), human services (12 percent), health (8 percent), public-society benefit (7 percent), arts, culture, humanities (5 percent), international affairs (4 percent), environment and animals (3 percent). The remaining 12 percent goes to foundations.[4]

Foundations focus their giving differently from the public at large. Some 2 percent ($468 million) goes to religious charities. Of the $52 billion in 2012 grant disbursements, 22 percent went to both health and education ($5 billion each); 16 percent ($3.5 billion) went to human services; 12 percent ($2.7 billion) went to public affairs/society benefit; 10 percent ($2.2 billion) to arts and culture; and 7 percent ($1.6 billion) to environment and animals. The remaining 11 percent went to a combination of international affairs, science and technology, religion, and social sciences.[5]

Most giving by individuals and foundations flows to large well-established educational institutions, hospitals, and arts organizations. Only a very small percent — estimated at 3 percent to 5 percent — goes to organizations serving the most needy and disenfranchised. And very little money goes to "change not charity" efforts to address the structural roots of some of our biggest social challenges: growing inequality, collapsing wages, ecological destruction, and youth at risk.[6]

One troubling aspect of the charitable industrial complex is the warehousing of wealth. At this point, an estimated $600 billion is sitting in charitable foundations and endowments waiting for distribution.[7] Even more sits in donor-advised charitable funds at mega mutual funds like Fidelity Investments.

Self-Interested Charity

There's a lot of positive publicity about the notion of the wealthy "giving back," largely through charitable giving foundations and other vehicles where they designate the donations. We are encouraged to celebrate this generosity — and anyone who criticizes the limitations of such charity is considered a skunk at the garden party.

Yet too much of the money that passes through the charitable industrial complex is given to reinforce the elite status and privileged interests of the giver, failing to address fundamental problems. And some charitable activity exacerbates inequality rather than alleviates it.

Philanthropy is failing to address our society's most vexing problems, including growing inequality and ecological destruction. From my three decades of viewing the limitations of philanthropy from a front-row seat, I've witnessed the good, the bad, the lazy, and the reckless.

Let's start with the bad. I have gotten to know family foundations that are vanity institutions, serving as public relations projects and hobbies for wealthy families. Such foundations operate as part of a constellation of family-wealth preservation strategies aimed at reducing tax liabilities and preserving status.

One family foundation flew me to a mountaintop resort in Colorado to speak to their eight trustees. I joined them for a "chuck wagon" western-themed breakfast on a broad wooden balcony overlooking a mountain range and rushing river. What I learned was that their charitable foundation essentially funded two family reunions a year, in luxurious surroundings, with a couple of hours of trustee meetings to justify the expense.

"We all donate our time but get our expenses covered," explained the 70-year old matron of the family, with a sacrificial look on her face. She was wearing cowboy boots and a broad-rimmed hat.

After a little sleuthing, I estimate that it cost $45,000 to $50,000 to fly eight trustees and their extended families to Colorado, and lodge and feed them for four nights at an exclusive resort. If the massages, guided wild-flower hikes, and golf green fees are included, the cost was even higher. Repeat that again at their winter meeting, when they decamp to a Caribbean resort, and they spend at least $90,000 to give away $200,000 in not terribly imaginative philanthropy. Half the funds go to alma maters. How difficult is that to figure out? And, remember, this is all done with funds that have been excluded from taxation.

These taxpayer-subsidized junkets are possible because the foundation covers the expense of trustee meetings and no one is watching. By statute, qualified foundations must give away 5 percent of their assets. But they can include overhead expenses, such as meetings, travel, and offices, in this "payout."

There are, of course, efficient family foundations that are purposefully lean and move significant money out the door to qualified charities. And some foundations have professional staff and nonfamily board expertise, and do very strategic and high-impact funding. But few of these institutions deviate from the herd in terms of funding; they stick to the safest forms of traditional philanthropy. Most don't surpass the minimum 5 percent payout requirement, treating it as a ceiling rather than a floor.

Almost every billionaire today has their own charitable foundation and multiple charity conduits.[8] While some adopt specific causes – my Cranbrook School classmate Jon Stryker funnels millions to LGBT rights and great ape conservation in Africa – others use charity as an extension of their influence and interest network.

Often the line between self-interest and charity is blurred. Steve Forbes, the wealthy heir to the Forbes fortune and editor of *Forbes* magazine, gave substantial money to fund a tax-exempt think tank that created his policy platform for his 2000 presidential run. Politically engaged donors, both left and right, skirt the intent of charity law by spending tax-exempt charitable funds alongside "hard money" electoral contributions to influence political issues and elections. For example, the donor network created by the Koch brothers advances their political objectives with tax-exempt donations to research institutes and think tanks and 501(c)4 advocacy groups, in coordination with outright contributions to political action committees and electoral candidates.

Many wealthy families give to their private high school and college alma maters, land trusts that preserve their views and buffer their private property, and cultural charities that they immediately enjoy. Many donors have the best of intentions, but default to give to charities based on social obligation, friendship, and familiarity instead of a strategic problem solving. As a result, they end up donating to "backyard" causes where they and their communities are the primary beneficiaries – and where they are appreciated and recognized for their gifts.

Gifts to private education institutions often preserve legacy admissions access for a donor's children and future generations. Since access to elite colleges has replaced land wealth and primogeniture as a means of promoting aristocracy, wealthy families use charitable gifts to guarantee slots for their children, provided they meet minimal admissions standards. Donating money – what journalist Daniel Golden calls the "wealth effect" on college admissions – opens doors not only for legacies but also for new wealth holders.[9]

Gifts to land conservancies, which receive the lion's share of environmental funding, protect beautiful places where donors live, including, in some cases, their personal property. Where my family has spent years along the coast of Central Maine, wealthy families will donate the land surrounding their homes to a conservancy, taking huge tax deductions for its appreciated value and removing the properties from the tax rolls. Often these holdings have no public access, so they effectively create a taxpayer-subsidized buffer zone.

Wealthy art patrons donate artistic works to museums, taking a full tax deduction for their appreciated value. I spoke with an anonymous employee at a major urban art museum in their "Advancement Office," one of the many upscale euphemisms for begging the wealthy. He described a cozy self-interested world that exists among the museum, major art collectors, art appraisers, and law firms. Their shared mission is to stretch the limits of the tax code and reduce tax obligations on behalf of wealthy clients and art patrons. They work collectively to inflate the value of artwork and then donate it to the museum, taking the maximum tax benefit. He described collusion among collectors who bid up each other's artwork at auctions, so that the purchaser can turn around and donate the piece with inflated tax benefits.[10]

This museum employee described the museum's practice of giving enormous perks to "benefactors" (privately curated programs, opportunities to handle art objects not on display, free valet parking, gala events), based on promises of future art donations that trickle in based on a tax avoidance schedule created by tax planners. He described how patrons donate a collection, have it fully deducted as a gift, but then fail to deliver all the promised art. While "booking" the entire collection as donated, museum employees begin the awkward process of trying to extricate the missing donations from the homes of the benefactors. One donor of expensive jewelry retained a right to wear it to an event, even after it was museum property.

In all these transactions — whether they are donations of land or art — there is no one sitting at the table saying, "What about the taxpayer?" There is no one representing the children of the elementary school that is a few blocks away, asking, "Is this really the best use of taxpayer money?"

Under our current tax system — and the definition of an acceptable charity — donations to all these organizations have the same tax benefits as a contribution to feeding needy children in Baltimore.

Reckless Stewards

The problem with mainstream philanthropy is bigger than the issue of where the money goes. The entire "charity industry" is expanding rapidly around us — with abuses of power and staggering inefficiencies. Money that should have been distributed, working to improve the lives of millions of everyday people, is sitting warehoused in family foundations, and bank accounts controlled by "family-friend" lawyers.

People bellyache about government waste, yet the charitable sector skates by without scrutiny. Should there be greater oversight of foundations to limit abuses? Should foundations live forever and be oriented toward wealth preservation? Should they "protect their principal" — like wealthy individuals?

$\diamond$

In 2002, I knocked on the unmarked door of the Paul and Virginia Cabot Charitable Trust. I had been researching local foundations and no one at the trust had returned my calls or queries. So I decided to drop by their nondescript Boston office building in search of a real human being.

A woman wearing stylish skinny eyeglasses cracked open the door about eight inches and peered at me.

"I'm here to get information about the charitable trust's grant making," I said, after introducing myself.

"We don't have anything written," she replied, eyeing me up and down.

"Well, could I meet with someone about the foundation?" I asked.

"I'm sorry, no," she said, closing the door. "Thank you."

"How can I . . . ?"

Click.

I never got any information, but a year later there was an exposé about the Paul and Virginia Cabot Charitable Trust in the *Boston Globe*, conducted by the same "Spotlight team" that exposed the Roman Catholic Archdiocese of Boston clergy-sex abuse scandal.[11]

The trust was established by Paul Cabot, a tweedy Boston investment banker and Harvard treasurer who died in 1994 at the age of 95. He was known for his Yankee thrift, frayed collar shirts, and a modest lifestyle. The trust at the time was administered by his son, Paul Jr., who was in the news for throwing a $200,000 wedding for his daughter in Boca Raton, Florida.

Lavish weddings are not news. But what was newsworthy was that Cabot Jr. paid himself $1.4 million from the trust. In his own words, he "gave himself a raise to help pay for the wedding."

According to the *Boston Globe*, between 1998 and 2002, Cabot paid himself more than $5 million from the trust's funds. The median salary for heads of foundations of a similar asset size at the time was $59,750. During the same period, the Cabot Foundation made an average of $400,000 in grants per year, primarily to the same charities each year. When the *Globe* investigative reporter asked directly if the foundation paid for the wedding, Cabot replied: "Yes. No question. The foundation pays for anything I do."

I find the idea of charitable nonprofit foundations paying their trustees to be truly bizarre. Over twenty years, I've served on fourteen different nonprofit boards without compensation. In fact, most foundations I've applied to for funding will disqualify a charitable organization with paid trustees.

But it turns out the practice is far from unusual. Of the eighty-six thousand charitable foundations that operate in the United States, 28 percent of them compensate their trustees. And thirty-eight of the fifty largest foundations paid trustees a total of $11 million in 2014.[12] Tax returns show that at an alarming number of foundations, the principal beneficiaries are trustees and lawyers, not external grant recipients. And there are no guidelines or legal parameters of what constitutes a reasonable fee — or what is inappropriate.

In 2013, the Minnesota-based Otto Bremer Trust gave out $38 million in grants and paid their three trustees a total of $1.2 million to make the decisions. Two of the trustees, Brian Lipchultz and Daniel Reardon, paid themselves over $465,000 each.

"It's just an outrageously high level of compensation for trustee service," said Aaron Dorfman, executive director of the National Committee for Responsive Philanthropy.

"These institutions get tremendously preferential tax treatment," he told the *Pioneer Press*. "And because of the tax-exempt status they enjoy, the rest of us pay higher taxes and, in effect, subsidize nonprofit tax-exempt charitable foundations."

Serving as a paid trustee for a foundation has certain legal duties but it is not heavy lifting. For example, the charter of the George Jr. and Harriet

E. Woodward Trust of Philadelphia dictates that the same seven charities receive the same-sized grants each year out of the $28 million trust. These trustee meetings can't be very demanding. Yet two Woodward trustees paid themselves fees averaging more than $100,000 a year.[13]

Should a gift that helps provide relief to Hurricane Sandy victims be weighted the same, from a tax deduction point of view, as a gift for a video-production facility at a private high school for privileged children? Should wealthy people be the ones deciding for the rest of us what social causes are worth investing in, essentially what's best for our society?

If a government official were found practicing such forms of compensation abuse — paying $2,400-per-hour fees and wasting millions on overhead — there would be investigations, oversight hearings, censures, and firings. But not in the opaque world of foundations, where these practices are legal and the IRS audits only about one hundred foundations a year.[14]

The "charity industry" lobbies vigorously for minimal scrutiny and keeps guidelines, such as those governing trustee fees, vague. Just as global corporations lobby against regulation, the charity industry argues for voluntary norms and self-policing. Their general attitude is "leave us alone, we know best."

Change Not Charity

There are many examples of how generous and well-considered philanthropy has stimulated social progress throughout our country's history. John D. Rockefeller's donations catalyzed massive advances in medical research and teaching. Andrew Carnegie's donations built over two thousand public libraries and advanced global peace. Today, the Bill and Melinda Gates Foundation has dramatically reduced childhood malaria while George Soros's grants in Eastern Europe have contributed to practices of open government and transparency.

The modest gifts of millions of people, most of whom don't take a tax deduction, have alleviated suffering after natural disasters and built great institutions of knowledge and culture, like the Boston Public Library.

In a book I co-wrote, *Robin Hood Was Right: A Guide to Giving Your Money for Social Change*, we encouraged readers to distinguish between social change solutions and traditional philanthropy — and look for giving structures that share power with people who didn't come from privileged circumstances, like community foundations. In one section, we gave examples of the difference between giving to change versus traditional charity.

Charity: Fund Toys for Tots during the holidays
Change: Fund organizing for a living-wage campaign so parents can afford to buy toys for their own kids

Charity: Fund a scholarship for one high school student to attend college
Change: Fund a student association organizing to ensure that higher education is affordable for everyone

Charity: Donate to cancer research
Change: Donate to a group organizing to clean up the toxins in our environment and to pressure polluters that dump carcinogens

Charity: Donate a dollar a day to help one child in Guatemala
Change: Donate to organizing to stop corporate free trade policies that undercut local economies and wages

Traditional charity plays an important role in maintaining institutions and providing direct services. But our challenge was to go further, to look at the power relationships that contribute to social problems.

It is not enough to fix philanthropy. We need to intervene in a system where the wealthy use philanthropy as a tax avoidance strategy. We need to change the rules governing charitable giving to increase transparency and accountability. And when charitable giving worsens inequality, we should ask some very hard questions about its role in a democratic self-governing society.

Wealthy donors and others may ask: Shouldn't people be able to do whatever they want with their money? Shouldn't government and the rest of us "butt out"? Read on. In part two of this examination of the shadow side of philanthropy, I examine why society has a claim and should have a say.

CHAPTER 11

When Charity Disrupts Justice

Never give in charity what is owed in justice.

POPE JOHN XXIII, 1965

Much of current philanthropic giving, by foundations and individuals, neither meets the needs of our charitable organizations nor addresses some of our most urgent public needs.

PABLO EISENBERG[1]

"Oooohh! You are as wealthy as you look!" says the auctioneer, who is dressed in a full Scottish kilt. He is stunned by the bids that have just been made.

The first auction item at the Weston, Massachusetts, school charity event is a two-night stay at a Vermont country inn. The auctioneer opens the bidding at $200. A few minutes later, the winning bid closes at $5,000 just as I'm about to sample my plate full of "Mediterranean treats." My mouth drops open.

I flash back to fund-raisers I've helped organize at my daughter's public elementary school in Boston. Our entire annual fund-raiser — with silent auction, raffles, and games — raised about $4,000, less money than the first auction item here at the event of the Weston Educational Enrichment Fund Committee.

I'm an undercover observer at this fancy charity event where, despite the early-April chill in the air, some of the wealthiest citizens of Weston wear sleeveless dresses, reenacting the staggering inequalities of the Gilded Age.

Mary and I purchased our tickets to this "Step into the Roaring Twenties" fund-raising gala for the minimum entrance fee, $185 each. Other participants are at the $2,500 Diamond supporters and $1,000 Sapphire donors.

Weston is the most affluent community in Massachusetts, with a median income of $177,000 and median home value of $1.34 million. This gala will raise money for the Weston public school system, already one of the best in the state.

In Roaring Twenties spirit many of the men have dressed as characters from *The Great Gatsby* — with summer suits and straw hats — and the women have dressed with feather boa scarves and flapper headbands and hats. As we entered, a woman in classic cigarette-girl garb — with a box fastened to her waist — offered us the opportunity to buy a raffle ticket, the prize being a bejeweled necklace worth $3,000.

"How much?" I asked.

"Twenty-five dollars and the lady gets to wear one of these." She pointed to the large diamond rings — plastic, with flashing lights embedded in them — in her box. Mary declined. But around the room dozens of women wear large blinking bling.

The third auction item concludes: A week in Umbria, Italy (airfare not included), goes for $8,000. I get up and wander down the rows of tables where silent-auction offerings are displayed. Two of them catch my eye. First is "Graduation Without the Stress," four reserved front-row seats at the high school's June graduation. Second, a "Ride to School with Weston's Finest." The blurb entices, "Your child and a friend can arrive at school in a police cruiser driven by one of Weston's police officers."

Two women dressed as 1920s flappers with large feathery hats debate whether to bid on the front-row seats. "You won't have to wait for hours to see the graduation," one advises the other.

I wonder if the planners of this gala in the state's richest town paused to consider whether it was poor taste to celebrate the last period of extreme and ostentatious wealth inequality in the United States. The Roaring Twenties were not so great in Jim Crow black America. But apparently 1920s style is back in vogue, a sort of nostalgia for Gilded Age chic. Or maybe it was fueled by the over-the-top cinematic remake of *The Great Gatsby*.

My intention is not to parody these partygoers. Weston is very much like the affluent Michigan town I grew up in. And the participants are supporting a public school system. The super-rich of Weston send their children to private schools, bypassing the public system entirely.

But I am here to experience firsthand a troubling trend — the use of charitable funds to compound the existing advantages of the wealthy. Tax-deductible charitable giving, as designed by our tax system, should not worsen existing inequalities; rather it should reduce them.

The co-chair of the evening's events, Allyson Jaffe, thanks all those attending and reminds them, "Every dollar we raise tonight directly benefits your kids."

The pattern is this: Affluent school districts are setting up charitable educational foundations to receive tax-deductible donations. The Weston Fund even allows donors to designate which specific school in the town their donation will go to.

It's probably a biological impulse to help one's children. As Stanford's Rob Reich writes, "Who could fault wealthy parents and townspeople for wanting to do best by their children and local institutions? That their efforts may widen the gap between their own children and children growing up in more disadvantaged districts is an unfortunate, yet unintended, side effect of their generosity."

At the state level, Massachusetts has worked to reduce the alarming disparities of education funding rooted in an antiquated system of paying for education entirely through municipal property taxes. That rusty old funding mechanism has meant that areas with high property values have traditionally had higher educational budgets than those with low property values, which struggle to provide adequate educational opportunities. But now these charitable education foundations are popping up all around. And they effectively bypass the state's attempt to foster educational parity. By reducing their state and federal tax bills with donations to their children's schools, these partygoers are worsening the gap.

Down the road, another pair of affluent communities, Dover and Sherborn, are throwing an annual "casino night" at the Dedham Polo Club. The tickets are too expensive for me to investigate. Between Roaring Twenties inequality and casino economic policy, I find the fund-raisers unseemly. I'm aware that most parents, moved to do something for their kids, don't connect the dots to understand how they are essentially diverting tax dollars back to their own families. Nor do they dress up like a flapper thinking, "Tonight I'll celebrate inequality!" The danger lies in the fact that all these undercurrents and dollar diversions go unnoticed – even by the donors and celebrants themselves.

In Hillsborough, California, one of the wealthiest communities in the United States, parents are asked to make a $2,300 annual charitable contribution to the Hillsborough Schools Foundation, supporting the *public* school system. In 2012, contributions amounting to $3.45 million were deployed, according to the foundation, to reduce class size, and add librarians, art and music teachers, and installation of smart technology in every classroom.

Stanford's Reich, who has studied school foundations, writes, "Private giving to public schools widens the gap between rich and poor. It exacerbates inequalities in financing. It is philanthropy in the service of conferring advantage on the already well-off."[2]

Tax policy effectively subsidizes wealthy parents who donate to their own children's schools. Donors to school foundations decrease their taxes, reducing what the state and federal government would have collected – and distributed to all schools. Most state charitable donation laws track the federal rules, with both deductions diminishing funds for education, infrastructure, and other public goods described in the previous chapter. As Reich observes, "Tax policy makes federal and state governments complicit in the deepening of existing inequalities that they are ostensibly responsible for diminishing in the first place."

My Money, Our Money

On a frigid winter day, I rent a Zipcar and take a ride out to the Boston College Law School to talk to Ray Madoff, a law professor who has written a lot about charitable giving and tax policy. I find her sitting alone in her book-lined office, actively perched over her computer.

I'm curious what she thinks. Are these trends in philanthropy any of our business? Does it really matter what wealthy people are doing with their private money?

In Ray's view, tax breaks for charitable giving are effectively government subsidies for individuals and corporations that make donations and create foundations. For this reason, society has a legitimate responsibility to supervise these donations and ensure they serve charitable purposes.

"The actual tax subsidy is much larger," she explains, with evident passion. "If you include lost estate tax revenue, it is closer to 50 percent." In other words, for every dollar donated by the wealthiest households, taxpayers contribute half in lost revenue.

In her research, and in books like *Immortality and the Law*, Ray explores how the dead dictate to the living through trusts and charitable entities. The charitable deduction and the perpetual charitable trust are two mechanisms that require, in Ray's words, "American taxpayers to subsidize the whims of the rich and fulfill their fantasies of immortality."[3]

The wealthier you are, the higher your matching subsidy. And when very wealthy people create foundations, they also reduce their taxable estates over time. Affluent households are also more likely to itemize and deduct charitable contributions. Only about half of taxpayers earning between $50,000 and $75,000 claim itemized deductions, but nearly 100 percent of taxpayers earning above $200,000 itemize.[4] Middle- and working-class people give a higher percentage of their income to charities, including religious congregations, but are less likely to get a tax benefit.

There are two reasons why the philanthropic choices of the super-wealthy are everyone's business. The first reason is a generic concern about concentrated power — when a small number of people have disproportionate power to shape our culture, our democracy, and civic life. Over the last several decades, many government services have been privatized and shifted to the charitable sector, so there is a greater public interest in how these funds are allocated and used.

Second, and more specific to this chapter, most philanthropic activity, especially among the wealthy, is subsidized by everyone else. In 2014, a congressional panel estimated that individual charitable deductions would cost the Department of the Treasury $43.6 billion in forgone revenue.[5] This doesn't include lost state revenue and the cost over time of reduced estate taxes from the creation of foundations.

Some people will complain this isn't the government's money.[6] I understand — it is private money. And in a free society, people should be able to donate their money wherever they like. But if they want a government tax subsidy, then there is a public interest. If anyone feels that this public interest is government encroachment, the answer is simple: Don't itemize your deductions, don't take the resulting tax break, and spend the resulting post-tax dollars however you'd like.[7]

If I donate $100,000 to a conservation land trust so the nonprofit can purchase the open space next to my house — and my income is over $450,000 — then my donation will reduce my taxes by almost $40,000. In other words, the government kicks in a matching subsidy, giving $2 for every $3 I contribute. All to protect my private view.

Or what if my daughter attended an elite private high school and I gave $500,000 to create a state-of-the-art computer lab there? US taxpayers would effectively be chipping in $200,000 of that donation. Is this the most appropriate use of taxpayer funds? And if I'm making donations instead of paying taxes, doesn't that shift the tax obligations onto others? Someone else is picking up the bill for military defense, highway construction, national park protection, and other services.

I think of a conversation I had with a billionaire. "I'd rather give my money to charity than pay Uncle Sam, who will just waste the money," he explained to me. "I'll make better decisions and be more efficient."

It's a common view among the wealthy. But should we subsidize the pet charities of the very wealthy — in the face of tremendous unmet needs? Probably not. Nor should we provide matching funds to charities that *worsen* the economic divide.

What Charity Can and Can't Do

Since most people are dubious about taxation and government solutions, there are high hopes that philanthropy and the independent nonprofit sector will solve our problems. But can charity address our most pressing problems of extreme inequality and ecological degradation?

I appreciate the "research and development" function of good philanthropy. It allows us to explore new territory, incubate ideas, and pilot test programs that might eventually be brought to scale. But there is a dangerous delusion that somehow philanthropy is going be a replacement for effective government at the local, state, regional, national, and global level.

As I walk from Boston's Longwood Medical area toward the Mission Hill neighborhood, the reason becomes startlingly clear. Here one can see the dizzying gulf between charity-funded projects and public-infrastructure investment in my city. In Boston's Longwood Medical area, there is a building boom. Cranes reach toward the sky, fueled by charitable gifts to hospitals, universities, and museums. Boston's Museum of Fine Arts is adding a new wing, and four major hospitals are each having a construction renaissance.

I wander through the campus of the Harvard School of Public Health with sleek glass buildings that form a quiet buffer from the bustle of city traffic. An underground sprinkler soaks a lush green lawn. Nicely detailed signs say "No Smoking" even in outdoor spaces. Sturdy wooden benches adorn the walkways, with researchers and medical students in scrubs sitting in conversation.

I arrive at the corner of Huntington Avenue and Worthington Street, the dividing line between institutional properties and a low-income neighborhood. A Green Line train, part of Boston's antiquated subway system (the T), screeches to a stop, metal on metal. The light turns green and the rusting train lurches on, clanging its bell and looking more like a nineteenth-century streetcar than a modern transit system. During the many winter storms of 2015, the T effectively shut down, the result of decades of infrastructure disinvestment.[8]

As I cross into the Mission Hill neighborhood, I'm in a different world. What grass there is has become parched and patchy. Block after treeless block is filled with low-rise cinder block public housing. Farther up the hill are several potholed streets with yardless brink tenements and sagging wooden triple-deckers, badly in need of repair.

Down Route 95 from Boston, in the city of New Haven, the disparity between charity-funded building projects and disinvested infrastructure is equally striking. Louis Uchitelle, a reporter at the *New York Times*, chronicled how billions in charitable donations to Yale University is fueling a building boom with over seventy construction projects. Meanwhile, New Haven's public infrastructure is in deep distress.[9] Near the campus, aging bridges are closed to traffic.

Uchitelle's exposé, "Private Cash Sets Agenda for Urban Infrastructure," described the way that "private spending, supported handsomely by a growing number of very wealthy families, is gaining ground on traditional public investment."

While New Haven used to be the largest per-capita recipient of federal urban redevelopment funds, public investment has now been surpassed by private investment. This is mirrored in national trends. Government spending on transportation infrastructure has declined to 1.6 percent of the gross domestic product, from 3 percent in the 1962. Philanthropic giving jumped from 1.5 percent of gross domestic product (GDP) in 1995 to 2.5 percent today. Most of this money is coming from wealthy individuals.[10]

From a policy point of view, we cannot substitute charitable dollars for tax dollars. The priorities are different and they pay for different things. As Uchitelle writes,

> *Philanthropic spending adds mainly to the nation's stock of hospitals, libraries, museums, parks, university buildings, theaters and concert halls. Public infrastructure — highways, bridges, rail systems, water works, public schools, port facilities, sewers, airports, energy grids, tunnels, dams and levees — depends mostly on tax dollars.*

This shift from public money to private wealth is reshaping our cities. The American Society of Civil Engineers gave the United States a "D+" grade for the state of our national infrastructure, arguing we need to invest $3.6 trillion by 2020 just to maintain the infrastructure we have.[11] There are no charitable foundations funding infrastructure projects. No foundation has the resources to rebuild Flint, Michigan's water system. Only government, with its taxing authority, can make such deep and long-term investments.

To address the growing inequality in our midst, we have to address deficits in both our public infrastructure and our civic infrastructure, also known as opportunity. The reason the American Dream is more attainable in Canada than the United States is because of public investments in early childhood education, early interventions in health care, and a greater commitment to debt-free education, from K–12 through college. This level of investment will not happen through charity — and certainly not charity with its current priorities.

Government spending to alleviate poverty — through Medicare, the food stamp program, emergency shelter, and so on — is at too large a scale for charity. The Supplemental Nutrition Assistance Program — popularly known as "food stamps" — provided food for forty-five million people in 2015[12] at an estimated cost of over $75 billion.[13] The total amount donated by foundations to everything in that same year was just under $49 billion.

Within the current system of virtually unregulated tax deductions, donations will change little and, despite the fact that many are given with good intentions, they will serve to sustain wealth status.

Fixing Philanthropy

Periodically, someone in Congress wakes up to these philanthropic abuses and tries to reform the system. In 2000, Congress introduced foundation reform legislation that included a provision to exclude administrative and overhead costs from the disbursements that foundations are legally required to make each year. That mandatory annual payout is just 5 percent of the foundation's assets. This would have removed one incentive for overhead abuse. More important, this wave of the wand would have put an estimated $20 billion more out onto the street in grants to nonprofit organizations. The Council on Foundations and other "charity industry" lobbyists vigorously fought the proposal and defeated it.

In 2013, the Senate Finance Committee released a comprehensive white paper on suggested reforms.[14] Other organizations, such as the National Committee for Responsive Philanthropy, have pressed for change, too.[15]

Here is a sampling of my favorite ways to reform the philanthropic sector to reduce some of these abuses and steer more resources toward reducing inequality. Those of us in the 1 percent — and our charitable entities — should take the lead in pressing for these reforms.

Link Excise Tax to Payout Distribution. In a *New York Times* piece, Ray Madoff wrote, "The 5 percent rule was enacted to provide a floor for charitable giving, but most private foundations use it as a ceiling as well."[16] When foundations simply meet this requirement, they pay the standard 2 percent federal excise tax on any income their investments earn in a given year. When they give more than their historical average, they pay just 1 percent. Madoff proposes restructuring the excise tax to encourage larger annual disbursements — reducing it to 1 percent for foundations that pay out between 6 and 8 percent, and outright eliminating it for those that pay out more than 8 percent in grants.

Increase Distribution Payout Percentage. Foundation assets have grown substantially over the last thirty years, paralleling the wealth expansion at the top. But foundations have resisted policy proposals aimed at raising the minimum payout rate. Foundations have complained that this would lead to an erosion of capital and the ability of foundations to exist in perpetuity. But a number of studies have shown foundation assets would not decline, even with a payout of 7 or 8 percent. And more important, we should not assume that foundations should live forever. As Pablo Eisenberg observed, "There is nothing sacred about perpetuity."

Exempt Foundation Overhead. The foundation payout requirement should exempt foundation overhead. This would reduce the incentive for lavish internal spending on salaries and other administrative costs.

Eliminate Compensation for Trustees and Board Members. There is no research indicating that public performance of foundations improves with paid trustees. As two nonprofit consultants observed, "Compensation turns board members into 'insiders,' a status that weakens their ability to act on behalf of the public and, when necessary, to dissent." Charities can always hire outside experts, but hired experts shouldn't vote on organizational matters.[17]

Require Independent Boards. If these are truly public interest organizations, they should not have boards composed entirely of family members and paid staff. Many states require 51 percent of corporation boards to be independent.[18]

Two-Tier Tax Benefits. Congress should establish two types of charitable entities and give them different tax benefits. Donations to qualified charities that alleviate poverty, reduce inequality, and address urgent social problems such as environmental degradation should receive the full deductibility under existing charitable tax laws. But donations to other types of nonprofits and associations should have their tax benefits reduced.

Sunset Foundations and Donor-Advised Funds. Foundations and charitable trusts should not live forever. Donor-advised funds should require distribution within five years. Foundation charters should have limited life spans, let's say ten to twenty years. This means big endowments — like the Ford Foundation and the MacArthur Foundation — should be spent down, directing them to focus on solving problems in the immediate term rather than focusing on long-term self-preservation.

Those of us with wealth to donate should support such reforms — including sunsetting — and lead by example. If you are a trustee of a family foundation, press for more rapid distribution and higher payouts. Suggest that the foundation "spend down" its assets over a decade, as the Atlantic Philanthropies recently did. Chuck Feeney, the donor who created Atlantic Philanthropies from wealth made from the Duty Free Shop franchise, never wanted to create a permanent philanthropic infrastructure. He also didn't want to burden his children. "Right from the very beginning, I felt this just would give them a destination in life that they hadn't earned per se and that I would be imposing on them," Feeney said.[19]

Feeney and Atlantic Philanthropies join a growing number of "giving while living" philanthropies that move money in a finite period. As philanthropic advisor Amy Markham and Susan Wolf Ditkoff write, "When you've fixed a date to turn out the lights, every grant is an attempt to make a lasting difference now — before the money runs out."[20]

Pay Your Damn Taxes

To those in the wealthiest 1 percent: Pay your taxes. Charity is not a substitute for taxes. Charity will not address the most fundamental needs for public infrastructure and economic opportunity.

We can all quibble about government waste or things we wish our tax dollars did or didn't do. That's an invitation for civic engagement, not a justification for tax avoidance. When we wealthy, who have historically paid substantial taxes, opt out of taxes by using massive charitable deductions, we disinvest from the public investments that created social mobility for past generations and the infrastructure we all depend on.

We can't pretend that charity is always virtuous when billions flow to pet charity projects with limited public benefits. No one is discouraging anyone's generous impulse to share. But if you must give to a suburban land conservancy or art museum or private school, don't deduct it. Don't ask the rest of us to pay for your priorities when we have other, more urgent priorities in our midst.

—◇—

If traditional charity is an insufficient response to our current problems, what is the way forward?

Up to this point, we've been talking about the barriers to engaging those with wealth and power to make a meaningful contribution to social change.

We are steeped in myths and stories about how wealth is created. We are drugged by privilege, which dulls our empathy and human response mechanisms. We misunderstand the basic physics of extreme inequality — so we fail to see or admit to the cumulative impact of class and racial advantages. The charity system falls short of intervening in the system.

In our current capitalist system, people are lavishly rewarded not just for their own labor or contribution, but for the full value of the commons that made their wealth possible. Mark Zuckerberg is metaphorically working in an ice cream parlor where he puts a cherry on top of an ice cream sundae. Not only is he rewarded with the full three-scoop sundae, but he lays claim to the entire ice cream parlor. We need a new system of rewards.

What is the next system? And what role can we all play in moving us there?

PART V

WEALTH, COME HOME

We can and must respond creatively to the triple crisis and simultaneously overcome dehumanization, economic inequality, and, ecological catastrophe.

VANDANA SHIVA

— CHAPTER 12 —

The Moment We Are In

We are dealing with issues that cannot be solved without the nation undergoing a radical redistribution of economic power.

DR. MARTIN LUTHER KING JR.

The eyes of the future are looking back at us and they are praying for us to see beyond our own time.

TERRY TEMPEST WILLIAMS

"Things are getting worse on many fronts," says Gar Alperovitz, an important friend and mentor. We are sitting in our usual back booth of the Beacon Grille, in Washington, DC.

"Income and wealth inequality, climate change, war, expanding militarism," he laments. "And we're going to see a real clamp-down in this country, a loss of liberties that has already begun. It's a very *nasty brew*, where we are going."

These are sobering words from a man whose perspective I have valued for nearly thirty years.

I was 28 years old when I first read an article by Alperovitz in *Sojourners*, a religious magazine focused on social justice. At the time, in 1988, I was living in Greenfield, Massachusetts, and working for an organization that assisted local community development projects. Part of my job included helping tenants in mobile home parks, like Harlan and Mary Parro in Bernardston, buy their parks and manage them as resident-owned cooperatives.

Alperovitz was the only person I had come across who was talking about the important role of local community development, the stuff I was doing, and how it fit into larger system changes.

"Who is this guy?" I remember thinking, as I sought out his books and talks. In the decades since then, I've gotten his advice on a wide range of topics, often in the same back booth at the Beacon Grille. I'm not big on labels — capitalist, Christian, socialist, Buddhist, anarchist. When pressed, I'd say I'm an Alperovist.

So it is even more alarming, this dire talk of "nasty brews."

"The system has run out of options," he says resolutely. "That means either it will get *really* nasty or there will be fundamental change. I think it's going do both: It *will* get nasty, and there's a possibility of fundamental change in a new direction. It's a very strange moment — and an important time to be engaged."

The Moment We Are In

I see the same gruesome picture. The twin problems I'm most active with — climate change and growing wealth inequality — appear to be cascading out of control.

As 2016 begins, I'm struck by the horrific floods in the Midwest and England, the droughts in Africa and the US West, and the fruit trees prematurely blooming in my backyard. I'm also steeped in the new statistics of inequality, having just released a series of reports about wealth concentration trends.

Yet our political system, captured at the national level by the rule riggers and game fixers of the wealth- and corporate-elite classes, is incapable of nimbly responding to these challenges.

And as wealth concentrates exponentially, the rule riggers will further use their concentrated wealth and power to block reforms we urgently need for human survival and well-being. This creates a downward spiral for both equality and ecology. Mix in a little war and terrorism and I can concoct my own foul-tasting brew.

At the grassroots level, our collective response is fragmented, incremental, and divided. Most social movements operate in silos: environmental, human rights, electoral politics, labor and economic populism, democracy reform. Much of this activity exists below the radar of what remains of traditional media, rendering it invisible. Meanwhile, the wider culture is absorbed in a range of distractions, from celebrity culture, to gladiator spectator sports (as opposed to participatory sports), and shock and awe presidential politics.

Yet, this is the moment to act, and the 1 percent has an important role in helping this transformation to happen. So let's take a look at the possibilities for change and the role that wealthy people can play in these movements. These roles range from working as policy advocates, as funders of campaigns, and as stakeholders in system change, to accompanying those without power to do what needs to be done.

Averting Climate Catastrophe

The climate crisis is unfolding in front of us, with new dimensions revealing themselves every week in the form of weird weather, superstorms, droughts, floods, ocean disturbances, and disease. It is worth quoting directly from most recent report of the Intergovernmental Panel on Climate Change:

> *Human influence on the climate system is clear, and recent anthropogenic emissions of greenhouse gases are the highest in history. Recent climate changes have had widespread impacts on human and natural systems.*
>
> *Continued emission of greenhouse gases will cause further warming and long-lasting changes in all components of the climate system, increasing the likelihood of severe, pervasive and irreversible impacts for people and ecosystems. Limiting climate change would require substantial and sustained reductions in greenhouse gas emissions which, together with adaption, can limit climate change risks.*
>
> *Climate change will amplify existing risks and create new risks for natural and human systems. Risks are unevenly distributed and are generally greater for disadvantaged people and communities at all levels of development.*[1]

As Pope Francis says, we must "care for our common home."[2]

The large fossil fuel companies — big oil, gas, and coal — possess four times more carbon reserves than can safely be burned without raising Earth's temperature past 2 degrees Centigrade. All rational parties agree that 2 degrees Centigrade is the maximum temperature rise our planet can attain without catastrophic climate change. In fact, at the December 2015 Paris climate summit, delegates from 186 countries set the target lower to 1.5 degrees, even as they failed to forge binding agreements to lower greenhouse gas emissions to meet that target.

To compound the absurdity, the big fossil fuel corporations are spending over $600 billion a year to search for new oil, gas, and coal reserves, carbon assets that we hope and pray will never be extracted and burned.[3]

The carbon-burning machine is on autopilot, with powerful corporations driving the extraction — but also using their considerable political clout to block legislative remedies that would alter the course. If carbon emissions continue on their current trajectory, we are heading to a climate reckoning.

Escalating Inequality

As we confront a planetary ecological crisis, we are also facing down poisonous social inequalities. We've seen, in earlier pages, how those inequalities manifest in the everyday aspects of our lives. But let's take a look at what this means in numbers.

In the United States, the pace of extreme inequality has been steadily increasing. Real wages have been stagnant for over three decades, even as productivity gains have surged. For most working families, this translates into working more hours and going deeper into debt.

The share of income flowing to the top 1 percent of US households is now 22 percent, up from 9 percent in 1978. The wealthiest 1 percent saw their share of US wealth increase to 42 percent in 2012. Most of this change accrued in the top one-tenth of 1 percent (0.1 percent), whose wealth share rose from 7 percent in 1978 to 22 percent in 2012. Since 2009, most of the growth in wealth has flowed to the top one-tenth of the top 1 percent. In other words, the big winners are the top one-in-one-thousand households.[4]

Vast amounts of wealth have pooled at the very pinnacle, the *Forbes* 400 and the global billionaire list. The combined net worth of the *Forbes* 400, an estimated $2.34 trillion in 2015, is now equal to the bottom 62 percent of the US population. The wealthiest twenty US billionaires — few enough to fit on a plush Gulfstream G650 luxury jet — now have as much wealth as the bottom half of the US population, according to a study I co-authored, with Josh Hoxie, called "Billionaire Bonanza: The Forbes 400 and the Rest of Us."[5]

The richest 100 now have as much wealth as the entire African American population, over 42 million people. The richest 186 individuals have as much wealth as the entire Latino population, over 55 million individuals.[6]

As mentioned in the introduction, French economist Thomas Piketty argues in *Capital in the Twenty-First Century* that unless we intervene in the current workings of the economy, wealth inequality will continue to grow. Drawing from centuries of historical research, Piketty shows that when the payout to owners of capital vastly exceeds the rate of productivity and the payout to labor, wealth concentrates in fewer and fewer hands. This results in what he calls "patrimonial capitalism," or a society governed by hereditary wealth and power. With 10 percent of the population holding more than 70 percent of the national share of wealth, Piketty observes, "the conditions are ideal for an 'inheritance society' to prosper — where by 'inheritance society' I mean a society characterized by both a very high concentration of wealth and a significant persistence of large fortunes from generation to generation."[7] Each day that inequalities deepen, so do hopelessness, deprivation, and the injuries of poverty. We must intervene in this system powerfully and urgently.

Engaging in Policy Campaigns for Change

We know what needs to be done to address both the climate crisis and extreme inequality. To avert climate cataclysm, the United States must make investments in energy conservation, green buildings and transportation infrastructure, and renewable energy generation and transmission. We need to put a price on carbon, which will create a huge incentive for these investments and generate some of the revenue required to make them. And we need to do this in a way that doesn't penalize one sector of workers or increase economic burdens on lower- and middle-income households. Yet it is hard to envision our society making these changes commensurate with the speed of climate change — in part because the US Congress has been captured by the fossil fuel industry.

So our challenge is this: How do people with advantage help shift this dynamic? As powerless as any of us may feel, people in the top 10 percent of the US public have more agency than almost anyone else on the planet to shift the outcome.

We can fund the organizing movements working for a just transition. We can support campaigns to put a price on carbon and invest in conservation and renewables. We can divest from the fossil fuel sector, making a public statement. And we can reinvest in renewable energy and the transition to relocalized economies that not only shrink their carbon footprints by meeting their food, energy, and many of their other basic needs regionally but also can build resiliency better than our current economies when facing challenges brought on by climate change and inequality.

What about the role of the wealthy in campaigns to reduce inequality? Both in US history and in other countries around the world it is possible to rewire capitalism to share prosperity and ensure healthy opportunities for all.

From my tale about visiting the World War II veterans in Norwood, Massachusetts, you may recall that the United States made a number of public investments in education, housing, infrastructure, and technology that fueled the 1945–1975 expansion of the white middle class.

Other industrialized countries, such as Canada, Denmark, and Germany, have much less inequality than the United States because the rules of the economy promote shared prosperity. We need to raise the floor, level the playing field, and break up concentrated wealth.

Raise the Floor. Establish stronger social safety nets, below which people cannot fall. Stop the cycles of deprivation and insecurity by ensuring basic income, health, and opportunity. This includes higher minimum wages, universal and affordable health care, and, when full employment is not possible, a guaranteed minimum income. As the nature of work changes and jobs vanish thanks to technology and globalization, more advanced industrial societies are establishing basic income support programs that are more robust than US-style disability and unemployment programs.

Level the Playing Field. Institute fair rules that don't give one business or segment of society preferences over another — but that also deal with historic inequalities. We should have fair tax policies so that two competing companies, such as Federal Express and United Parcel Service, are taxed at the same rates. (Instead, thanks to aggressive tax dodging and loopholes, FedEx pays an effective corporate tax rate of 4.2 percent while UPS pays 27.5 percent.)[8] Our political system must also be shielded from the "wealth effect" that allows a few billionaires to have disproportionate political influence, effectively disenfranchising millions of voters. We need campaign finance reform without loopholes.

Societal investments must ensure genuine equality of opportunity, such as access to early childhood education, school preparation, decent schools, and training that prepares us for participation in the economy of the future.

These are not new ideas, nor are they "radical" to the majority of Americans. So why haven't we been able to put them into effect? A lot of debate and policy campaign resources go into rule changes to "raise the floor" and "level the playing field." In 2014 and 2015, there were successful campaigns to raise state-level minimum wages for low-wage workers. But in today's world, such advances don't seem to make the kind of differences we expect them to make: They don't truly level the playing field or raise the floor. That's because they are overwhelmed and undermined by the power of concentrated wealth.

For example, past efforts to reduce the influence of money on politics have failed. Campaign finance reforms, such as McCain-Feingold, were trumped by *Citizens United* and other rulings that opened the spigots of private money. Concentrated wealth subverts boundaries like water running down a hill. You can put up a dam, but eventually the water finds a way around it.

So, fair rules are necessary, but we are spinning our wheels if we don't tackle concentrated wealth first. *It's the only way to protect our democracy.*

Reduce the Concentration of Wealth. There are essentially two sets of rule changes that could intervene in the destructive cycle of concentrated wealth begetting more concentrated wealth. One set of rule changes are "redistributional," such as progressive income, wealth, and inheritance taxes. Another set of interventions are "predistributional," such as broadening the employee ownership of enterprises that spread around the wealth, advancing living wages, and increasing access to opportunity.

Rule changes that reduce the amassing of wealth are the most controversial. Conservative politicians and pundits equate any talk of "inequality" or "redistribution" as part of a "politics of envy" and "class war," even though we've just lived through several decades of upward redistribution, in which workers produced more and more but endured flat wages while CEO and executive pay rose dramatically from the fruits of their labor. Recent years also saw working- and middle-class tax dollars bail out corporations deemed too big to fail when their speculative behavior brought the economy to its knees in 2008. These conservatives would rather talk about "equality of opportunity" than the existing imbalance of wealth and power. But as we know from previous discussions, too much inequality undermines opportunity and social mobility.

The United States has experienced these levels of extreme inequality before, during the first Gilded Age that spanned, roughly, from the 1880s to 1915. Leaders from across the political spectrum decried the threat to our young self-governing republic. Movements emerged to challenge concentrated wealth and its distorting influence on society.[9]

Then and now, the already wealthy helped break through the stuck pattern of political discourse. In the early 1900s, members of the wealthiest 1 percent, such as Andrew Carnegie and Theodore Roosevelt, supported progressive tax policies, including establishing a federal estate tax.[10]

Henry Dearmest Lloyd, the publisher of the *Chicago Tribune* and a member of the richest 1 percent, wrote an exposé, *Wealth Against Commonwealth*. Lloyd argued that private wealth and large corporations such as Standard Oil were undermining the "commonwealth."

In Lloyd's day, four hundred families dominated wealth and culture, alongside a handful of powerful trusts and corporations that monopolized whole sectors of the economy. As we enter a second Gilded Age, the 1 percent has an important role. Like Henry Dearmest Lloyd, we need to stand with the commonwealth against the forces of predatory wealth.

Facing the System Problem

"Unfortunately, a lot of political activity does not get at the underlying systemic change we need right now," says Alperovitz, back in our Beacon Grille booth.

"Too much of politics is a distraction, soaking up all the attention from the real business at hand. I'm not dismissing politics, especially at the state and local level. But we have to face the limits of our political system in fixing the underlying system drivers right now."

What Alperovitz is saying here is that our current system can't fix our current problems. Even though his message is unsettling and could even be depressing, he seems every bit the happy warrior. In fact, today Alperovitz seems radiant, glowing with vitality. He mentions that he is turning 80 soon, which I find hard to believe. He's in terrific physical shape. I know he swims almost every day at a neighborhood pool. He's been married for over forty years, and is engaged with younger activists who adore him, dozens of whom attend the monthly discussion group he organizes through The Democracy Collaborative, which he cofounded. He writes prolifically, and keeps up a rigorous travel and lecture schedule.

Alperovitz tells me he had his own dark night of the soul facing the deep systemic crisis around us. In his early 50s, he was much in demand as an economist. He was on *Meet the Press*, the premier serious news show of the period, and interviewed on other talk shows. He was regularly quoted in the *New York Times*. He was on the lecture circuit. But he felt something was off.

"I was riding high and enjoying it," he confesses. "It was remunerative and flattering. And then one day, I didn't believe it anymore. I didn't know what to do. I went upstairs and started reading and scribbling. I stopped taking media calls and stopped writing for newspapers. Just cold, boom."

Alperovitz began to reorient his work and practice. "The important thing to remember is none of this is easy. Facing the deeper system drivers requires commitment."

I ask him, "What is the role of wealthy people in bringing about these system changes?"

After a moment of thought, Alperovitz answers, "I start with, what's the role of anybody? First, we have to get perspective. We don't quite realize what an important moment we are in. So much of what we must do is lay the groundwork. My heroes are the civil rights workers in Mississippi in the 1930s and 1940s. That's when the groundwork was done, the hard stuff. It's easy to join a movement once it's moving.

"The other piece that is important is about community," he continues, invoking the importance of place. "We need to reconstruct genuine community, come out from isolation, and build relationships and institutions. It's both psychological and institutional. How do we build institutions that nurture community?"

Alperovitz points out that the conventional American theory of change is rooted in the last century's model of the 1930s New Deal. We think we can put together a labor–community coalition that will create a countervailing power to corporate domination. But the period influenced by New Deal policies and organized labor, 1940–1970, was an aberration, he stresses. Today, labor is so much weaker and corporations are so much more powerful. Now add in the climate crisis to the mix.

"We are talking about challenging the most powerful corporate capitalist system in the history of the world. And there are movements laying the groundwork for its transformation, which I believe is possible."

To work toward the next system, we need to understand the current system, its nature and drivers. Alperovitz and new economy thinker Gus Speth have teamed up to co-chair the Next System Project, to seed new ways of thinking about the future. Speth writes, we have "unleashed a virulent, fast-growing strain of corporate-consumerist capitalism." We are in a phase of hyperextractive capitalism that is thrusting its wealth-extracting tentacles into every aspect of human endeavor, including areas once thought sacred and beyond the market.

"In its ruthlessness at home and abroad, it creates a world of wounds," continues Speth. "As it strengthens and grows, those wounds deepen and multiply, with especially severe impacts on America's black and other minority communities."[11]

So what is the next system? And what role can advantaged people play in ushering it forward? Alperovitz is animated about the localized efforts that are building a checkerboard of social ownership across the country, efforts to build "institutions, workplaces, and cultures concerned with democratizing wealth," as he puts it. Such work is under way in many US cities.

"There's all this stuff the newspapers don't cover. But now you can find impact investing, cooperatives, community land trusts for housing, people taking over public utilities, taking over public broadcasting systems, socializing neighborhood land trusts. There is a movement for public banks and municipal banks in Philadelphia, Santa Fe, Denver. These are no longer experiments. We are long past that."

Key components in all these initiatives are institutions that democratize and broaden ownership of wealth. It's not just a return to Main Street economies, it's a rethinking of the way business is done and who benefits from it. Economist Marjorie Kelly calls this emerging economic model "generative capitalism," which is the opposite of extractive capitalism.

Accompaniment

Over the course of our discussion, I tell Gar about the Patriotic Millionaires, the more than two hundred wealthy business leaders engaged in policy debates around wealth and income inequality. And we also talk about impact investing and the Divest-Invest movement, where people shift their wealth out of investments in fossil fuel and into clean energy and ventures that support strong local economies.

This is one way for wealth to come home, engaging in place and in projects that are building the next system. Many wealthy people live in cities and metropolitan areas that have become increasingly polarized in the last decade, especially along racial lines. What if they stepped up?

I ask Alperovitz again, "What would it look like to fully put a stake in these communities and commit to community wealth-building initiatives?"

"Get your hands dirty," Alperovitz advises. "Be part of democratizing wealth and building a community-sustaining economy from the ground up. It may be tricky to show up as someone with money — because you just want to be a person rather than be viewed as a person with money. But be part of the experiment.

"This is not to say it's easy," said Alperovitz. "It's actually quite hard. And there is no single blueprint. Sometimes the thing to do is *accompany* others in the journey and find out what happens."

Accompany. Alperovitz has said a word I had not heard since my days in Central America in the 1980s. Working at a refugee camp in El Salvador, my colleagues and I described our role as "accompaniment."

We had the privilege of holding US passports, which meant that when we were in the United States, our role was to lobby for a just foreign policy. But while in El Salvador, living and working alongside people affected by our government's policies, our job was to be present, to accompany. As Dr. Paul Farmer wrote, "To accompany someone is to go somewhere with him or her, to break bread together, to be present on a journey with a beginning and an end."

As a white person working in the civil rights movement and later an attorney working in the labor movement, Staughton Lynd describes his work as "accompanying." He quotes another colleague, saying, "Sometimes all you can do for another person is stand in the rain with them."

I feel this way when I've showed up at a rally of hotel workers who've been illegally fired or at an eviction blockade where neighbors stand with a person whose home is being foreclosed on. I don't have any specific power or role. I'm there as a witness. I'm accompanying other people in their struggles against injustice, and in the process, I'm allowing myself to be touched and moved and changed.

Sometimes all you can do is accompany, risking awkwardness and judgment. Alperovitz and I talk about our mutual friend Jodie Evans, who went to Ferguson, Missouri, after the shooting of Michael Brown. She is white with flaming-red hair, and it was probably pretty obvious that she was not from Ferguson. But she showed up and said, "How can I help?"

"The thing about Jodie is she is genuine, so people can hear it," Gar observes. "If it's not genuine, people can hear that. For some, like Jodie, it is showing up and being present that counts most."

People are struggling to figure this out. Not just people with wealth, but with any kind of advantage. Many of us are pained by runaway inequality and the dangers of the climate crisis, but don't see a path to system change. We hunger to be part of something bigger.

In policy campaigns, we need to leverage our privilege to help as messengers and advocates. Other times, we should move capital to support community-based businesses or donate to advocacy and electoral campaigns. But we should also accompany others as they engage in their struggles.

The final section of this book explores what these different roles might look like, with no rigid blueprint or program. What does it mean to come home, to establish a stake in a place? What does it mean to accompany others? How do we fully devote ourselves to the change we want to see?

Alperovitz invokes a phrase from Napoleon, which roughly translates from French as, "You engage and then you see."

"You learn by engagement, not by hanging back," he says, smiling. "And it's in those risk-taking leaps that we find the excitement, the meaning of life."

— CHAPTER 13 —

A Stake in the Common Good

Sometimes resilience means surviving long enough to get out, to build something new somewhere else. But sometimes, it means staying put.

KRISTEN MOE

"We have to take a shower before we get in the pool," I said, pointing to the sign on the locker room wall.

My 7-year-old daughter Nora and I were in the men's locker room at our local community center pool.

"That's silly," Nora replied, preening in front of the mirror in her pink one-piece bathing suit. "We will get wet in the pool."

The locker room was a smelly mess, with large gritty puddles, boot tracks, soiled towels, and the fragrance of urine and overpowering chlorine. Nora didn't seem to notice.

It took fortitude to leave our warm house on a winter day and walk to the Curtis Hall Community Center for family swim hour. But Nora, like most kids, was a fish, eager to plunge into water. Once she was in the water, it was always hard to get her out.

"Well, it's the rules," I said, turning on the shower nozzle and waiting for the water to warm up. "We just need to look a little wet." The pool is sufficiently chlorinated to kill off almost any living organism, except hopefully the swimmers.

We ran around in the shower and then stepped out into the pool area. An adult swim hour was just finishing up and older women in bathing caps were climbing out of the pool and walking toward the locker room.

A mother and her two little girls emerged from the women's locker room, also freshly showered. Several other families stood patiently by the edge of the pool holding Styrofoam "noodles" and kickboards. I noticed that Nora and I were the only white people.

"Sorry folks," said a man in a maroon community center shirt, walking out of the office with a clipboard. "There is no family swim today."

All the children standing by the pool wore confused frowns.

"Why?" I ask.

"No lifeguard," he replied. "The last lifeguard has to leave, and we don't have anyone to cover."

"You don't have anyone in the building?" I could feel my temper starting to kindle.

"Nope, sorry, those are the rules." He turned and headed back to his office.

The other parents broke the bad news to their kids, collected their towels, and headed for the exits.

I met eyes with a Latino mother holding her daughter's hand.

"Bummer," I said to her, smiling. "We're all suited up, showered, and nowhere to go."

"Yeah, really," she said, smiling at Nora. "This happened at last Saturday's family swim too. It happens half the time we come here. No lifeguard." She shook her head in resignation.

"Really?" I was surprised. "Yeah, well, take care."

I stood there, dripping water and looking at Nora. She was staring at the empty pool. A mischievous smile appeared on her face, "Hey Poppy, why don't I just fall in."

"Hmmm," I said, appreciating her rebellious temperament. I glanced toward the office. "Probably not a good idea."

I felt the fury welling up in my chest. Why can't the community center get its act together? I didn't want to be another entitled white parent blowing his top at an underresourced community agency.

Other white upper-middle-class parents I knew had abandoned the community center long ago. They had joined private swim clubs or the West Roxbury YMCA, which costs $500 a year for a family membership. In the summer, families paid $600 a season to have access to the outdoor pool at the Park School, a local private school where we had been guests. It was always pristine, with plenty of lifeguards.

I approached the pool office and saw the man through the window. He was a younger black man, sitting in front of a computer terminal. I knocked and did my best to hold a friendly tone.

"Hi, I'm Chuck Collins — and this is my daughter Nora. What's your name?"

Slightly startled, the man looked up from his computer. "Oh hi, I'm Albert." He smiled and waved to Nora.

"I'm curious, one of the other parents said we've had a hard time getting lifeguards for the other family swims."

"Yes," he replied. "I'm not responsible for scheduling. But I have to break the bad news to people."

"Yeah, I bet that's no fun," I replied. "So who is responsible?"

"What do you mean?"

"Who hires and schedules the lifeguards?"

"Sandy Jordan is the recreation director."

"Is she around?" I was trying my hardest not be a pain in the ass. "Maybe we can help lobby for more resources from the city." I'm not a government basher. Most of the time the people running local services are stretched.

"Her office is on the second floor." He grins nervously. "I haven't seen her today."

"Thanks, Albert." I waved. "Take care!"

Nora and I dried off, put our clothes back on, and managed to stay dry while dodging the gray puddles around the locker room. As we left, I walked by the administrative offices. There was no Sandy Jordan to be found, but I did get her phone number.

Over the next couple of days, I called the number several times, listening to her voice mail and leaving polite messages. She never called back.

Over the next week, I ruminated about the pool. When I complained to my friends, they all repeated a sort of "can't fight city hall" mantra and suggested we join a private pool. We have the money, but it is the principle for me. What about all the other families that can't opt out and join a private pool? Shouldn't the public pool not only have a lifeguard but be a great place to go?

Opt In or Opt Out?

This is the privileged choice dilemma. We vote with our feet and money and engagement. Do we maintain a stake in the public services system? Or do we opt out for a privatized system?

There are dozens of these kinds of small choices every day, such as: Do I take public transportation or drive? Do I look for a book at the public library or buy it? Then there are huge choices: Do I send my child to public schools? Or opt for private schools? Do I live in the city or the suburbs?

And then there are medium-sized choices: Do I stick with the local public pool? Or do I give up and opt for a private recreational facility?

Wealthy people often don't just withdraw their tax dollars from public investments, they also disengage from the democratic process around spending priorities and the quality of public services. It may feel like we can't fight city hall or Congress, but if anyone has a fighting chance in our current system, it is the donor class, the people with the time, social networks, and capacity to help change happen.

As we've become a more economically and politically polarized society, we are doubly challenged by the fact that people with the most wealth, power, networks, and sense of agency do *not* have a stake in the functioning of the institutions and services that everyone else depends on. They opt out, privatizing their needs. The very wealthy have always done this, but the pace of disconnection is accelerating as inequality grows.

Instead of using the public park or town pool, the wealthy have backyard paradises, vacation houses, and private country clubs. In the town where I grew up, the City of Bloomfield Hills, there are no public parks. In a listing of recreation options, the city recommends visits to Cranbrook (private grounds with an admission fee) and four private clubs, Bloomfield Open Hunt (frequented by the horse people), Stonycroft Hills Golf Club, and Bloomfield Hills Country Club (where I was a caddy). Women can join the exclusive Village Club, founded in 1956 by "Marian Gilbreath, who after lunching at the Pasadena California Town Club, came home eager to see a similar club in the Birmingham area."[1] All social and recreation needs are privatized and exclusive.

Instead of retaining a stake in public schools, wealthy families create exclusive glide paths for their children that include private schools, tutors, enrichment classes, elite summer camps, music, and arts, all outside the public government-funded sphere. Like residents of gated communities that have private security, landscaping, and rubbish removal, they lose interest in public services. Eventually they lobby to opt out of paying taxes and favor budget cuts. Even the most civic-minded, who profess allegiance to quality public schools and services, contract an "out of sight, out of mind" malignancy when they don't have a personal day-to-day stake in a system.

As public services deteriorate, it becomes more rational to opt out. After the very wealthy pull out, upper-middle-class and middle-class parents try to follow behind. The less affluent stretch to pay for private schools and other opportunities for their kids, usually at a higher personal price of overwork, longer commutes, and mounting debt. In urban areas, with a larger population of low-income people, there is a "rush to the door" as upper-middle-class parents depart en masse from public services, leading to further service deterioration.

In our 2003 book, *Wealth and Our Commonwealth*, Bill Gates Sr. and I wrote:

> For those who are not born wealthy, however, opportunities depend on the existence of strong community and public institutions. The ladder of opportunity for America's middle class depends on strong and accessible public education institutions, libraries, state parks, and municipal pools. And for America's poor, the ladder of opportunity also includes access to affordable health care, quality public transportation, and childcare assistance.

Schools are the most salient example of the power of engaged stakeholders. Public schools lose clout if they don't have affluent parents with social capital. They lose music, arts, theater, and other enrichment programs, things considered special extras in public schools with austere budgets. Quality deteriorates without engaged stakeholders to hold politicians, school principals, and teachers to higher standards of excellence. The squeaky wheels get the grease — and in a public school system the grease is the resources, experienced teachers, and enrichment extras.

Growing inequality has exposed glaring disparities in the quality of recreation facilities and playing fields at urban and suburban high schools.

As a parent, I've attended high school sporting events around my region. Once I accompanied my bonus-son Caleb's wrestling team to a tournament in suburban Wayland. The Boston city boys were blown away by the amenities of Wayland's gym facilities, including enormous 15-foot doorways. Their coach wisely explained that this was where the Wayland home team rode in on their "high horses" and advised them not to be intimidated.

I live a few blocks from Franklin Park, a 527-acre public park designed by Frederick Law Olmsted, architect of New York's Central Park. At one time, Franklin Park was a public paradise for Boston's working classes. There was a first-rate zoo, walking and horse trails (with affordable horses to rent), and the nation's first public golf course. Sitting atop a bluff was a clubhouse, with a great veranda, 5-cent showers and towels, and toys for borrowing, including sleds, ice skates, and tennis rackets. Families with children flocked there on weekends, enjoying the recreational riches.

Today, the clubhouse is gone, the ruined stone steps covered with broken glass and weed trees. The park is desolate on many days. On my regular walks, I rarely see another soul. There is still a struggling zoo and golf course with a snazzy new clubhouse that is open to the public. But Franklin Park is a shadow of its former grandeur. An active neighborhood group, the Franklin Park Coalition, advocates for the park and organizes events to draw people to its attractions. But few wealthy people have a stake in Franklin Park, unlike the downtown Boston Garden that is surrounded by luxury housing.

Deepening a Stake

I knew that if I opted out from the Curtis Hall pool, it would have soon receded from my mind. I might have felt principled umbrage that hundreds of poor and working-class families didn't have a functional swimming pool. But I wouldn't have felt a deep and personal stake in fixing the inequity. My thoughtlessness would not have been rooted in malice, just in simple disconnection. The "privilege drug" would have altered my memory and leveled out my emotions about this civic injustice. I would have forgotten about the pool.

So I decided to opt in, with gusto. I adopted the Curtis Hall pool as a personal cause. I embraced my inner screechy privileged parent because no one else was stepping up. The other parents didn't seem to have the time, sense of agency, social capital, or entitlement to keep the pressure on.

I also understood community organizing — the process of bringing other affected parents together, developing leaders, analyzing the problem, identifying who has the power, and designing a campaign. As a parent with a full-time job, I wasn't going to do that. I was going to try a privileged shortcut.

After leaving several voice messages over the course of a week, I began to research the governance structure of the community center. I figured out who the director was at the city level and the local level.

The next time Nora and I went for a swim (and there was a lifeguard), I talked to Albert again and got a list of the dates over the last month when there was no lifeguard on duty — about a dozen incidents. I learned how much the lifeguards were paid, which is no different from the wages paid to lifeguards at the YMCA pool in West Roxbury, which managed to keep its pool fully staffed.

I talked to my Boston city councilor, someone I knew personally and whose campaign I supported with a contribution. I wrote a letter, summarizing the problem, and sent it to all concerned. I fought city hall. I became a squeaky wheel. I tried to keep my outraged entitlement at bay, emphasizing that I would do whatever was necessary to get the community center the resources it needed to have clean locker rooms and ample staffing. But as I waded into the weeds, I came to suspect that the problem wasn't about money. There was a management problem. Someone was falling down on the job.

My breakthrough moment happened accidentally. I ran into Tom Menino, then the mayor of Boston, at a community arts event. He was in a personable and chatty mood. I explained the no-show lifeguard problem. "Picture all those kids standing there in their bathing suits," I implored. This visual image upset the mayor, and he ushered over his number one helper at the event and passed me off to him. I gave him the details, got his card, went home, and emailed him a letter.

The next day my phone rang. It was the city's director of community centers. She had no idea about the lifeguard problem, she said; no one had complained to her. She gave me her personal cell phone and told me to keep her posted. And I did. The next time we had a no-show lifeguard problem, I called her from the locker room. I told her that twenty-two Boston children and parents were standing there wet and deprived of a family swim. She was incensed.

The squeak got some grease and the wheels turned. The no-show employee was relocated to some other patronage desk where she would do less damage, probably in the emergency preparedness unit (sigh). The locker room was cleaned, and the lifeguards were scheduled. A couple of years later, Curtis Hall received major renovations, including new locker room facilities. I was only one small squeak in making that happen. Curtis Hall is now the people's country club, which is as it should be.

My campaign probably took about ten to twelve hours in total, but few people have such slack. More important, I had the sense of entitlement to believe I could directly talk to Mayor Menino and demand accountability. Maybe someone else would have eventually taken on the missing-lifeguard problem, but maybe not. By maintaining a stake in the system, I used my advantage to make a system work for a wider group of people. I'm not bragging, because I understand how much of this is wired in place for me and is not some inherent or virtuous personal trait. I think the system is broken. In a healthy democracy, everyone would feel a similar sense of agency to make institutions work better, and everyone would feel empowered enough to ask for and think it was possible to achieve change.

My friend Scott has taken on a different campaign: to make the trains run on time. The general manager at the MBTA — the T — Boston's transit system, knows Scott by name, has seen his many letters, and has spoken with him on the phone. That manager has read the articles in the newspaper that Scott has provoked by directly communicating with reporters. He has been called by state representatives, responding to Scott. Scott is polite, respectful, and undaunted. But he is also a thorn in the general manager's side because of his high expectations. He doesn't opt out and drive to work or fatalistically accept the late trains or bad service. He follows through.

My daughter Nora went on to attend the Boston public schools from kindergarten to graduating from high school, spending one year at a private school. In the early years, I was very engaged in our school governance, participating in the parents' organization and teacher hiring. Parents wrote grant proposals, organized fund-raisers, and attracted various arts and supplemental program resources to the school. I watched how, even within the public school system, the schools with privileged parents got more goodies than the schools that didn't have affluent parents. These schools improved while others declined, and the cycle worsened as privileged parents advised one another to steer clear of certain schools and toward others.

For affluent parents, the public school choice is tough. No one wants to make a social experiment out of their child's one and only education. And there are often special circumstances — a child with a unique need — that justify in a parent's mind the choice of a private school. This may be compounded by a "too much money" situation — surplus income, inherited wealth, or grandparents willing to write checks — that make the private school choice irresistible. But I know plenty of affluent parents who keep their kids in urban public schools. If you have advantages and a stake in the system, you can be part of the solution. And by making it work for your kid, you make the school better for all kids.

Schools are not the only avenue to addressing inequality, though. There are many public services at the local level that need adoption and advocates. Public education, libraries, parks, public art, beaches, swimming pools, public restrooms, building inspectors, community policing, litter reduction, and more. Privileged whiners of the world, unite!

For every time I opt in, I confess to opting out of some public services, not having the patience to deal with underperforming systems. After many years of being a parent in the Boston public schools, I eventually got burned out. Let someone else tackle that problem, I decided. Same with Boston's building-code department, a hornet's nest of dysfunction, unaccountability, and patronage. We each have to pick our fights.

Opting in will have its frustrations. You will butt heads with city hall, experience the inefficiencies. You might end up standing wet in your bathing suit with nowhere to go. It will mean sometimes tolerating dysfunction, waiting in a line, or waiting for the bus. You will experience the no-show lifeguard or the ill-prepared substitute teacher. But you will also meet extraordinarily dedicated public servants, hardworking and spirited bus drivers, park rangers, teachers, mental health workers, street youth workers, public safety professionals — people who get up every day to make our community stronger. Thank them and celebrate them. Not everyone has the slack to appreciate and honor unappreciated public servants either. Your presence and stake in the system will improve the situation for all.

Coming Home, Near and Far

At the town or municipal level, an individual with time, treasure, and agency can make a huge difference. Transnational corporations have not captured the political system at these local levels as they have at the federal level. But we certainly can't give up on the larger democratic system and national politics.

I have worked for several decades to restore progressivity to our federal tax system, reversing sixty years of tax cuts to the most wealthy. Inevitably, when I talk to wealthy individuals about taxes, they will object, pointing to obvious examples of government waste and corruption or incompetence. It is hard to be enthusiastic about increasing taxes to pay for things like the F-35 fighter jet program projected to soak up $1.5 trillion in taxpayer money — a boondoggle one Pentagon official characterized as "acquisition malpractice."[2]

What I've come to realize is that we must attempt to separate the importance of maintaining a fair and progressive system of revenue from how the funds are used. They are two separate fights. One is for a fair and adequate revenue system. One is for a set of spending priorities buffered from powerful military and corporate lobbying.

As the wealthy use their political clout to opt out of taxes, we're shifting obligations onto present and future (thanks to debt) middle-class taxpayers. Wealthy people need to both be advocates for a fair *revenue* system and be engaged in fighting for proper *spending* priorities. If lobbyists for Lockheed Martin can spend $3.6 million a year lobbying Congress for $40 billion in contracts, who will serve as a countervailing force?

Coming home will require us to deepen our personal stake in a web of systems and services in our communities. It will inspire us to act, draw on our social networks, money, and sense of agency to make institutions more accountable, better resourced, and more responsive. We need the wealthy to opt back in to our communities, not from a charitable arm's-length distance but up close and personal. This is the pathway toward a truly more egalitarian society.

CHAPTER 14

Neighborhood Real Security

When I studied disasters past, what amazed me was not just that people behaved so beautifully, but that, in doing so, they found such joy. It seems that something in their natures, starved in ordinary times, was fed by the opportunity, under the worst of conditions, to be generous, brave, idealistic, and connected; and when this appetite was fulfilled, the joy shone out, even amid the ruins.

REBECCA SOLNIT, *A PARADISE BUILT IN HELL*

"I have about two months' rent in the bank," said Edith, holding a wide mug of coffee with both of her hands. "My job at the senior center is not very secure. The layoffs just started."

Edith and I were sitting in a coffee shop in Jamaica Plain. She is a friend from my congregation, First Church Jamaica Plain. At the time, she was in her late 40s, single and living in a small one-bedroom apartment. But until that moment, I didn't know how economically precarious her life was.

It was early October 2008 and the world was falling apart. A few weeks earlier, on September 15, the financial giant Lehman Brothers had imploded, and it seemed as if a bank a day were collapsing.

Fear was in the air. Already, layoffs were rippling through private corporations, particularly in financial services. Local government layoffs were starting to be announced. The stock market was in a free fall, plummeting 2,399 points between October 1 and October 10. Secretary of Treasury Hank Paulson pleaded with Congress to pass a massive bank bailout bill.

As President George W. Bush watched the $700 billion bailout bill fail to pass Congress, he exclaimed, "If money isn't loosened up, this sucker could go down."[1]

"I don't have much savings," Edith sighed. "After a couple months, my cat and I will be homeless."

"Don't worry, Edith," I said, in an offhand way. "You can always come live with us."

Edith looked up, her eyes welling with tears.

"Well, you can," I said more deliberately, meeting her fearful eyes. "We're not going to let you become homeless."

Edith covered her mouth, looked away, and sobbed quietly, tears streaming down her face. I touched her shoulder.

"As long as we have a home, you have a place," I added, reflecting the vulnerability all around us, including my own.

A few days later, I saw Edith at church during coffee hour. "I'm sorry I became so emotional," she said. "I'm embarrassed."

"What was going on?" I asked.

"You know, in my isolation, I had forgotten that I have friends that will *hold me* during tough times."

"We're not alone, that's for sure." We looked around at the room filled with people from our church. Wouldn't this group hold one another in the face of hard times?

That day after coffee hour, our pastor, the Reverend Terry Burke, invited us to talk about the economic meltdown. Over fifty people stayed for the discussion, breaking into small groups to talk about how they were faring. We decided to form a Resilience Circle, a sort of mutual aid support group.

I didn't know it then, but for me personally, this would become the ultimate connector, the point at which I became firmly rooted in a place. At that point, I had lived for seventeen years in the Jamaica Plain section of Boston, a community that had gone through a lot of economic change. In the 1970s, Jamaica Plain was a blighted urban neighborhood, struggling with rampant crime, arson, and disinvestment. At the age of 30, I put my stake here, buying a house, raising a family, and committing myself to a congregation and neighborhood that works for everyone. I started to feel the benefits of having stayed put.

Real Security

Fifteen of us from First Church started to meet one evening a week — and continued meeting regularly over the course of a year, shifting to twice a month. At each meeting, we went around the circle and checked in about how each of us was doing. I was embarrassed to learn things about the economic lives of people I thought I knew well. For example, my friend Heather, who had just turned 60, had no health insurance.

We did what we call "budget makeovers" for one another. It started when one of our members, Alice, brought copies of her budget — her income and expenses — to share with others. "I'm not making ends meet," she said frankly. "I could use some advice on how to cut costs."

The group brainstormed ways to earn and save money, and tips to reduce expenses. In the end, Alice decided to sell her car. After the discussion, she collected the paper copies of her budget. "I'd just as soon these not be floating around," she said, in a dignified way. After Alice took the risk to share something so private, three others stepped forward. "Me next! I want a budget makeover!" said Heather.

The Resilience Circle movement took off, with dozens and then hundreds popping up around the country over the next six months. My program at the Institute for Policy Studies played a support role to this emerging network, documenting activity and sharing lessons. Andrée Zaleska and Sarah Byrnes, my coworkers, created a facilitator guide of tools for start-up circles.[2] And I began to travel to different communities, from Maine and Maryland to Michigan and Washington State, leading workshops about forming Resilience Circles. In Portland, Oregon, four Resilience Circles sprung up in one neighborhood.[3]

After six months, we stepped back and realized that these Resilience Circles seem to serve three purposes — learning together, mutual aid, and social action. Participants were hungry to understand what was happening in the economy. They felt like they had trusted the "experts," the politicians and the bankers, but now had to learn for themselves.

The Resilience Circle network circulated articles, books, videos, and documentaries to help people understand the deeper roots of the debt crisis and the growth of the speculative financial sector. Our circle talked about the drivers of the mortgage crisis, growing inequality, and the ecological constraints on future growth.

Whatever individual self-blame that people in our group may have showed up with, they felt better as we understood the widespread and systemic roots of the economic meltdown. Together, we faced the reality that we were probably not going back to some kind of "glory days" booming economy.

The mutual aid work of Resilience Circles, which are still proliferating, helps participants recognize that we are not alone.[4] Through mutual aid, sharing resources, and holding one another through the tough times, we don't have to be passive and isolated in the face of economic and ecological change. This takes the form of concrete sharing and the formation of bartering exchanges, where people swap time helping each other.

The third purpose of our Resilience Circles — social action — is to organize together to build a more resilient and equitable economy. Individually, none of us can fix the root causes of the precarious and speculative economy. But we can build alternative ways to meet our real security needs through local businesses, credit institutions, and "sharing economy" practices.

Resilience Circles around the country move their money out of the megabanks like Bank of America and Wells Fargo that drove our economy off a cliff with reckless practices. They open accounts at local banks and credit unions that lend in the real economy of goods and services. They lobby for consumer protection and financial reform legislation, holding these "too big to fail" banks responsible. They form local community organizations inspired by the U.K. experience with "transition towns," engaging in community education, practical projects to strengthen community resilience and preparedness (to be discussed further in the next chapter).[5]

One of the activities that Resilience Circles do is an exchange of "gifts" and "needs." People write down at least three things they can offer the group — willingness to drive, help with chores, cook food, or babysit. Then they write down things they need help with — learning computer skills, language proficiency, and carpentry help. Immediately, there is matchmaking as the group realizes that they each have things to offer others. Informal exchanges begin. People help each other with yard work in exchange for babysitting or rides to doctors.

My friend Cecelia, a minister serving a congregation in a suburb of Seattle, shared a story from their Resilience Circle about a participant named Grace — a relatively new member of her congregation who had not made friends or rooted herself in the community. People were going around the circle, sharing their offering of gifts and needs. When it was Grace's turn, she shared, "I've been coming to the church for the last year, since my husband died. One of the gifts I have is his pickup truck. I've held on to it and paid the insurance, thinking it might be useful. But it just sits there in the driveway. The things I need are — " Grace paused, a little embarrassed. "I need help with things my husband used to do — putting up storm windows, standing on ladders changing lightbulbs, help moving things . . ."

There was a pause. And then one of the women in the Resilience Circle said, "You have a pickup truck?" The group laughed. Everyone could think of a time when they could have used a pickup truck. Within days, people were visiting Grace, bringing her meals to share, and bartering for use of the truck. Grace is now webbed into the community and congregation in a new way. And people's real needs are being met in a way that also saves them money.

In my Resilience Circle, we soon realized how much money can be saved by sharing tools and neighborly exchanges of help. We effectively became our own bartering network. Paul raked leaves for Jan. Jan drove Alice to the doctor. Alice cooked a meal for Paul on his busiest day, so he didn't have to spend money eating out. We noticed how a huge part of the economy depended on us staying isolated and not creating neighborly interdependence.

One member of our circle, Catherine, wanted to start a business helping people organize their stuff. She offered three people in our circle a free consultation session. In exchange, they allowed her to take "before" and "after" pictures and they wrote endorsement quotes for her brochure and website. Then members of the circle brainstormed marketing ideas and worked their networks to identify paying clients for Catherine. Her business took off and continues to this day.

Our members recognize the absurdity of forming a circle to do what communities naturally used to do for one another. One, named Dax, observes that we New Englanders don't share as readily as they do in the Caribbean, where he grew up. "In my town, if you have a ladder, then the community has a ladder," said Dax. "And people take care of something they borrow as if it were their own."

Eight years after its launch, the Resilience Circle movement is expanding, especially among the shaken or imploding middle class, those people who thought they were secure and self-sufficient before the economic melt-down. They often live apart from their extended family. There is a large segment of folks who have lost jobs and savings, but don't have the support network or the experience of asking for help, even when in dire need. They have internalized the cultural shame of asking for help.

Not everyone needs these circles. Some lower-income people and more recent immigrant groups have stronger interdependent communities because they are used to depending on one another to survive. They don't have sufficient income to pay people to care for their children, elders, or family members with special needs. When a car breaks down or someone needs a ride to the hospital, they can't afford to rent a car or take a taxi. They have to ask for help, which is the real human condition. As one black friend said to me, "We've had a Mutual Aid Committee in our church for 125 years. Our church never separated material and spiritual security." But these are rare. Most communities are fragmented and have weak webs of social support and insufficient public services to fill the gaps. Our middle-class congregations have little history of internal mutual aid, other than the "casserole groups" that bring food to people who are sick or recovering from accidents. What mutual aid muscles there may have historically been have atrophied.

The challenges of facing the economic collapse and its long tentacles that have shaped ensuing years are compounded by growing social disconnection and loneliness. The Resilience Circles have proved important to people who have no existing networks, including the growing number of people who live alone. According to a Duke University study, one in four adults is socially isolated, meaning they have no one they can talk to about their most important concerns. And another one in four has only one person they can talk to, typically a spouse. This is an increase from 1985, when fewer than one in eight adults were considered socially isolated.[6]

From our national perch of supporting the formation of these circles, we see emergent themes. Gift exchanges are distinct from "charity," which is often conducted at arm's length, disconnected, and requires no vulner-ability on the part of the giver. We learn how many participants have an easier time offering help, but freak out when it comes to receiving help and gifts. Resilience Circles become a place where participants practice asking for help and receiving it.

Behind this reticence, we find, are unspoken fears about being a burden on others or, on the other hand, being overwhelmed by the requests of others. There is a deep shame placed upon people with needs, even as we all have needs through our lives. And some people do have enormous hardships, the result of mental wounds and deprivations, which cannot be addressed through a simple mutual aid network.

Our unspoken fears of being overwhelmed reflect how badly our mutual aid muscles have atrophied, to the point where we are out of practice knowing how to ask for help or lovingly say, "No, I'm not able to help, but I will stand by you." Resilience Circles develop a number of simple maxims, such as "I may not be able to be your bank, your therapist, or shelter, but I can accompany you as you find ways to meet your needs."

When family systems cannot solve a problem, we need the mutual aid of community, congregation, or tribe. When these small communities cannot solve a problem, we need robust community and government systems — to address issues like mental illness, homelessness, and hunger.

My own family faced this after my younger brother's mental illness wore down our family's capacity to help. Like many families, we had exhausted our psychological and financial resources. My brother was in regular crisis situations and in and out of mental hospitals and private treatment programs. Eventually, we had to depend on county mental health services in Michigan to help us out. People who were initially complete strangers stepped in to ably care for him. This help lifted a huge burden from our family.

We cannot easily become a mental health system for one another. But there are so many ways that we can support and assist people that would be easy and joyful. That is the open space these circles fill.

Wealth and Connection

After our Jamaica Plain group had been meeting for a while, a couple that I knew to be quite wealthy joined our Resilience Circle. At one point, they offered to give money to the group to create a sort of mutual aid fund. But the group wisely decided not to accept the gift. "It's good to know it's there," one member said. "But I think it would change our dynamics." When I asked Daniel and Jane why they were in the club, they answered, "For authentic community." They may have been wealthy people who didn't have the same financial pressures as others in the group, but they understood that this was a moment when people were connecting around real needs and forming lasting bonds.

Without vulnerability, without the experience of receiving a gift, there is no authentic community. Daniel and Jane have material abundance. They have enough money that they never have to ask or depend on anyone, because money enables them to purchase what they need. As a result, however, they are isolated from authentic connections with others.

As the writer Charles Eisenstein observes, "Community arises from the meeting of needs. There is no community possible among a group of people who do not need each other. Therefore, any life that seeks to be independent of other people for the meeting of one's needs is a life without community."[7]

Many affluent people might as well walk around with signs that say, "I don't need you." I could understand this from my own life experience. Because we have enough money to buy most of our services, we don't have to express vulnerability and need. Even within our families and kinship networks, we don't ask for help, weakening the bonds of family.

Some wealthy people even celebrate the illusion of their self-sufficiency, counseling others to "be independent like me." But the perpetuation of this illusion is destructive, both to our society and to wealthy people themselves. It may be where some of the makers-and-takers rhetoric comes from.

I know hundreds of people who are very wealthy and deeply disconnected. Many of them hunger for real and heartfelt community. They find the social gatherings centered on food, entertainment, and talking about their latest vacation to be vapid and unsatisfying.

Indeed, one of the ways that wealthy people can come home is by participating in these gift economies and sharing in the joys of meeting local needs. Coming home may mean bringing money, time, and talents home. But it also means showing up with your needs and vulnerabilities. When you ask and receive, you break down the illusion of self-sufficiency, the cruel notion that there are makers and takers. You dismantle the stigma of need and the stiff arm of organized philanthropy and replace it with a culture of reciprocity, gift exchange, and the open hand of authentic generosity.

CHAPTER 15

Community Resilience

We can begin by doing small things at the local level, like planting community gardens or looking out for our neighbors. That is how change takes place in living systems, not from above but from within, from many local actions occurring simultaneously.

GRACE LEE BOGGS

Forming Resilience Circles in our community naturally led to the question: How do we make our larger neighborhood more resilient? Our personal resilience is interwoven with the health and resilience of the entire community. And there are limits to how prepared an individual can be if the overall community is not prepared.

This was one of the inspirations for forming Jamaica Plain New Economy Transition (JP NET) in 2010. We wanted to set Jamaica Plain on course to becoming a "transition town," inspired by a movement that began in the United Kingdom. The transition movement founders, including Rob Hopkins and Naresh Giangrande, have motivated a growing band of communities around the world to respond to global realities like climate change and the volatility of our energy systems and economy by building local self-reliance. In order to prevent catastrophic climate change, they remind us, we must transition away from a fossil-fuel-based energy system and toward greater community resilience.[1]

Several community leaders, including Andrée Zaleska, Dakota Butterfield, Orion Kriegman, Sarah Byrnes, and Carlos Espinoza-Toro, galvanized the formation of JP NET — inspired by transition organizing around New England. There were transition towns under way in the seaside town of Newburyport, Massachusetts, and also in rural Western Massachusetts, as well as in Montpelier and Putney, Vermont. But few were organizing in urban neighborhoods such as Jamaica Plain, with our racial and class diversity.

JP NET set out to build community resilience while bridging race, class, age, culture, and language. We held multilingual educational events and meetings, including an annual "state of the neighborhood" forum that now brings together three to four hundred neighbors to take stock of such issues as housing, youth, local energy, and small businesses.

Today, JP NET convenes over twenty potlucks and educational events a year on transition themes. Over the last four years we've explored how Jamaica Plain can power itself; we've had Bill McKibben talk to us about the moral and spiritual dimensions of climate change; we've heard how cooperatives can help us strengthen economic democracy in our neighborhood; we've invited permaculture leader Toby Hemenway to encourage more permaculture food production in our backyards and community gardens. Other sessions have explored whether New England can feed itself; what a resilient water system for Boston might look like; how our region might become net zero, supplying all its own energy through renewables; and how to create cities that work for all of us, with durable economies. We've had big-picture exchanges on emerging visions for a new economy, and working sessions on specific enterprise ideas, like bike-based businesses.

Reskilling and Doing Stuff

One of the practices of the global transition movement is, in the words of Rob Hopkins, the "power of just doing stuff." Instead of lamenting the bleak future and withdrawing to bunkers, the movement enlists people who are "hopeful and helpful" to build the new economy in the shell of the fossil fuel economy. Transition groups celebrate practical projects, including growing food, producing local energy, self-provisioning, helping neighbors, and strengthening gift economies.

For Hopkins, the big idea is "local resilience as economic development. . . . By taking back control over meeting our basic needs at the local level we can stimulate new enterprises — new economic activity — while also reducing our oil dependency and carbon emissions and returning power to the local level."[2]

The transition movement recognizes our need to "reskill" for the future. This includes learning craft or maker skills that our elders may have known:

growing and preserving food, sewing, repairing and making things we need. But there are new skills required, too, such as green building techniques, creating small-scale energy-generating plants, and advanced permaculture land planning and farming.

The emergence of "makers spaces" is a reflection of this movement. In nearby Somerville, the Artisan's Asylum took over 40,000 square feet of the former Ames Safety Envelope factory to house a wide variety of specialized tools and equipment for woodworking, metalsmithing, fiber arts, jewelry, electronics, digital fabrication (3-D printers), and more. Individuals join the organization, pay dues, and have access to tools and classes. In Jamaica Plain, JP NET is part of a local ecology of groups supporting the creation of the Boston makers space, which secured a location in early 2016.[3]

One hub of our activity is around the Brewery, a business incubator space owned by our Jamaica Plain Neighborhood Development Corporation (NDC), where the office of JP NET is based. The "incubation" of start-up businesses is helped by affordable space, business services, and technical assistance and financing from the NDC. This complex of buildings was built in 1870 as the Haffenreffer Brewery, one of thirty original breweries that served the area. Haffenreffer closed in 1965, and the buildings sat empty for more than a decade until our local NDC bought them. One of the first anchor tenants in 1988 was a small upstart craft brewery named Boston Beer Company, creator of the Sam Adams brand. Six days a week, tourists snake around outside our office to join brewery tours.

JP NET has served as an incubator for a number of projects, each with its own constellation of volunteer energy and activities. Projects and committees range from food to energy, support for local businesses, and preparedness — and several have spun off into independent organizations.

Building a Local Food System. Building a relocalized food system is central to many transition efforts and a magnet for volunteer energy. Like many urban neighborhoods, Jamaica Plain imports over 95 percent of our calories from outside the community. Our goal, over several years, is to grow and produce more of these calories in our neighborhood and region. Several institutions address this goal, including the Egleston Farmers Market that brings fresh produce and local food businesses to the underserved Egleston section of the neighborhood. A lot of intention is devoted to ensuring affordable access to food, including a wide variety of vendors and several programs to bring down food costs for working-class and low-income households.[4]

Now in its fourth year, the Egleston Farmers Market, which includes a winter market, is a hub of community activity and enterprise. Neighborhood producers of value-added products, such as jams, granola, pickles, cupcakes, and cheese, have gotten a boost with a stall at the Egleston Farmers Market. After its first year, one farmer reported that the market gave him the economic lift he needed to buy land in the region for a permanent farm site.[5]

The CommonWealth Kitchen, a licensed commercial kitchen based at the Brewery, is particularly helpful for start-up businesses still shaping their product and market. Over forty food businesses and culinary entrepreneurs lease space there, creating products that are sold in the neighborhood and at the Egleston Farmers Market. These include Seta's Mediterranean Foods, Voltage Coffee, Nella Pasta, OMG Nuts, NoLa's Fresh Foods, Frozen Hoagies, Sushi Dream, and Whoopie Monster. There is such a demand that CommonWealth Kitchen expanded to a second facility with more than 36,000 square feet in nearby Dorchester, another economically and racially diverse Boston neighborhood that is also facing gentrification pressures.

Community garden plots are expanding along with food projects like the Egleston Community Orchard and the Food Forest project, both growing fruits and vegetables and educating the community about the crops that are all around us and free for the picking. Neighbors help other neighbors construct raised garden beds or share garden plots with those who don't have access to sunny land.

Our work in the food sector creates jobs and livelihoods — and also enables existing businesses to expand or transition to the new economy and flourish. Instead of focusing solely on start-ups, JP NET works to boost existing businesses that are already rooted in the neighborhood. For instance, food activists have helped local butcher Harry Perez, owner of Plaza Meat Market, which serves the neighborhood's Dominican community, connect to the region's producers of organic grass-fed pork and beef. They've also been crowd-sourcing new customers for him, hoping to shift the demand to locally produced meat.

Strengthening Main Street Businesses. In the Egleston Square section of Jamaica Plain, there are dozens of immigrant-owned businesses, including automotive shops, beauty and nail salons, dry cleaners, restaurants, and more. These are "livelihood businesses," often owned by sole proprietors or extended families, that enable a family or two to pay their bills. They are not going anywhere, nor selling out to a chain store or moving offshore. They are rooted in the local economy. JP NET's approach is: How can we help them grow and flourish? How can we help them capture more of the neighborhood's spending dollars and demand for goods?

A key aspect of helping them expand has been mobilizing local businesses to better compete for residents' business. In 2012, JP NET convened a gathering of local business owners to learn about Cambridge Local First, a vibrant neighborhood business organizing effort just across the Charles River. In 2013, JP Local First was born. Membership has grown to over 175 businesses and the group publishes a directory, promotes events and activities, and communicates the value of locally owned and independent businesses in the community. They have helped many understand the powerful "multiplier effect" of local trade: For every $100 spent at a locally owned business, $48 will continue to circulate in the local economy. If you spend $100 at a multinational chain store, such as Walmart, Whole Foods, or Target, only $14 remains in the local economy.[6]

Creating a Cancer-Free Economy. One hope for this emerging new economy is that it will create healthy livelihoods. But many of these livelihood enterprises use highly toxic and, in some cases, carcinogenic chemicals. Cancer rates in Jamaica Plain are above the state average for surrounding communities. There are many reasons for this, but one factor is increased exposure to environmental risks.

So, Carlos Espinoza-Toro and I, both involved in JP NET, teamed up with some public health organizers to create a cancer-free Jamaica Plain initiative. We researched toxic exposures, including chemicals used in nail salons, and degreasing cleaning fluids used in automotive shops and restaurants. We brought in an expert to show the neighborhood's many artists how to reduce toxic exposures. But our first challenge was to help a dry-cleaning business transition away from using toxic chemicals.

Myra and Ernesto Vargas immigrated from Guatemala and Colombia and bought J&P Dry Cleaners more than fifteen years ago. "The chemicals were so bad," Myra tells me, "that I avoided the shop when I was pregnant." Most dry cleaners use a known carcinogen, perchloroethylene or "perc," in their dry-cleaning process.

JP NET introduced the Vargas family to organizations in Massachusetts that specialize in professional wet cleaning, a completely safe alternative. The Vargas family decided to take the leap, which required investing in new equipment. JP NET helped them get a $15,000 state grant and run a Kickstarter campaign to raise another $18,000 to help pay for the transition. A number of affluent Jamaica Plain residents quietly contributed to the campaign, one giving $1,800. Just as important, we educated consumers and crowd-sourced customers from the community. And we reached out to local hospitals, hotels, nursing homes, and other anchor institutions in the community to steer their business to J&P Dry Cleaners.

In September 2014, when J&P had a grand reopening to celebrate becoming one of the first truly "green cleaners" in the city of Boston, Myra was glowing with excitement as Boston officials and her family cut the ribbon. The city celebrated J&P with a Greenovate Award, and J&P became a powerful example of a rooted neighborhood business making a transition to a healthy alternative and positioning itself for green market success.

Building on this achievement, Carlos worked with a local auto body shop, Saucedo Auto, to stop using lead weights in tire balancing, removing 80 pounds of lead each year from the environment. The community celebrated Saucedo's decision with a fiesta, with local elected officials and neighbors. And we pressed other auto shops to do the same.

Supporting Neighborhood Leaders. Many residents knock on our door at JP NET, asking how to be connected. They are searching for meaningful jobs, new skills, and connection to the transition movement. We have no money to pay them. But Carlos Espinoza-Toro and Sarah Byrnes have created a Community Leaders Fellowship program where people can formally participate, volunteering fifteen to twenty hours a week in exchange for training, mentorship, and personalized coaching sessions. Four years after the program began, a number of these fellows had already started businesses or found work in the new economy and transition spheres.

We know there is a generation of young people who realize our society is entering into a deep shift, and that none of their schooling or jobs have adequately prepared them for what lies ahead. What if we could connect them to empty nesters in the neighborhood who could provide free housing and mentoring? What if we could deploy their considerable energy into local projects, such as staffing the Time Exchange, the Food Forest, or the Co-op Power project? JP NET is working toward this vision.

Preparedness and Pie Parties. In 2014, JP NET was nationally recognized for our work on emergency preparedness. Over the prior couple of years, our community had been tested, especially by severe winter weather. We watched Hurricane Sandy head our way, only to veer at the last moment and plow into New York and New Jersey. Then the 2014 Boston Marathon bombing and city lockdown exposed us to another vulnerability.

At the local level, we organized emergency preparedness "pie parties" so that people could get to know their neighbors better. These pie parties continue today, and our motto for them is, "In case of emergency, your neighbors are your first responders." At the parties, people meet each other and spend an hour mapping their block, identifying vulnerable neighbors and shared resources. Then people eat pie and socialize. The city of Boston supports this effort, supplying emergency crank battery radios to participants. And FEMA promotes our effort as an innovative approach to neighborhood preparedness.

In February 2015 we faced another test: It snowed steadily for a week, accumulating over 25 inches of white powder. Our homes, buildings, and public infrastructure were straining. Our subway line shut down completely, leaving tens of thousands of people without a way to get to work. Structurally weak buildings were evacuated and some collapsed. As the weekend approached, the forecast was grim: more snow, changing to rain. Everyone knew this was a critical moment. People did everything they could to get snow off rooftops and buildings. But most were ill prepared. Fortunately, the temperature never rose above freezing, and the rain never fell. But if it had — soaking the snow and weighting it down — things could have quickly turned from winter inconvenience to a life-threatening emergency situation.

A week later, snow still thick on the ground, JP NET organized "Burning Snow Man," a meetup at a local restaurant. People were invited to walk, sled, ski, snowshoe, or find another way to get to Doyle's Cafe — and share one-minute stories of the good, the bad, and the ugly of the storm. Over sixty people trudged out and fifteen folks shared poignant and funny stories about neighborly connections, selfishness, and hardship. Many lingered late into the night, and Doyle's was thrilled to have customers. The event put the "community" in "community resilience."

Making Energy a Priority. A number of Jamaica Plain projects are focused on helping community members boost energy efficiency and reduce energy bills. The Home Energy Efficiency Team (HEET) has worked to support a number of "barn-raising" energy retrofits, where neighbors get together to help one another do energy assessments and button up their homes through conservation retrofits. JP NET has hosted a number of programs on energy efficiency, including workshops with Co-op Power, a consumer-owned cooperative that assists in installing solar hot water and solar electric systems in residential and commercial buildings.

Keeping Capital Local. A growing coalition of people is interested in finding ways to keep capital in the neighborhood and redirect it to local projects and businesses. Boston Community Capital borrows and lends funds for local housing and small business projects. The JP-based Boston Impact Initiative (BII) provides three types of financing — equity, debt, and grants — to high-impact social enterprises, and Balanced Rock Investment Advisors helps investors evaluate projects. Several local banks have a commitment to local lending — and community organizations have rewarded them with deposits.

Time Exchanges and Building the Gift Economy. JP NET's Time Exchange is a barter network where the unit of currency is an hour of one's time. It's like our Resilience Circle, with the exchange of gifts and needs, only at a larger scale. Over three hundred members exchange a wide variety of goods and services, such as cooking, sewing, rides, health care services, child care, companionship care, computer repair, language instruction, yard work, dog-walking, and carpentry. Participants don't need to do direct one-to-one exchanges. When they do a service, they record a deposit in the time exchange, via computer. When they use a service, they register a withdrawal.

At monthly orientation sessions, participants learn the benefits of joining the JP Time Exchange, including saving money, living more ecologically, and sharing undervalued skills (knitting, baking, chain saw help, organizing, party planning). Professionals can reach new clients and spread the word about their services. People meet neighbors and build community. The mainstream economy isn't working for many people, so the JP Time Exchange is a way to build an alternative economy to meet our real needs.

In the transition to a new economy, there are many examples of the emerging sharing economy and gift economy, including barter networks, time banks, and bicycle-sharing networks. Tool-lending libraries and other networks help people make the shift from solely owning things to providing periodic access. A neighbor who only infrequently needs a car or a gardener in search of land to grow food are matched up to owners through peer-to-peer car-sharing groups and yard-sharing networks.

Wealth in the New Economy

In our organizing efforts at JP NET, we have consciously reached out to people of all economic circumstances, inviting them to the table to build community resilience. At many of our meetings, I see young people in the community connected to Resource Generation, a network of high-net-worth people under age 35.

Several of them enjoy being at a table that views them not as philanthropists, but as neighbors. One wealthy woman explained to me that she has lots of superficial communities in her life that are based on co-consumption but not on mutual interdependence. "We go to restaurants or share entertainment — maybe even travel together — but we don't really depend on one another," she explains. In these circles, it's only when someone has a real need — such as a medical emergency — that a potential for a real bond of interdependence emerges.

As Charles Eisenstein writes, "Intimacy comes from co-creation, not co-consumption." An economy of gifts is the cornerstone of a vibrant community of connection.

> *Community is nearly impossible in a highly monetized society like our own. That is because community is woven from gifts, which is ultimately why poor people often have stronger communities than rich people.*[7]

We all depend on one another to survive — and this reveals our fundamental vulnerable and dependent state. But money masks this dependency, fostering an illusion, especially among the wealthy, of self-sufficiency.

In today's market system, according to Eisenstein, "Built-in scarcity compels competition in which more for me is less for you." In a gift economy, the opposite is true.

People in a gift culture pass on their surplus rather than accumulating it. Your good fortune is my good fortune: more for you is more for me. Wealth circulates, gravitating toward the greatest need. In a gift community, people know that their gifts will eventually come back to them, albeit often in a new form.

Wealthy people miss out on a key part of the human experience, the connections that come through vulnerability and needing help — and the gift exchange that comes from reciprocity and people helping one another. Alternatively, wealthy people "opting in" can make a huge difference in building a local resilient economy.

As Rob Hopkins observes, "If we wait for governments, it'll be too little, too late. If we act as individuals, it'll be too little. But if we act as communities, it just might be enough, just in time." Of course, local community responses can't change the world on their own. To fix the future, we need activities at all levels. But as Hopkins writes, it is in this middle terrain, between individual action and larger government and institutional responses, where we have room to move. "The community engagement, the new enterprises, the internal investment opportunities, the skill-sharing, the potential of communities owning and developing assets: the potential is vast."[8]

I see privileged people participating in the barter network, exchanging rather than buying services, offering their own time and skills and gifts and receiving from others. As early stakeholders, they are boosting the gift economy, setting a different tone of generosity, and inviting greater generosity.

I watch wealthy individuals bring their spending home, shopping at the Egleston Farmers Market, taking their laundry to J&P Dry Cleaners, and patronizing JP Local First businesses. Some bring their capital to local banks or impact investment funds to invest in locally owned or cooperative enterprises. By putting their stake in fostering a local economy that works for everyone, they are improving their lives and lifting up others as well. After all, creating resilience isn't just about preparing for and surviving challenges. It's about the joy and happiness that come from connection.

CHAPTER 16

Bringing Wealth Home

Community wealth building begins with loyalty to geographic place. If globalization is the hallmark of today's mainstream economy, relocalization is the hallmark of the alternative. Globalization works well for capital, which can move across borders with a computer keystroke. But the real economy of jobs and families and the land always lives someplace real.

MARJORIE KELLY AND SARAH MCKINLEY[1]

B ringing wealth home has multiple meanings. On the one hand, vast amounts of wealth are ricocheting around the planet in our globalized financial system. Trillions of wealth is booked in secrecy jurisdictions, hidden from accountability, oversight, and taxation. Wealth is also on Wall Street, invested in the fossil fuel sector and transnational corporations. What does it look like to bring wealth home?

Wealth Out of the Shadows: Jacques Leblanc

"The offshore system is a global scandal," says the man I will call Jacques Leblanc. "It is where the hidden wealth of nations resides."

Leblanc has agreed to meet me at a restaurant a few miles from the San Francisco airport. I cannot use his name. I cannot use a tape recorder. When I arrive at the restaurant I see his Lexus parked in a far corner of the parking lot. He is already seated at a table, next to an enormous colorful fish tank.

"I grew up in a wealthy and visible family in France," Leblanc explains, leaning forward in his seat, glasses on his nose. "Our treasure was stashed in Luxemburg, Switzerland, Monaco, Isle of Man. We banked in all these secrecy jurisdictions, all for the purposes of avoiding French taxes."

Leblanc speaks four languages, attended the École de Paris, and worked for a decade in Europe. But he found love in America and moved here twenty-five years ago. Over time, he came to understand the fuller picture of the offshore system.

"It is the system that is bleeding Africa of its wealth, taking food from the mouths of children," says LeBlanc. "For every dollar of aid that flows into Africa, ten dollars leaves through secrecy jurisdictions."

The offshore system refers to secrecy jurisdictions that enable wealthy investors and transnational corporations to create shell corporations and bank accounts that don't disclose the real human beings that benefit from them. Some sixty countries could be characterized as tax havens, with no or very low taxation and little transparency in terms of reporting bank holdings and investments. Several US states, notably Wyoming, Delaware, and Nevada, are themselves tax havens. In these jurisdictions, the process of getting a library card or a fishing license — where you have to prove identity and residency — is more rigorous than creating a corporation and bank account, where you don't have to disclose "beneficial ownership."[2]

In April 2016, massive leaks from a Panamanian law firm that specializes in shell corporations — the so-called Panama Papers — focused a bright spotlight on the global abuses of this offshore system. While not always illegal, the offshore system is often abused to dodge taxation, launder funds from criminal activity, and allow public officials to conceal assets from publicity and scrutiny.[3]

Growing scrutiny is focused on US-based transnational corporations that incorporate subsidiaries in tax havens and pretend, for tax purposes, to generate profits in these countries. In 2013, 358 of *Fortune* 500 companies operated at least 7,622 subsidiaries in tax haven jurisdictions and avoided an estimated $620 billion in US taxes. Most of these companies have subsidiaries in Bermuda or the Cayman Islands, two of the most notorious tax haven countries, where subsidiaries simply need to incorporate and maintain a mailbox. The worst offenders include Apple, American Express, Nike, PepsiCo, Pfizer, Morgan Stanley, Google, and Bank of America.[4]

The wealth of individual investors is harder to track, as nations and banks refuse to report account information. Economist Gabriel Zucman estimates that 8 percent of the world's individual wealth is hidden in tax havens, an estimated $7 trillion in 2015. This leads to a minimum of $200 billion in lost revenue each year at the global level, but it is probably significantly more.[5]

There are clear policy solutions that US lawmakers can enact to crack down on tax haven abuse. They could end the incentives for companies to shift profits offshore, close the most egregious offshore loopholes, and increase transparency by requiring corporations and bank account holders to disclose their real owners and beneficiaries. Banks could be required to report individual holdings and major transactions to the countries where account holders are citizens. Those of us in the United States have tremendous leverage and responsibility to fix this system, first by closing our own state tax havens and then using our status as a financial power to enforce transparency throughout the system.

"Our nations are not broke," says Leblanc. "All these governments around the world plead poverty, propose austerity measures, and take on debt. But the absurdity is, the money is hidden in plain sight.

"This system emboldens corruption," says Leblanc, his eyes on fire. "These are mechanisms that allow the illicit flows of drug dealers and terrorists. But the capitalist class wants to keep it this way. It's how they hide their money.

"The more I learned — and the more I understood my own family's role — the greater the shame I felt," Leblanc recounts. "I believe the Republic of France made our wealth possible.

"I didn't know what to do. Should I blow the whistle? Should I cut family ties?" he says, his hands open in a plea. "I felt tremendous love and conflict."

Leblanc took the opportunity to change his family's practices. When it was his generation's chance to run the family enterprises, he forced parts of it to come aboveground and pay taxes. "I urged our family to take responsibility and let the sun shine in."

Leblanc has become an activist, speaking out about the offshore issue in general, funding transparency organizing, and supporting researchers and advocates that are exposing the tricks.

I'm moved by his story of taking personal risks to change the corrupt offshore system. "Can I tell your story?" I ask.

"It is risky," says Leblanc. "Some segments of the family are still in the shadows. There is a lot of money at stake. And people will go to extreme measures to protect this wealth. You can tell the basic outlines of the story. Don't use my name."

Dissonance and Divestment: Lisa Renstrom

"Why should people divest from the fossil fuel sector?" Lisa Renstrom laughs. "I'm a terrible salesperson." She pauses and thinks. "Let me count the ways."

"We want to revoke the social license of the fossil fuel industry to destroy our planet," she declares, in an unwavering resonant voice. "The fossil fuel industry — big oil, gas, and coal — is undermining Earth's habitability for future generations. They have lied to us and used their political lobbying power to block alternatives. They have committed crimes against humanity."

Lisa Renstrom and I are the founding co-chairs of the campaign to engage individuals in the divestment movement. Divest-Invest is a national network promoting divestment from the fossil fuel sector and reinvestment in renewable energy and a just transition.

Divest-Invest formed to boost the individual and philanthropic pledges to divest from the fossil fuel sector. But we also realized the power of the reinvestment — the "invest" part of the equation. Divest-Invest keeps track of the total global amount of divestment pledges and promotes investments in renewable energy and the new economy.

Renstrom grew up in Omaha, Nebraska, daughter of a hardworking Swedish immigrant who created several patented hair curlers, including a popular pink, foamy hair roller that gave bounce to a generation of women's hair before and after World War II. This led to the formation of Tip-Top Products, a company that was so successful that it enabled Renstrom's father to finance the development of a number of resorts in Acapulco, Mexico.

Renstrom was studying business administration in 1981 at the University of Nebraska when her father died. She immediately stepped in to manage three of those resorts. "I got my MBA by fire in Mexico," she told me. Though she spoke fluent Spanish, it was challenging as a young, blond female to venture into a rough-and-tumble Mexican business environment. The resort managers fraudulently claimed an ownership interest and Renstrom refused to back down. They filed criminal charges against her.

In Mexico's "guilty until proven innocent" justice system, Renstrom spent six months in Reclusorio Oriente, a sprawling women's prison in Mexico City, separated from her 10-month-old infant daughter, Alex. Renstrom believes her prison time was invaluable. "It was an unbelievable experience that I wouldn't trade for the world, even though at the time I didn't know if I would be swallowed up in the system."

For four months she didn't see her daughter. "It was painful to hear her name, knowing I couldn't see her," Renstrom said. After that, Alex was allowed to visit her in prison on weekends.

"You're not facing your death, but you're certainly facing limitations — the loss of your freedom, the loss of being able to live the life that we take so much for granted: showers, cleanliness, friends, family." Eventually, the plaintiffs dropped all charges, and Renstrom sold the resorts in 1993.[6]

"After that, not a lot of things scare me," said Renstrom. "The experience of jail made me less patient with injustice than I was before."

Working with Renstrom, I could feel her tenacity to address the climate crisis. Divest-Invest first gained attention in September 2014, when we joined a press conference to announce $50 billion in divestment pledges from individuals and institutions, including philanthropic foundations, colleges and universities, and local governments. Rockefeller Brothers Fund, built with money from the Standard Oil company, pledged to divest its endowment of $860 million.[7]

South African Archbishop Desmond Tutu, a champion of the antiapartheid movement that deployed divestment strategies, addressed that press conference by video.[8] "The destruction of the earth's environment is the human rights challenge of our time," said Tutu. "Time is running out," he implored. "We are already experiencing loss of life and livelihood because of intensified storms, shortages of fresh water, the spread of disease, rising food prices, and the creation of climate refugees. The most devastating effects are visited on the poor, those with no involvement in creating the problem, a deep injustice."

In the antiapartheid movement, Tutu argued against corporations profiting from investments in South Africa. About fossil fuels, Tutu said, "No one should profit from rising temperatures and seas, and human suffering caused by the burning of fossil fuels.

"We are on the cusp of a global transition to a new safe energy economy. We must support our leaders to make the correct moral choices." For Tutu, this includes freezing further exploration for new fossil fuels and discouraging politicians from accepting money from a fossil fuel industry that blocks action on climate change. "Divest from the fossil fuels and invest in a clean renewable energy future," said Tutu. "Move your money out of the problem and into solutions."

The actor Mark Ruffalo, who played the Incredible Hulk in a recent release of the superhero movie *The Avengers*, joined Renstrom and I at the press conference, too. There, he called upon all the "Avengers" — including the actors who played Captain America, Iron Man, Black Widow, and Thor — to also divest from fossil fuels.[9]

A little more than a year later, as delegates gathered in Paris for the December 2015 Climate Summit, Divest-Invest issued an update: Over four hundred institutions and forty-six thousand individuals worth $3.4 trillion had pulled their investments out of fossil fuels.[10] "It's a tribute to the movement," said Renstrom. "More people are taking the step. And the risks of investing in carbon burning are playing out in the marketplace."

For Renstrom, divestment has a political objective, to weaken the legitimacy of the fossil fuel sector in order to regulate and put a price on carbon emissions. It is also a deeply personal choice.

"If you are truly aware of the global impacts of climate change, they compel you to take personal action and 'be the change.' It is not easy in a world that is just beginning its shift to renewable energy. I do small things, compost and grow food, ride my bike, buy secondhand clothes — small acts of personal witness. The 'aha' moment came when I realized that I could move my money, withdraw it from the legacy industries and invest in the companies of my future. That is when I felt power and the dissonance began to lessen."

For Renstrom, being invested in the fossil fuel sector, profiting from an association with this nasty industry, was added "dissonance" in her life. "To live out of alignment with one's values and knowledge is bad for your health. It's like having an annoying noise — a bell or a tuning fork — ringing in your head all the time." So, she pulled out; then she became interested in motivating others to do the same.

"It is hard to live in this world with integrity. I think it must be like growing up Hindu in a culture that holds cows sacred and then being forced to be around people eating beef all time. On some very basic level, it physically hurts to be out of alignment with your values and beliefs."

Renstrom's interests don't stop at divestment. She also wants to better understand how to democratize finance and invest locally in projects that make our coming transition a just one. "It's not enough to move money into the renewable energy sector," she stresses. "We also need to redirect our economic system so that it aims towards goals and metrics that support life, and a common good."

This additional layer of purpose isn't something that everyone under-stands — yet. "I was sitting with a group of hedge fund guys," Renstrom says. "We all know we need to move $30 trillion in capital to the renew-able energy sector by 2050. When the finance types talk about an energy transition, it is a conversation about rearranging the chairs at the top of the economy. That will not work long-term. We need a transition that democ-ratizes finance and broadens ownership, bringing the excluded to the table. If the transition favors the few, they lose eventually and we all lose."

What does it look like, to bring wealth home to the most local level? Sometimes it starts with a food scrap.

People, Planet, and Prosperity: Deborah Frieze

It is dawn and the chirping of morning birds is interrupted by the beep-beep-beep of a large disposal truck backing up to an America's Food Basket market in the Dorchester neighborhood of Boston.

Tim Hall pops out and attaches the truck's levers to a jumbo 20-gallon green plastic bin, hoisting it up and tipping its contents into the truck.[11]

"That's about 700 pounds of food waste," says Hall, wearing black glasses and a black sweatshirt. Hall works for CERO, a worker-owned commercial waste management company, based in adjacent Roxbury.

He empties a dozen containers into a custom-built compost collecting truck. "Someday this food waste will return to the neighborhood as healthy compost for gardens."

CERO was founded in 2013 to take advantage of then-new Massachusetts legislation on commercial food waste. The law requires establishments with more than a ton of food refuse a week to compost the waste rather than ship it to landfills. CERO provides "one-stop shopping" for restaurants, hospitals, universities, and grocery stores — handling organic waste along with other recycling and garbage. Their clients lower their waste-disposal bills while supporting a green, locally owned, worker-owned company.

Compostable organics make up more than 25 percent of the state's commercial and household waste. Instead of creating dangerous methane gas in landfills, CERO shifts this part of the waste stream to compost. "CERO diverted 350 tons of waste from landfills and sewers in 2015 and we expect to double that in 2016," according to Lor Holmes, a cooperative worker-owner and business manager. "We're about people, planet, and profits."

On the side of the truck are names of sixty CERO investors who were the first to support a crowd-sourcing campaign to raise funds for the company's start-up.

The CERO cooperative is a compelling example of "bringing wealth home." Its owners are primarily black and Latino, based in Roxbury, providing the ultimate in green business services. But they struggled to find access to capital. Fortunately, pioneering financiers are blazing the way toward shifting capital out of Wall Street and into local community economic ventures.

"We didn't have access to capital," explains Holmes. "We had a business plan, but it took two years for us to get start-up financing. We couldn't get financing because none of our members had money. We went to banks and were turned down. We had to look elsewhere."

"Fortunately, the Boston Impact Initiative and the Coop Fund stepped up to provide patient capital," said Holmes. "They were wicked important."

"CERO is the sweet spot for us," said Deborah Frieze, cofounder of the Boston Impact Initiative, or BII as it is called locally. The company was one of the early investors in CERO. And Frieze is an example of a person coming home, bringing her personal stake, talents, and financial resources to a place.

Putting Down Roots

"I've spent the last two weeks getting really intimate with thousands and thousands of oak leaves," says Frieze, sitting at her kitchen table, looking out at her backyard. As she speaks, she cranes her neck to look up at a towering oak tree. "A lot of oak leaves," she laughs. "I've been tending this half acre, preparing for winter."

You could forget you are in a city here, with its large open sky and century-old trees. Four years earlier, Frieze moved to the Jamaica Plain neighborhood after more than a decade of life in the fast lane.

Frieze grew up in a business-oriented family in the Boston area. "On my father's side of the family, the men were entrepreneurial and good at making money, and the women were engaged in radical politics and giving the money away. I wanted to do both." Her great-grandfather founded Gordon Brothers, a wholesale liquidation company located during Frieze's childhood on Bromfield Street, in the heart of Boston's retail district. "When I was old enough, I worked summers, sorting jewelry."

After graduating from Harvard Business School, Frieze cofounded Zefer, an internet consulting company. Riding the wave of growth on the upside of the high-tech bubble, she also lived the downside. "We went from being a boutique firm with a vision of democratic access to content, to drinking the Wall Street growth Kool-Aid." When outside investors approached Zefer, wanting to pump $100 million into the company, Frieze was outvoted. "In came the middle-aged white guys to manage the company. But when the bubble burst, I found myself having to be the one to face people as they were laid off.

"I witnessed an ugly form of capitalism," says Frieze, shaking her jet-black hair at the sour memory. "Maximize return to shareholders at any cost, growth as an end rather than a means, efficiency as more valuable than people. I'm not against capitalism; it's just that the form we've been practicing is corrupt. Capitalism itself may still have potential."

While repulsed by extractive capitalism, Frieze hasn't given up on the possibilities of enterprise for good. She's excited about what she and others call generative capitalism, with broader worker and community ownership. "Capitalism, if we accounted for its real costs, could be a great system. But in business school the only time we talked about negative externalities was in accounting — and how you didn't have to book the externalities of pollution or underpaid workers needing food stamps."

Frieze walked away from Zefer and did consulting work with a variety of businesses. She joined the staff of the Berkana Institute, exploring how systems work and change. She visited communities in Africa, India, and South America that had opted out of extractive capitalism and were working to build new systems of vibrant local gift economies and healthy commerce.

"Many of these communities experienced economic collapse," observes Frieze. "When systems start to unravel, we have a choice. We can struggle to fix the current system or we can create new alternatives. When enough people 'walk out' of the old system — and the beliefs that hold it in place — there is a shift."

In collaboration with Meg Wheatley, Frieze wrote *Walk Out, Walk On: A Learning Journey into Communities Daring to Live the Future Now*. It chronicles seven communities around the world and the people who have walked out of limiting beliefs and assumptions and "walked on" to create healthy and resilient communities. In it, they profile the "walk outs" who use their ingenuity and caring to figure out how to work with the community's existing assets and talents and create what they need.

Frieze spent a couple of years on the road, promoting the book and conducting trainings on the "walk out, walk on" practice. Her message is, "All change is local, and it is through intimacy with place that we create the conditions for new systems to arise." But when people asked her, "What are you doing locally?" — her answer was, "I'm not really at home much."

Frieze believed her life would have ebbs and flows, from global to local. "We also know that large-scale change is trans-local, meaning ideas and practices are local, but they need to connect and travel from place to place to create conditions for change." At some point she knew she would reground in a place and put down roots.

In 2012, she bought a house in Jamaica Plain that had an old garage, and built the Old Oak Dojo, a gathering place for exploring how to build resilient and inclusive communities through discussions, movement, celebrations, and retreats. "It is a place where I could experiment with gift culture and grounding the values I wished to live in a place."

She began plans with her father Michael, who had worked all his life in the family business, to bring together their complementary skills and shared interests in entrepreneurship and grassroots social change to create a better future for urban communities. This led to their founding of the Boston Impact Initiative and an initial commitment of $5 million to enterprises in Greater Boston that meet social impact goals such as broader ownership, sustainable development, and racial equity.

For Frieze, community is not just her immediate neighborhood; it's anyone in the region who is excluded from access to capital. "I'm interested

in place, but also in bringing a racial justice lens to this work. So our definition of community includes Brockton, Framingham, and the low-income
neighborhoods of Boston."

Most capital investment vehicles put the type of capital at the center
of the discussion. "We put the relationship at the center of the discussion—and try to be flexible with the forms of capital." BII provides loans—
often at low interest rates and flexible terms—equity investments, and
grants. The same project, at different stages, might tap all three types
of capital.

"In our geographic place, we're looking to build a thriving local living
economy," says Frieze, talking about BII's investment criteria. "So we're
asking different questions about prospective communities and borrowers.
Are they locally owned? Who owns them? What kinds of products and
services are they providing to the community? Most significantly, what is
the relationship among them? If we think of them as an ecosystem of relationships — are they buying and selling from each other? Are we supporting
each other locally?"

Frieze also looks at the macro economy and how to substitute local production for things the community is importing. "How do we start closing
the loop on the production side? It's not just about whether we're selling
it in Boston, but are we producing it here? Are we growing or producing
the raw material? How much are we moving toward this ecosystem mind-
set — that our system can produce most everything it needs? And where it
doesn't — for example, we're not going to grow coffee here — can we buy
and sell from other businesses that share our values?"

Going Off the Wall Street Grid

Frieze and BII are interested in transforming the system of finance, moving
beyond the practices and beliefs of Wall Street finance. "My hope is that BII
will invite people to walk out of Wall Street, where finance is at the center,"
says Frieze, "and have capital be in service to a system that puts place and
community and justice at the center."

The Wall Street system of finance is complex, opaque, anonymous, and
based on short-term outcomes. What would happen if the financial system
was built on direct, transparent, personal practices, based on long-term
relationships?

For Frieze, this means walking out of Wall Street and walking on to emerging fields of impact investing. She's inspired by groups like RSF Social Finance that are going "off the Wall Street grid."

"In the dominant Wall Street system, we don't actually make many direct investments in businesses, but participate in a complex system of trading equities. Eventually, there may be a business involved, but getting capital to them is mediated through layers and layers of transactions. With impact investing, it is a direct relationship, as in 'I'm a lender and you're a borrower,' and the interest rate is set through a conversation, not tied arbitrarily to the LIBOR float that has nothing to do with us."

Capital Coming Home

The work of impact investment funds, such as those of BII, marks an evolution in finance, from remote extractive capitalism to more direct lending. For hundreds of years, people have applied ethical criteria to lending. Some religious investors screened their investments to avoid tobacco and alcohol. Others used their power as owners to engage and attempt to reform corporations. In the 1960s, the Sisters of Loretto, an order of Catholic nuns, bought shares of the Blue Diamond Coal Company to protest strip-mining practices. Dubbed the "stinging nuns" by the coal industry, the sisters showed up at shareholder meetings to press their case.

In the 1980s, the movement to divest from corporations operating in apartheid South Africa rapidly expanded the field of applying "negative screens" to securities. Whole mutual funds emerged with socially screened investment criteria, excluding the most socially injurious corporations.

The 1980s also witnessed the parallel emergence of a "community investment" sector. Between 1982 and 1992, I worked for the Institute for Community Economics (ICE), supporting community groups attempting to get control over their local land, housing, and enterprises through cooperative or community ownership. Projects like our Bernardston mobile home park cooperative couldn't get access to traditional bank financing, at least initially. So we had to tap alternative investments.

ICE created a revolving loan fund to borrow from individuals and religious congregations and lend to these local projects. By 1990, we had over $14 million under management with no loan losses. We attributed our successful track record to our intimate knowledge of the communities we were working in and a technical assistance working relationship with our borrowers, which greatly lowered risk.

The community investment sector expanded, with the creation of other intermediary loan funds. ICE served as an advisor to several of these start-ups, including Boston Community Capital, the New Hampshire Community Loan Fund, and the Reinvestment Fund of the Philadelphia and Delaware Valley region.

These loan funds, together with local venture funds and community development credit unions and banks, formed a community investment sector. The larger socially responsible investment (SRI) world embraced these community capital institutions, in part because we brought compelling human-interest stories of local transformation. But the share of capital actually flowing through these local intermediaries was a drop in the bucket. The vast amount of "socially responsible" capital remained in the equities market universe and the high financial returns, between 1980 and 2000, were hard to resist.

The SRI field evolved rapidly, moving beyond negative screens to proactively make investments in companies with affirmative environmental, social, and governance qualities. Traditional investors found that companies with strong sustainability practices, transparent governance, diverse boards and managers, and a commitment to human rights were also strong financial performers. As a 2007 financial risk study revealed, "There is increasing evidence showing that superior performance in managing climate risk is a useful proxy for superior, more strategic corporate management, and therefore for superior financial value and shareholder value-creation."[12]

By 2014, over $6.5 trillion was managed with social criteria, according to the Forum for Sustainable and Responsible Investment, a trade association of socially responsible investment funds, advisors, and investors.[13]

The community investment sector also grew and evolved. Federal legislation in 1994 established a federal designation and funding program for community development financial institutions, now know as CDFIs.[14] By 2014, two decades later, there were over 800 certified CDFIs, including 492 loan funds; 177 community development credit unions; 176 bank holding companies, banks, or thrifts; and 13 venture capital funds. In 2013, this sector made over twenty-four thousand loans or investments totaling $2 billion. According to the CDFI Coalition's twentieth-anniversary report, this capital financed over seventeen thousand units of affordable housing and sixty-five hundred businesses and created an estimated thirty-five thousand jobs.[15]

As the community investment sector has grown, so has the pool of investors. After the 2008 economic meltdown, a growing number of investors of all sizes sought ways to shift their money out of the Wall Street casino and into the local economy. The impact investing field is the latest incarnation of this evolving community investment sector. "As a term, 'impact investing' is about as meaningless as the phrase 'natural food'," says Frieze. "Lots of people, including some 'impact mutual funds' composed entirely of public equities, use the label."

Another system change, at the core of the BII, is the broadening of ownership, supporting models of worker and community ownership. "We know how unequal wealth is. Expanding worker ownership concretely broadens the distribution of wealth and control."

They are less concerned about the product or service, as long as it's not causing any harm. "We put ownership at the center — who owns the company, who is coming into ownership, who is building assets and wealth." Frieze points to the problem of persistent wealth inequality, particularly the low asset base of black and Latino households. Worker ownership has a track record of building equity and wealth for low-income people.

Capital to CERO

"The CERO project had it all, embodying everything we believed in," says Frieze. "Of our seven investment criteria, the only criterion they were missing was financial viability. We weren't initially sure it would succeed financially."

BII took the risk, providing early financing to CERO, starting with a $10,000 loan at zero interest that they were prepared to lose. This enabled CERO to do the first stages of planning and undertaking an Indigogo crowd-funding campaign to raise $16,950 from 252 contributors in one month.[16] This helped finance their initial public offering.

When CERO did their direct public offering, raising $370,000 in equity from eighty-three investors to launch the company, BII bought equity shares. Later, the initiative was the lead investor alongside two other partners to loan CERO capital for larger-scale capital expenditures, including trucks and equipment.

"It continues to be an incredibly high-risk venture," acknowledges Frieze. "But this is where grassroots organizing meets entrepreneurship in a beautiful way. CERO understands how to organize where they don't have assets. Unlike privileged people, they can't just bootstrap through friends and family. They have to reach out further to build community alliances, and they've done a brilliant job at it."

BII has made over $2 million in investments, including loans to more mature businesses looking to expand. With start-ups like CERO, the initiative's ability to provide a mix of grants, loans, and equity investments is what makes it distinct from other types of investors.

Now, BII is figuring out how to be a patient investor with businesses going through transition from sole proprietor to worker ownership. "There are a significant number of enterprises owned by baby boomers that are ready to retire," says Frieze, talking about a niche BII has identified. "These are viable local businesses that could either be lost to outside ownership or become worker-owned and locally rooted. You need patient private equity capital to hold it, not for the big exit to some multinational buyer, but for the slow arduous exit to workers. We need impact investors to come in and hold that equity so the owner can move on and retire but make sure the company stays in the hands of the worker-owners to be."

$$\diamond$$

It is twilight under the oak trees, but the yard is bustling with voices. Friends and neighbors are gathering at the Old Oak Dojo for a film screening. There is a bustle of talk and children's voices around an open fire pit.

"Auntie Deborah," says one young boy tugging at Frieze's sweater. "Auntie Deborah, can we have popcorn?"

"It's all ready," says Frieze, pointing to several large bowls. "Find a cozy seat. We're going to start the movie soon."

Frieze has found tremendous satisfaction in work that roots her in the region. But she is also part of a national and international community of practice, people in other regions creating impact investment funds.

"There is an amazing community of people doing this work," says Frieze. "When I traveled, I had close friends and deep connections. But there is nothing quite like the interweaving of lives and continuity of relationships that happens at the local level."

"Is this the vision of what you wanted for the dojo?" I ask, impressed by the mix of people and ages gathered.

"It's unfolding," she says, finding the precise words. "I can't predict or accelerate what will happen with this place. I'm following its lead."

She sits down on a chair, and several children pull up chairs and blankets next to her. Other adults find their chairs and sit down as the movie begins, beaming images from another corner of the planet onto the walls of the Old Oak Dojo.

— CHAPTER 17 —

Openhearted Wealth

A person's world is only as big as their heart.

TANYA A. MOORE

I want you to meet a few more people, with widely varying stories. But what each of them has in common is that they are openhearted and open-minded to the predicament of having more than they need.

The Billionaire Buddha: Dariel Garner

Dariel Garner laughs freely, a joyful and inviting laugh. More than once, I've heard him say, "Wealth does not buy happiness. Wealth becomes a barrier that keeps you from the true happiness that comes from your heart."[1]

Garner sits on an Adirondack chair, on the porch of our Vermont cabin. His life partner, Rivera Sun, is sitting next to him, also grinning. We are all eating oatmeal and fruit, squinting into the morning sun. They are far from their home outside Taos, New Mexico.

At one time, Garner was worth hundreds of millions of dollars. Over his life, he started and owned over forty businesses on four continents with thousands of employees. His enterprises included the second-largest agribusiness exporter in Mexico, a tech company that created software for banks, and companies as diverse as golf courses, ski parks, and natural health care products.

A decade ago, he was the developer and co-owner with his former wife of a vast resort in the California Sierra Mountains with projects under way that had projected profits of $750 million. Then he had a change of heart.

Today, Dariel has none of this wealth. At the age of 67, he lives on a modest $900 a month from a Social Security check.

"I've never been happier," he says with a smile. "Today I am penniless and have far more than I could ever imagine existed. Each day I am awakened to the joy of being connected and part of all of life around me. I am able to be with other people and with nature in a way that was impossible for me when I was wealthy."

"Don't forget to tell him the part about how you got the girl, too," Rivera says. She has long red hair and a quick smile. She has recently written and published a novel, *Billionaire Buddha*, that tells a fictionalized version of Dariel's story.

Business Success

Most journalistic accounts would call Garner a "self-made" multimillionaire. His mother grew up in a poor sharecropping family in rural Arkansas, and his family moved to California in the 1930s, part of the great western migration. They worked stable jobs in war industries, and Garner was born and raised there.

He attended the University of California at Berkeley, both as an undergraduate and as a graduate student. Early on, he was interested in computer science and resource economics. His curiosity for environmental issues was rooted in the happiest days of his childhood, visiting Yosemite on vacation and wandering in the forests.

His first business venture was entirely accidental. A tremendous freeze killed off hundreds of eucalyptus trees in the Berkeley Hills. He and two friends — "three guys, three briefcases, and a pocket calculator" — created a business to harvest the trees and ship them to a pulpwood market in Japan.

"At that point I got my first and only job as an employee." He smiles. "I worked for someone else for three months, as a financial consultant. I learned a great deal about finance, insurance, and the operations of small banks." He quickly realized he could go out on his own and opened up a small office, working with banks and businesses in California's Central Valley. He identified a business niche, creating computer spreadsheets for local banks to analyze lending. This was before Lotus and Excel and other software systems became popular. Banks hired Garner's company to develop and install software.

Garner's company expanded and he sold it to the US subsidiary of a large French bank, Société Général. At age 31, Garner had become a multimillionaire. More important, he had learned to trust his vision and instincts.

"I got into the fast-changing software business, with lots of different platforms. IBM, Sun, NCR, Apple, Smith Corona — they all needed different software." It was a time of intense competition and innovation. Garner went into a big deal with General Electric that ended in disaster, and they took over his company.

At this point, in the 1980s, Garner was quite wealthy, living with his wife in a beach house in La Jolla, California. They decided to move to Mexico, starting several ventures in Northern Baja, the most successful being growing and exporting agricultural products. California cuisine was taking off — and winter vegetables from Mexico were in high demand.

"We had three years without any real competition and made a lot of money," says Garner, in an even voice. His ventures produced flowers and 140 varieties of fresh and frozen vegetables, and he shipped wood to Japan. At one point his companies had 7,000 acres under cultivation and he was the second-largest Mexican food exporter, after Dole Foods.

After a decade of business in Mexico, Garner sold out and moved back to the United States, looking for the perfect place to live and eventually getting into resort development. He and his wife couldn't find the ideal place, so they decided to develop one.

After creating a resort in Idaho, the Garners returned to California, building the second-most-expensive recreational subdivision in California, in the Lake Tahoe region of the High Sierras. They named it Gold Mountain and designed a mountaintop subdivision and golf course. Frank Lloyd Wright had designed a clubhouse for a Madison, Wisconsin, golf resort that had never been constructed. The Garners acquired the plans and built it.[2]

The *Tahoe Quarterly* described the undertaking: "Rising out of the top of a hill near Graeagle, an hour north of Tahoe, is America's newest Frank Lloyd Wright masterpiece, finally completed 42 years after his death. Exact in every detail to the master's plans — from the fabric on the pillows to the landscaped grounds — the Nakoma Resort and Spa is an instant architectural attraction, a 'museum' for lovers of Wright's work from throughout the world."[3]

By 2004, Garner was at the pinnacle of wealth and accomplishment. "My perspective on wealth kept shifting," Garner chuckles. "At first I thought $5 million was wealthy. And then I couldn't tell how much I was worth within $5 million. Another time, I thought, 'Wealth is when you have more than your weight in gold.' I did a calculation and realized I was really wealthy."

Turning Point

One day Garner's physician said, "Dariel, I really envy you because I can imagine you up on top of the veranda of your resort having a cocktail with your beautiful wife. The only problem is you won't live to see it."

Garner thought to himself, "Well, that's fine with me." He was deeply depressed. He weighed 365 pounds and was, in his words, "committing suicide by eating."

He kept eating and feeling numb. Then one day he was entering the private dining room at his resort. The hostess touched him gently, as she steered him to a table. "I hadn't been touched by anyone other than my wife for years. Because people don't touch rich people." That gesture moved him and shook him. "It was like the touch of God. I realized that I could love and be loved. I was floored."

The next day, Garner stopped eating. He went on a long lemon juice fast, losing weight.

"I decided to live."

His demeanor shifted. He felt lighter and friendlier. A few months later he overheard a comment that wasn't meant for his ears. The wife of his comptroller said, "You would hardly know Dariel anymore. He has a heart."

"I thought I had always had a heart," Garner says. "People were seeing a change. I'd lost 180 pounds and some people couldn't recognize me, but more importantly I was becoming human again. My heart was growing."

Garner was connecting with people, enjoying life more. "I had lost track that people were people — not just part of the production process: employees, customers, homeowners. I was very disconnected.

"I remember sitting at my desk and signing paychecks for people who would make in a year what I made in an hour. And these were people making $20,000 a year. I began to recognize the vast difference of income and wealth.

"I turned my back on the money. I felt there was something wrong with one person having so much more than others. At a certain point I felt the money was ill gotten, taken from someone else."

Through several years of giving, spending, divorce, and loss, the money went away. He and his former wife gave away millions through a family foundation. Garner donated a huge development project to a small California city, after creating the infrastructure. His ex-wife took over the Tahoe resort.

Garner moved down from the Sierras to coastal Big Sur. He started reading more and reconnecting with his body and reconciling his interests in spirit and science.

"Then I met Rivera," Garner says, smiling at his partner. "We met in a teahouse and together we have learned a tremendous amount about wealth, social change, and spirit. I met so many people from very different circumstances, people I would never have met if I had been buffered and suffocated by my wealth."

Self-Made Man?

Garner objects to the misnomer "self-made." "I got a lot of help along the way. I got a free education at the University of California, in the days when school was virtually free. Governor Ronald Reagan's signature is on my diploma!

"Wealth is the fruit of a culture, of an economic system," he came to realize. "If someone says they are self-made, they are being disingenuous. There are roads, technological infrastructure, rules, and structures — all the goods of the entire system. The problem is just that a few people have been able to benefit from the system and keep most of the fruit."

Once he was among the keepers of that fruit, Garner says, the game was rigged in his favor — "from tax breaks and doors opening to financing." In the process of creating a golf club, he discovered a loophole provision in the 76,000-page federal tax code that allowed private golf club developers to treat membership sales as nontaxable income. "I thought, 'Wow, I'm going to make $15 million, and I don't have to declare the income!' Someone had come before me and lobbied for that perk." And that is just one of many examples.

Says Garner, "The system is designed for someone like me to succeed. The first million is the hardest to make. But then the doors fly open. A whole 'wealth defense' industry rises up — lawyers, lobbyists, politicians — that enable the already advantaged to rise and stay on top. The tax laws are written by the wealthy for the wealthy. At the other end of the spectrum — for the poor and disadvantaged — the doors are closing."

When Garner was in business school back in the late 1960s, he read a case study of General Electric and how they hadn't paid federal corporate income tax in decades. "Well here we are, fifty years later, and GE still doesn't contribute to federal tax obligations.

"We have a culture of wealth, separation, extraction — which is the foundation for most of wealth of this country. We are living a myth that needs to be pierced through scrutiny — to look at the truth of our interconnection. As Gandhi said, 'There is enough for everyone's need, but not for everyone's greed.'"

Changing the System

Garner's decision to give away hundreds of millions is extraordinary, but not unprecedented. Yet he has no regrets. "I am one with people and the Earth, no longer the dominator, no longer separate and alone, not idolized, idealized, or loathed for being rich. I am filled with the true love for the self and others that comes from the recognition that we are all equal in the heart of creation."

Garner recognizes his choice was more renunciation, a shedding. Like the weight he lost, he also shed millions. If he had the chance to do it again, he would do it differently. "Although I would willingly give my wealth away again today, the way in which I would give it away has changed. I wouldn't just turn my back and walk off. I wouldn't fritter it away on diamonds and thousand-dollar bottles of wine. I wouldn't give it to charities that simply put Band-Aids on the sicknesses of our society.

"Instead of giving it away," he says, "I would give it back. I would give it back to the society that created it: the workers, inventors, teachers, artists, families, and communities. I would try to protect our natural systems, the whole interconnected web of creation that is the basis of all wealth in this world. I wouldn't stop there, either. I would, as I am doing today, join with others in building a movement to share the wealth, to fix the systems that create inequality, and help others rejoin the human family.

"Our global society is reaching a crisis where the greed of a few is stifling the flow of resources and limiting our ability to confront the challenges our world faces. Currently, a few individuals are hoarding huge reservoirs of wealth for their personal enjoyment while the planet and the people are suffering to make them even richer. This is an unsustainable situation, and we must resolve it."

Thanking Pete Seeger: Arthur Cornfeld

Dariel Garner's story is powerful and unusual. But it is only one path toward "coming home." I've also met plenty of people who choose not to renounce or radically share their wealth, but are powerfully openhearted in the way they live their lives. One of them is a man named Arthur Cornfeld, the patriarch of a New York City real estate business he has built over the last thirty-five years.

"We were poor, but I didn't know it," says Cornfeld, sitting in his office in a high-rise next to Carnegie Hall. I've been asking him about his childhood growing up in a vibrant working-class neighborhood in the Bronx. "We had a close-knit community where I played all kinds of stickball, baseball in a schoolyard democracy. We worked it out, with the bigger guys yielding the court to the younger ones."[4]

Over the years, I've met Cornfeld for lunch once or twice a year when I'm in New York City. Sometimes he brings along his business partners, who are all very, very wealthy. They have a spirited banter, batting ideas around. And they like to bat me around when I visit. But there is something different about Cornfeld. He seems to have his full empathy faculties intact, his heart open to the suffering and goodness of the world. I'm curious how that can be.

Cornfeld was born in Palestine in 1935; his family fled to the United States before World War II to work in the garment industry. As a young man, home from the University of Michigan for the summer, he worked as a busboy at the Lido Beach Hotel on Long Island. "It was the Jewish Four Seasons," he quips. "There were fat guys sitting around playing poker and I disliked their elitism and privilege. I used to laugh at them."

His first entrepreneurial venture was producing folk concerts: "Josh White, Odetta, Rambling Jack Eliot, New Lost City Ramblers — many of the greats." Later he went to Harvard Law School, worked at a law firm on intellectual property issues, and started a medical education company. He got into real estate originally as an investment and for the tax breaks.

"My life is one lucky thing after another," he recalls. "First, escaping Nazism, then enjoying the good fortune of my neighborhood. The timing of my investing in New York City property was lucky — things just exploded.

"I may have made money," he says, "but I always felt hardscrabble. I still feel like an underdog. And I really like helping people."

Cornfeld lives on Fifth Avenue, and daily sees an almost surreal level of prosperity all around him. "I don't have a plane, though some of my partners do," he says. "All around us are huge buildings going up — luxury retail, residential, commercial — going for unreasonable prices."

Yet he hasn't lost sight of how unusual his circumstance is: "I don't forget the people who really run the city, who get up at 5 a.m. and make the trains run and the electricity stay on, and they get paid crap. Other people fall by the wayside, becoming homeless, struggling for medical care. I often think about them.

"I don't know why I feel this way," he says. "I have a brother who I love dearly, but he couldn't care less. He won the lottery and is like, 'Too bad for the others.'"

Cornfeld is not a religious man, but he had a near-religious experience meeting up with the folksinger Peter Seeger about two years before Seeger died in January 2014. He had met Seeger as a young man in the 1950s, producing concerts for the Weavers and Seeger at summer camps in upstate New York and the annual Forest Hills music festival.

"He was such a strong and honest man. I remember watching him before the House Un-American Activities Committee. He was dignified, standing up for his rights against the bullies. Seeger was questioned about his affiliations and performances, at which point he said, 'I have sung in hobo jungles, and I have sung for the Rockefellers, and I am proud that I have never refused to sing for anybody.'[5]

"So about three years ago, I called him up and made a date to talk to him in person. I drove up to Beacon, New York, to meet him." Cornfeld stops and wipes a tear from his eye. "During our visit, we went out and stood with an antiwar sign at a vigil in Beacon.

"I offered him a gift of $100,000. His wife Toshi was quite sick, and I thought it would make his life easier. It was my way of showing him the enormous respect and gratitude I had for him. Seeger always struck me as a man who lived very simply but with great integrity. He had a moral compass that is hard to find these days."

Seeger turned the money down. "I offered to make gifts in his honor," Cornfeld remembers. Seeger thought about it and then pulled out a piece of paper and wrote down a list of a dozen organizations, including the Clearwater Sloop, the boat and environmental education center that Seeger cofounded, and several indigenous rights groups. One contribution in his honor went to *The American Songbook* project.

"He didn't care about money," says Cornfeld. "It was a holy moment — and I'm not a religious man. It was one of the most transcendent moments of my life, getting to thank Pete Seeger."

Risk Telling the Truth: Abe Lateiner

Abe Lateiner fills a small plate of Indian food from a restaurant buffet and sits across from me.

"I don't like to waste or overeat, so I keep my helpings small," says the lanky red-haired 33-year-old former Boston public school teacher. He does not appear to be at risk of overeating.

Like Arthur Cornfeld, there is something striking about Abe Lateiner, which is his piercing honesty and openheartedness. I first met Abe when he reached out to talk about privilege, and we've had many conversations.

"I thought I was going to be a career teacher," said Abe, about his public school teaching years. "But after a decade, I hit bottom." He was mostly teaching in inner-city schools and every day saw the barriers his students faced. He had some positive experiences that uplifted him. "But I wasn't very resilient and I kept losing my footing," he says.

After he stopped teaching, he took advantage of his savings, which were enabled by his family's wealth — made from a Pennsylvania industrial tube manufacturing company — to take a break and not immediately get another job. He took the space to read and talk to people, and engage with others in Resource Generation, a network of people under age 35 with wealth.

Instead of hiding from privilege, he started to ask himself, "How can I use this privilege? What am I uniquely positioned to do that the world is asking for — not in a superhero way — but what does the world, including me, need?" The answer, reflected in Lateiner's choices, is to be fully himself and connected with the world.

"In my home in the Port neighborhood in Cambridge, I'm a gentrifier," says Lateiner. "I came in with money, but I didn't have a network here. I didn't know who was in my neighborhood." Over the course of many conversations with new and old neighbors, Lateiner cofounded a pay-what-you-can community meal called the Port Café, a space where neighbors come together over shared food, across differences of race and class.

Through the Port Café, Lateiner got to know his neighbors and made friends. "Throughout the process, I was completely up front about who I was. I explained to people that my life has been limited by having access to money, that I've missed out. I used to believe that the only wealth is money. There are many types of wealth and my neighbors have nonfinancial wealth that I don't have."

Lateiner is making an important insight. Many wealthy people see their privilege and believe they should be more charitable. But what Lateiner is saying is, "I'm not whole, I'm missing something." And that other people, who live without privilege, hold an essential piece of the puzzle. As Felice Yeskel used to say to me, "You owning-class people don't understand — I have stuff you need. You're ill equipped in some fundamental ways." This is the first step toward reciprocity and away from a charity framework. Lateiner reflects this understanding.

"I feel as though I've experienced poverty of the spirit. I was confronted with a rough situation," says Lateiner, referring to his teaching years. "It crushed me, partly because I hadn't built up a resilient spirit."

Lateiner also feels he has experienced a poverty of intellect, the inability to see the systems of privilege and oppression that surround him.

"It is humbling to admit this, but this is what I was born into," he says, his lunch plate empty. "When I tell people about my circumstances, they are surprised or shocked by my honesty. But the positive responses out-weigh any negativity. The people who have responded harshly also tend to share a privileged identity. We are most vicious to people who remind us of ourselves.

"I've been able to make friends with people from very different back-grounds. But I had to develop an ability to be honest in a sustained way. I'm the person that others have good reason not to trust. I was born into the dominant race, class, gender, and sexual identity. The only thing that allows me to be part of justice work is honesty. Honesty is the number one offering that I have."

In the spring of 2014, Lateiner had a breakthrough moment when he went on a road trip. He invited a former student to Wisconsin to visit the coordinator of the after school program they had both been a part of. Lateiner also invited his father-in-law, Hernan, to join them.

"We were a sight to behold," says Lateiner, grinning at the memory of three of them setting off for Wisconsin in a gray 2007 Prius. "There was me, the white 31-year-old privileged guy, my 23-year-old former student from Cape Verde, and my 76-year-old Peruvian father-in-law who speaks very little English."

As people encountered the unlikely trio, "People had no idea what to do with us," says Lateiner. "We would stop at a gas station, and we noticed a magical energy that seemed to follow us everywhere. People would just start smiling when they saw us, which had never happened to me. We went out dancing at a salsa club in Madison, and we were invited to dinner by people we had just met."

Lateiner felt like the universe was telling him: "You are on the right path."

"The three of us were connecting with each other and strangers and being honest with people. It was a transformational experience."

Lateiner recalls a moment, driving down rural highway in Wisconsin. It was snowing and the trees were barren and they were singing and listening to music and dancing in their seats, a bubble of vibrancy traveling through a cold and gray world. In that moment, Lateiner thought to himself, "How do we keep this going? How can we bring this traveler's energy back home with us?"

One insight was the importance of honesty, of not pretending to be someone else. "Honesty has been my guide," he says. "Honesty is scary when I show up with so much privilege. My identity, my ways of being, the way I look at the world — all of these things are potential minefields because they have been born out of supremacist mentalities."

Another formative moment for Lateiner was the eruption of the Black Lives Matter movement. "I'm sitting in Boston, reading James Baldwin, and then Michael Brown is killed in the street by a white police officer," says Lateiner, recalling the 2014 shooting that sparked fury in Ferguson,

Missouri, and beyond. "Things explode and a people's movement emerges into the mainstream consciousness. For me it's a gift to have the opportunity to be part of this movement and act on what I'm learning and see things emerge in real time."

When the killers of Eric Garner — also black, and who died after police put him in a chokehold in New York City — were not indicted in November 2014, Lateiner joined thousands of others at a Black Lives Matter demonstration in Boston. They walked past the South Bay Correction Facility and saw prisoners pounding on the glass and bars. Thousands of people in the street began chanting, "We see you! We see you!"

"I've never had any formal religion." Abe wipes tears from his eyes as he tells the story. "It was the first time I felt part of something. I was in it. Going up Massachusetts Avenue, we were stopping traffic both ways, people cheering, horns honking. We were alive.

"My upbringing as a white person means my understanding of race is constructed completely upside down, as James Baldwin pointed out," he says. "I don't look at race as more important than other types of oppression. But I see it as a fulcrum of American delusion and illusion, a justification for maintaining power."

Lateiner feels like he is living in the movie *The Matrix*. Everything he's been taught is not true, in regard to both race and class. "I've been fooled, used as a tool of atrocity, given goodies to keep me silent and ignorant about the oppression that happens in my name. To ignore that truth is to kill something inside myself.

"As teacher" — Lateiner smiles — "I did not have time to have my world turned upside down. I have had to surrender to be able to see things outside the conditioning of my gender, race, and class and to let go and learn." Lateiner feels humbled by how much time people have invested in him so he could learn awareness and begin to understand whiteness.

Lateiner seems to be called to do this work around white privilege and wealth advantage. He started a blog, called *Risk Something*, to explore the way forward, away from guilt and into true solidarity. "I feel like I can harness and boil down some of the lessons, to offer a path to white people seeking a way out of silent complicity.

"How can I hold space for people to come to a place of surrender? Surrender to the fact that we are born into complicity, that it's not our fault, but that it is our responsibility?" he asks. "This is not about facts or arguments. It is fundamentally spiritual work. I think our spiritual survival is hanging in the balance. Through our complicity with the violence and physical harm toward people of color, our souls are destroyed."

Lateiner is working with a group of other white people on an experimental curriculum that gets at this. "Grief is the first step in my becoming useful as a white person," he reflects. "We have to go through grief at how we've been acculturated and dehumanized to play the role we are playing. This is our liberation, our saving ourselves.

"Once I surrender, I can accept the truth that the foundations of my advantage have been built on land theft, genocide, rape, and slavery. There's blood on everything. As a parent it is particularly bracing to know that some of that blood is children's blood. You can't unsee that. How do I ignore that unless I'm a monster?

"Once I realize: Who can live with that kind of lie? Surrender is a precondition for being able to do the work," he says. "On the bright side, now I get to show up with everything I have. I have inherent value. I don't think I'm worthless because I'm an oppressor. I'm positioned to do valuable work, but first I have to surrender."

Alignment: Jenny Ladd

"I feel the pain of the trashing of the planet very deeply," says Jenny Ladd. We are walking on a leafy path through a tall hardwood forest.

"Humans might be shortsighted and greedy, but do we have to take down this beautiful planet? Such a waste, such a horror," Ladd says.

On cue, we approach a flowering tree, its buds opening around the winter solstice in New England. The seasons have gone haywire, a combination of El Niño and climate change.

Ladd and I are at Temenos, a rustic retreat center in Western Massachusetts, where she often stays in a cabin and goes on silent retreats. I've been looking forward to my visit with her. She is someone who "walks the walk" as a person with wealth who is deeply aware of the economic and ecological moment we are living in and has made thoughtful decisions and lives her values. It's her last day here, and we're spending the afternoon together, walking outside and then driving back to her home.

"We are facing a transition," Ladd says, patting the trunk of the tree with concern. She is wearing a gray wool sweater and hiking boots. Though in her early 60s, she seems unchanged from when I met her over twenty-five years earlier — youthful, funny, lively, and grounded. But in this moment, she is dead serious.

"I don't want to act based on fear, but I see how fragile the institutions are around us. Things could suddenly change. I listen behind the headlines to the trends in the news, the signs of our societal decomposition. There are many ways we should prepare for the transition, and connecting with neighbors and local people is key."

Jennifer Ladd grew up in a wealthy family, an heiress to the Standard Oil fortune. She was raised without any formal religion, but was instilled with a deep interconnectedness with nature. "We spent many weeks each year camping and hiking in the White Mountains. And we had an old lobster boat with two bunks, and we would bounce around out at sea. For me, being involved on issues of the environment and climate change is easy."

At the age of 21, she inherited just under $1 million that she has mostly given away over her lifetime. When she was 40, she "came out" to people about having money and made a plan to give away substantial assets. "That was upsetting and destabilizing to some people, because they were attached to me having money and being a source of support to them." Decades later, Ladd is deeply engaged in supporting the transition to a just and resilient local economy in Western Massachusetts.

"Fossil fuel oil was a great achievement in the 1860s, but we have to move quickly to a new energy economy." One of her ancestors, Charles Pratt, worked with the founder of Standard Oil, John D. Rockefeller, to refine the process of oil production. Ladd's mother died in 2012, and she inherited an additional bundle of 1924 Standard Oil stock, now ExxonMobil. She gave all of it away to fund organizing around climate change.

"It was the perfect thing to do," she says. "I used the money to heal the wounds caused by the way the money was made. I felt part of the historical moment spurred by the Divest-Invest movement. Giving the money now, in terms of its impact on these movements, is more important than ten years from now. Don't wait."

Ladd and I arrive at a hand-pump well next to a large rock outcropping. This is the source of water for all the cabins. We fill up a few water jugs at the pump. I ask Ladd how she felt divesting from Standard Oil and funding organizations addressing the climate crisis.

"GREAT!" She laughs. "It felt clean, good, like defragging your computer. It's like I closed a loop. I felt in line."

"In line?" I ask.

"It felt in line with my deepest values. It's liberating. I feel like I played my part in a relay race. I got the baton, ran my leg of the race without tripping, and passed it on."

Ladd explains she has held on to some money, placed in socially responsible investment funds, to cover her future needs. "I'm single, and we'd don't live in Scandinavia where I know I'd be taken care of with dignity in my old age," she says, and she has no regrets about using the rest to create change. "It feels better to me not to hold back and to instead be part of a movement to create a better society. I do trust that one thing leads to another, that money can be a catalyst."

Ladd has spent more than a decade working with people as a coach and advisor, especially with those with substantial wealth. She has accompanied many people in their process of figuring out money and how to use it effectively.

"I believe how people give, the spirit of giving, is as important as the gift," she says, hoisting up two jugs of water. I carry another two, and we walk on another path to her car.

"The best giving is out of gratitude, when you feel like you are in the flow. Listen for a 'yes' in your heart and mind."

She has given money to friends, but instead of asking them to pay her back, she asks them to make contributions to organizations or pass the gift along. She helped one friend who was unable to finish her schooling because of money. "I gave money to her with the understanding that she would pay it back as a gift to another woman over 40 finishing her education. That gift has been passed on many times."

Ladd has done creative giving and watched others do it as well. "It opens up the flow of giving and generosity. Others have the experience of being givers, as well."

From her coaching and advising work, she knows the inner barriers and demons that some wealthy people face in the process of aligning their lives with their values and hopes. "It is not easy," she says. We arrive at her car and begin driving back to her house in Northampton. "We live in an insecure world. And many people don't have a sense of family and community they can depend on. If very wealthy people feel this vulnerability, think what it's like for the rest of the society?"

Like many others I've talked to over the years, Ladd understands how wealthy people can miss out on the interdependence and community that is formed by people helping one another. "Why ask someone to help you with gardening if you could hire a gardener?

"The wider community reinforces this dynamic, thinking it strange or cheap that someone wants to be in relationship other than a paid relationship," she says. "So then all the relationships this wealthy person has become transactional rather than reciprocal. If you never have to ask, only pay, and are never vulnerable, you miss out on a fundamental part of the human experience."

Ladd describes many wealthy people who are locked into disconnected situations. They live in large houses at the end of long driveways or in the countryside. This might be a family house or land, so it has meaning to them. But it keeps them apart. "They can't see their neighbors, so they have less interaction. They don't really get to know them, so the bonds of community are weak.

"It's less of a problem if you live in a neighborhood like mine," Ladd says, pulling onto her street in Northampton, a neighborhood of modest bungalows and mature trees. Her block is a tight row of older single-family homes on small lots, close together, without fences. No one is building McMansions here. Neighbors see each other on a daily basis, adding to a sense of community security, well-being, and resilience.

"When I had a fire in my house, I stayed with two of the families on my street who were very welcoming. Another family on the street let me stay in an apartment they had, so they really helped me out."

We are standing in her driveway, looking up and down the street. Neighbors drive past and wave. Ladd points at different houses, each with a story. "See those neighbors park their cars across from each other, creating a sort of speed bump. People are reminded to slow down because of all the kids.

"My neighbor Peter snowblows my sidewalk when he can," she says. Another neighbor worked with her to take down large weed trees on their shared lot line, opening up more sunlight for gardens. Together, they planted blueberry bushes between their houses that both families share. There are lots of kids on the street and lots of shared family activities and potlucks. "We help each other out," she says. "We have a book group that turned into a movie group.

"This is my neighborhood," says Ladd. "But I consider my community to be this wider valley, including Springfield and Holyoke. My stake in this area includes communities that have been excluded from prosperity." Ladd is part of valley-wide initiatives to bridge racial and class divisions, create local jobs, and invest in local enterprises, similar to the Jamaica Plain New Economy Transition. One group, Invest Here Now, is an impact investment fund moving capital to local projects.

We venture inside and take off our boots. Ladd puts on slippers and pads into the kitchen, putting a teakettle on the stove and assembling a plate of cookies. Her small house is compact but warm. There's a woodstove in the living room, but we don't need it on this summer-like winter day. We sit at her dining room table.

"There are a wide variety of barriers for wealthy people trying to come home, in addition to the fear of the unknown," Ladd says. She describes one family that is locked into needing to hold on to millions because they own multiple homes and now the next generation of grandchildren all attend expensive private schools. "They are used to having a lot of space," says Ladd. "And caring for all these things takes inordinate time and energy. You see people trapped by the expectations of a high standard of living and by all their belongings and properties. The wealth owns them rather than they owning the wealth. And there's still a sense of scarcity, of not having enough.

"Sometimes the people who have the hardest time are those with the most money," observes Ladd. "I know people with over $100 million and they feel they are unable to change their situation. I realize it's hard to give away that much money." She pauses and thinks. "If I had that much money, I'd find a way to give it to small-town governments."

One challenge of "coming out" — being known as someone with resources — is facing the tremendous deprivations in our communities and people asking for money. "This is one of the ways we experience the great inequalities of our time," reflects Ladd. "No one wants to be regarded as a 'walking wallet,' but sometimes we are. Where else are people going to get money for community organizations and social change projects? Foundations are hard to reach. Corporations and governments aren't a source of funds. It's going to come from individuals."

Ladd says part of being open and your whole self in community is to develop systems to share money that give boundaries. For example, you might say *Send me a letter, I only give twice a year*, or *I only give through this intermediary that has a community board*. "But just remember," she advises, "this experience is the result of great inequality. And our experience is considerably less intrusive then being a low-income person on welfare, with everyone questioning your choices."

There is no cookie-cutter approach to working through the barriers. Her advice is, "Get over yourself. Find a role. Do stuff. Don't hold yourself back. Don't wait for the perfect organization to support."

Ladd also advises working in collaboration with others — not trying to save the world yourself. "Play your part in the orchestra. Ask yourself: How can I be a portal for the flow? Can I add value and enthusiasm to movements? If you're stuck, there are plenty of people willing to help you, who don't want to rip you off.

"For some people it's hard to feel like they are part of something bigger," says Ladd, pouring us each a cup of tea. "One thing that moves people is a powerful vision and plan. People get stuck when they are disconnected from community and social change movements. Or they don't see anything inspiring. People need a supportive community of others who are coming home, investing money, and giving boldly. I've seen people create a plan and program, with others, to move substantial resources — and they do it."

An important first step is making a plan. Figuring out what you really need to live on and what you can easily give away.

There are huge benefits to sharing wealth and coming home, according to Ladd. "You don't feel separated. You are not stuck in fear and cynicism. I think it's good for your physical health. Coming home to community is alive, joyful, and puts you in authentic relationships.

"There are struggles and pain — and the dynamics of interacting with others in community is not always easy. But at least you're in the dynamics. You're not in some sterile nonfeeling zone watching everyone else through a glass window." Ladd acknowledges knowing what that sometimes feels like as a person without children. "Engagement can be messy, but it's engagement."

Homeward

One thing I appreciate about "coming home," after talking to these individuals, is that it is not a sacrifice. Coming home satisfies a hunger for more — a more personal, connected, and meaningful life — closer to one another and the sacred.

When someone chooses not to live in a big house, but live in proximity to others, it is not out of austerity and deprivation. It is a choice to be more connected to community, to nature, to others. "The same goes for the rest of the modern consumer lifestyle," writes Charles Eisenstein.

> *We will put it aside because we can no longer stand the emptiness, the ugliness. We are starving for spiritual nourishment. We are starving for a life that is personal, connected, and meaningful. By choice, that is where we will direct our energy. When we do so, community will arise anew because this spiritual nourishment can only come to us as a gift, as part of a web of gifts in which we participate as giver and receiver.*[6]

To fully come home is to live into this new story. The feelings of scarcity and deprivation give way to constant awareness of abundance and sufficiency.

PART VI

THE INVITATIONS

Privilege is not in and of itself bad. . . . Privilege does not have to be negative, but we have to share our resources and take direction about how to use our privilege in ways that empower those who lack it.

BELL HOOKS, *HOMEGROWN*

CHAPTER 18

Wealthy, Come Home

The most remarkable feature of this historical moment on Earth is not that we are on the way to destroying the world — we've actually been on the way for quite a while. It is that we are beginning to wake up, as from a millennia-long sleep, to a whole new relationship to our world, to ourselves and each other.

JOANNA MACY

Wealthy friends and neighbors, it is time to come home.

Our challenge is to use our special privileges to eliminate special privileges and build healthy communities and an economy that works for everyone.

We are living between stories, as Charles Eisenstein observes. The "old story" of wealth, economic well-being, and deservedness has run its course. This story has brought us to the brink of ecological ruin and violent divisions. We are in the process of creating a "new story" that describes the deep interconnection between humans and nature. Wealthy people can aid in this transition to a new story and system.

How do we let go of the "old story" way of living and begin to live in the "new story"? What should I do? Where should I live? Where should I give my money? And how much do I want to give away and how much should I keep? Where should I invest? What practices might I undertake? These are some of the questions that should be considered, not alone but in small groups or associations. What follows are ten elements of a program and thoughts on a way forward.

1. Root Yourself in a New Story

Not surprisingly, the first step in the journey is to root ourselves in a new story. We can choose to act from fear and scarcity or from gratitude, acknowledging the enormous gifts around us.

One part of this practice is to open our eyes and hearts to see the web of people, nature, ancestors, and our community that has made the positive aspects of our lives possible. This means acknowledging that our wealth comes, in large part, thanks to a commonwealth that includes the gifts of nature and society around us.

"No one does it alone," as Bill Gates Sr. said. "We all benefit from the contributions of our ancestors who have established the fertile ground for opportunity and wealth creation that we have inherited." The challenge is for us to notice these gifts every day, celebrate our good fortune, and ensure they are a birthright for all.

Keeping our eyes open also means seeing the horrific damage caused globally by powerful, wealthy, and disconnected people. As George Pillsbury told me, it would be a problem if we didn't *feel* something in the face of this. Among the powerful emotions we might feel are both paralyzing guilt and motivating empathy. But we shouldn't lose touch with a basic truth: None of us asked to be born into a world with such grotesque disparities of wealth, power, opportunity, and suffering. It's what we do with our lives that will influence the future.

2. Tell True Stories About Wealth

You are invited to help demystify the confusion about wealth, success, and privilege — by telling true stories. Like Martin Rothenberg, tell the truth about society's role in your individual good fortune — and the ways that privilege and advantages and luck have worked in your favor. It is important to include your own individual choices and contributions, but not disproportionately glorify them.

There is no shame in acknowledging the reality that any wealth held in your name is the result of the ecological commons plus your efforts or someone else's hard work, combined with the fertile ground that previous generations and today's workers and taxpayers helped to build. Your own personal story of help will provide a powerful counternarrative to the "I did it alone" stories that dominate our culture.

By telling true stories we can help demystify the dynamics of inherited advantage that are undermining equality of opportunity and worsening inequality. Young people born without family wealth face a challenging and sometimes dismal future. Think of the four 21-year-olds — Miranda, Marcus, Tony, and Cordelia. One of them will be vaulted into the wealthy classes while the rest will struggle. Is this really the kind of society we want to live in?

3. Help Redefine Wealth and See the Commonwealth

You are invited to help redefine wealth and steer the culture away from a narrow definition of wealth as property, money, and financial capital. Real wealth includes a healthy ecological commons, a web of community institutions, and security based on authentic and caring relationships. This is the wealth that money cannot buy but that is being degraded by predatory capitalism and narrowly defined financial wealth.

Our cultural challenge is to see the commonwealth and commons that surround us — that make our life and private wealth possible. Other societies recognize and protect their commons. But the United States has a particular blind spot when it comes to seeing and protecting our commons.

Business leader and author Peter Barnes defines the commons as "all the gifts we inherit or create together":

> *It is shared wealth writ large. It includes innumerable gifts of nature and society, from the atmosphere to the Internet, science to children's stories, soil to community strength. We inherit these assets jointly and hold them in trust, morally if not legally, for those who come after us. These assets are essential to the human and planetary well-being as well as to the functioning of our modern economy. Yet to economists and others, they are stunningly invisible. Economists fail to see the commons because its contributions are difficult to monetize.*[1]

Our commons include ecosystems, language, music, money, law, mathematics, parks, and so much more.[2] Life is sustained by the ecological commons, including water, soil, air, and seeds. An invisible socially created commons is integral to private wealth. Its aspects include regulated capital markets, intellectual property laws, the Internet, and accounting systems, to name a few.

True wealth is not in the size of our bank accounts or asset holdings, but resides in the quality of our relationships, the interconnectedness of our community, and the overall health of the society. The reason for our being is not to accumulate the most toys before we die. It is fundamentally about connection. For us to be in authentic connection and community, we will have to feel vulnerability, practice mutuality, and depend on others. All the walls and security systems in the world will not protect our families from the fragmentation and breakdown that will occur in an extremely unequal and ecologically degraded society.

4. Put a Personal Stake in a Place and Work for the Common Good

Each day we cast votes for the kind of future we want. Coming home means voting with your feet and life commitment, bringing your time, treasure, and talents to a place. Like my small campaign to get lifeguards at my local pool, I invite you to engage your stake in the smooth functioning of societal institutions, starting at the local level.

Resist the urge to privatize one's needs through the creation of private recreational paradises, private education and transportation, or gated or enclave communities. Instead develop a personal stake in quality public education, livable communities, and healthy ecosystems. If we make personal choices that reflect this, it will have a positive ripple effect on the whole society.

Planting your stake in a place will engage your social capital, your time, money, and insight. Democracy requires engagement with other people, making your case, winning, losing, and compromising. Often wealthy people, when we don't get our way through the democratic system, pick up our ball and leave, creating private institutions and unaccountable systems. Mature societies require all members, especially those with wealth and power, to accept compromise while remaining committed to the whole. We are called to be a voice for policies and investments that will expand, in the words of forester Gifford Pinchot, "the greatest good for the greatest number."

Make a commitment to ensure that the lives of all children are as good as the lives of the children in your extended family. This includes advocating for public investments in early childhood education, enrichment, early intervention health care, and quality schools. But it also means deescalating the inherited advantage arms race of assistance to our own children and families.

We may be wired to protect our own children and ensure they are safe and flourishing. But when we inadvertently direct all manner of privileged advantages to them, we both undermine their own development and exacerbate disparities in opportunity. We can thoughtfully shift this dynamic. We can prepare our descendants to live in a more equitable society.

5. Bring Wealth Home

The wealthy control trillions in capital, money that has been chasing speculative financial returns at the global level. It's time to bring this wealth home and redirect it to enterprises in the real economy. If money is stashed in the shadows, in the offshore system or special trusts, bring it back into the light. This hidden wealth of nations must pay its fair share of taxes.

One starting point is to divest from the fossil fuel sector. As Lisa Renstrom says, "We want to revoke the social license of the fossil fuel industry to destroy our planet. Their business model will lead to catastrophic climate change."

Jenny Ladd, an heir to Standard Oil, was thrilled to publicly move her money out of the fossil fuel sector. "I'm moved by the right action at the right time in the right place." This is the time to enlist friends, family, family-controlled enterprises, and charitable institutions to divest. Use your leverage as an alumnus and donor to other endowed institutions to demand the same.[3]

Another step is to break the cycle of extraction and exploitation represented by vast accumulations of wealth in traditional financial markets. Wealth sitting in traditional stock market investments represents a lost opportunity to redirect capital to the generative life-giving enterprises of the future. The current money system of usury — money making money with interest — destroys nature and degrades people. It extracts value and energy from our communities and forces non-capital-owners to toil with little to show.[4] This cannot be fixed through "socially screened investing," trading one group of securities in socially injurious corporations for less offensive investments. The alternative is to reinvest in the new economy sector.[5]

As Deborah Frieze has described, we should walk away from Wall Street as much as possible and walk toward building an alternative economy. The owners of substantial capital can reduce the demand for the exotic financial returns delinked from local communities and the meeting of real needs. Frieze urges us to move investment capital to real productive enterprises, rather than financial speculation, even when the financial return is less. There is a range of options, including opportunities in the community investment and Slow Money movements that are investing in community financial institutions and high-impact investments.[6] A substantial shift in wealth will create new capital markets that steer resources toward an equitable and sustainable economy.

As Frieze argues, ownership matters if we care about spreading around wealth ownership and agency. Impact investors are moving money to businesses like the locally owned and operated waste management company CERO rather than absentee-owned businesses.

6. Catalyze Change Around the Ecological Crisis

We are living in a time of separation — most of us are separated from both people and nature. We should see ourselves in a natural web, not apart or destined for dominion. Many children suffer from "nature deficit disorder," but the same can be said for many of us. Taking time to reconnect with nature is key, and it also helps us take steps to reduce our impact on it.

A good first step is to reduce our own consumption. The carbon footprint and consumption demands of the wealthy are huge drivers of extractive capitalism and contributors to climate change.

While poor people around the world may need to increase their energy consumption to have decent lives, the wealthy should power down. We must adopt the credo, "Live simply so that others may simply live." Wealthy people in the global North need to reduce our depletion of the world's natural resources so that those who have been excluded have the opportunity for a decent life.

We must reduce our overall energy consumption, not just shift to green technologies. We can help shift investment by being early adopters of renewable energy technology, paying more in some cases so that the systems can come to scale.

This means less jet-setting and being more geographically rooted. People in the top 10 percent of US income and wealth holders are incredibly mobile, moving around, flying on airplanes for work and pleasure. This may be challenging because our affluence has enabled families and loved ones to be dispersed over several time zones, requiring huge expenditures of energy and resources to remain connected. We must do all we can to reverse these patterns, encouraging rootedness and family and community building to be as local as possible.

7. Share the Wealth

The invitation is to give away wealth, deeply and boldly. In spite of the earlier discussion about the limits of charity, well-targeted social change funding is critical to transformation. This requires navigating the problem of wealth holders having disproportionate power. One step in shifting this is to expand decision making and support reforms to the philanthropic sector, as discussed in chapters 10 and 11.

Each of us is immersed in cultural assumptions about giving and charity. Whatever the message, it is probably possible to be bolder. Some of us were told, "Don't give from assets, only income." But many of us will live good lives, even if we share assets. Get help thinking about your giving—but then give deeply.[7]

Don't let the perfect be the enemy of the good. Many donors are sitting on vast treasure, waiting for the strategic moment or the perfect organization. The bad news is you will not find this perfect leader or organization. Practically speaking, a huge warehouse of private wealth will be less useful to us in five years than it is today—as we continue down irreversible paths of human deprivation and hopelessness, and ecological points of no return. The good news is, you can have a tremendous impact on the future by giving today, boosting the next generation of leaders and organizations.

It is not necessary to reinvent the wheel when it comes to giving. Wealthy people suffer from a tendency to want to create and control their own institutions and intermediaries for giving. But this is an inefficient use of resources. There are plenty of existing channels, intermediaries, and outlets that are sufficient for giving. If Warren Buffett can give his money through another guy's foundation (in this case, Bill Gates's), there is no need to create duplicative intermediaries.

There are real and understandable barriers to moving substantial wealth. For example, many people are held back by such practical questions as, "What do I need to live on?" and "How much can I give away?" Or they've been told, "Never give from assets, only income." The good news is there is now a very experienced network of advisors, community foundations, resource books, and seasoned elders who can guide and support you in this journey. And there are insurance policies to guarantee against the worst-case scenarios.

The more money you have, the more you are surrounded by people urging you to move slowly and cautiously, including a wealth defense industry of investment advisors, professionals, and lawyers. In this context, my advice is, "Jump." Look first, but then jump. Buy a parachute if it makes you feel better, but be bold and generous.

8. Pay Your Taxes

The most democratic means of redistributing wealth and power is through taxation, especially at the state and local levels. As imperfect as our government systems are, there is still greater accountability in the use of funds compared with charity. The priorities of the federal government have been hijacked by global corporations and the military-industrial complex. But even here, a good chunk of our taxes also pays for public infrastructure, scientific research, and environmental protection. We should pay our fair share of this, without question.

There is waste, fraud, and abuse in the public sector, just as there is in private business and the charitable sector. But aggressive tax avoidance (including creating new charitable entities) is not a legitimate response to government ineptitude and misdirected priorities.

There are millions of trustworthy stewards working in the public sector. We often only notice them when things go wrong, like the water contamination crisis in Flint, Michigan. What about the hundreds of thousands of public works employees who quietly bring clean water to your tap? Who is up before sunrise to plow the roads or start up the trains? We have an important role in celebrating these people who hold the public trust and manage our local commons.

I invite you to resist complaining about government in an unconstructive and generalized way. Instead be engaged as an advocate for effective and efficient government. Explain to others that no matter what size or function of government, we must have a fair and equitable revenue system — where those with the greatest capacity to pay should pay more. A previous generation of wealthy put their full stake in "good government," ensuring that public institutions worked well rather than opting out and walking away.

We need your voice to defend and expand the progressivity of the tax system at all levels. The moral rationale for a progressive tax system is, as Bill Gates Sr. said, that those with great wealth have disproportionately benefited from society's investments — and have a special obligation to pay back so that others have similar opportunities.

Taxes at the state and local level should be fully paid and celebrated. And wealthy people who live in states with highly regressive tax systems, where low-income people pay a higher percentage of their income than wealthy people, should enthusiastically support reform movements.

We need higher-income taxpayers to speak out for a fairer tax system and to pay their taxes without aggressive tax-avoidance schemes. The tax code is now porous for the wealthy, thanks to systematic lobbying by antitax groups. As a result, the percentage of income paid in taxes by the wealthy has dramatically declined over the last four decades. Just because we don't like every activity of government — or have concerns about government inefficiency — does not justify our withdrawing our funds from the system or dodging taxes.

We should take the lead, like Jacques Leblanc, in bringing hidden wealth out from the shadows. The world's wealthy are avoiding taxes and accountability through the elaborate uses of complex legal trusts, sheltered corporations, and offshore tax havens. Trillions of dollars are circulating through this system beyond the reach of accountability and taxation. Make a personal decision not to use aggressive tax-dodging techniques, such as GRAT trusts and others.[8] Refuse to use the "offshore system" of secrecy jurisdictions to hide wealth from taxation and accountability. Work to eliminate these systems as a matter of global justice and fairness.

9. Support the Leadership of Others, Especially Working-Class People

We have an important role to support movements led by others who are organizing for a fair and equitable economy. There will be some "letting go" required, as these movements and efforts may not always look or sound the way you want them to. They may appear rough-edged or lacking in strategy or a coherent message. There may be a "class war" tone in their rhetoric. This is not a reason to withhold support. In the wise words of one radical philanthropist, "Have a little faith."

We are surrounded by working-class people who are resourceful and have a lot to teach us. Our liberation is tied to our ability to be humbled by these neighbors. Seek them out, befriend them, support them, and follow them.

Participate with humility. Our role is not to withdraw nor is it solely to be a faucet of resources for others to deploy. You hold a piece of the puzzle in terms of what it means to be human. Class privilege and distance sometimes bring insights to the process of change. At the same time, bringing money to the table is fraught with risk in terms of having too much power and say in decision making. The role of the 1 percent is to be engaged without dominance or manipulation. As Jenny Ladd says, "Play your instrument in the orchestra, with others."

10. Organize Your Peers

You are invited to reach out and engage others from our class background. Who else will organize them? These include friends, family, classmates, and other social networks. We need to overcome whatever gets in the way of engaging fully with these potential allies, as it is one of the most important and strategic things we can do.

There are real opponents, such as the powerful cabal of wealthy people who deploy the "dark money" machinery to influence our political system. There is the "wealth defense" industry of professionals who create trusts and shell corporations to protect the already advantaged. But there are allies to be found.

Resist the tendency to blame "other" rich people. The desire to deflect anger and animosity onto others is understandable, but we must try to rise above this. Instead, consider other members of the 1 percent as siblings and cousins, potential allies and other wounded souls that share an interest in a more vibrant, equal, and ecologically habitable world. There are, of course, differences between "Billionaireville" and "Lower Richistan," but if we understand we have a common dilemma, it is impossible to blame others.

Be alert to the workings of anti-Semitism. One of the historic deflections in Western cultures has been to shift responsibility onto Jewish people. Learn the history of how anti-Semitism has been used to deflect blame onto Jews during periods of upheaval and class tension.[9] Interrupt any talk along these lines.

The most compelling way to move our allies in the 1 percent is through your own emboldened example. When people see your energy, passion, and connectedness, you will become a walking invitation for people to ask you questions and consider changes in their own lives. Through your truthfulness and vulnerability, others will be inspired to follow suit. Through your compassion, forgiveness, respect, and love, you will draw others in.

Changing these systems is fundamentally heart work. Our larger project is about cracking hearts and minds open, starting with our own. Notice the moments when your heart is beating, when the goose bumps flow down your back, when the connections happen with other people. Savor them and make more of them happen every day.

Forming Small Groups

None of us can figure this out alone. We know that to change and transform ourselves, we need inspiration, support, challenge, accountability, and respect. We need regular reinforcement of the new story that we can live into.

We need our siblings and cousins in the 99 percent to generously extend to us an invitation to the table, to break bread and sit together. We need to be invited home, welcomed at the door, and offered a role and place, not at the head of the table, but among the respected.

It may be helpful to form small groups to support one another to take bold action. Whatever we call them — affinity groups, praxis groups, Resilience Circles — they are places where we can share our true stories, learn with others, break out of isolation, strategize, and set intentions with support and trust.

Moving from our small groups, we can "co-create" this movement, spark creative actions within one another, and encourage each other to change our ways of thinking. Forming such a group is critical to being able to move forward with any specific programs and ideas.

Where do we find such people? Who can we trust? They are probably right nearby — if not geographically, by telephone. They may not be our closest friends, but they are living parallel lives to us. Not everyone has the slack to participate in a group — but most people can find the time to meet at least monthly with a group of peers.

We wealthy people are busy, busy, busy. We have our commitments, our meetings, travels, and properties to take care of. But because this is fundamentally about our own liberation, I urge you to slow down and make the time. Form a circle, a small group of more than three people and less than a dozen, that can ideally meet face-to-face — or on the phone or via Skype. The network Resource Generation has already begun to pilot these groups and engage hundreds of individuals.[10]

Patriotic Millionaires

Another important role that wealth holders can play is as advocates and messengers. Over the last twenty years, I've cofounded several networks of high-net-worth individuals, including Responsible Wealth, Wealth for the Common Good, Business for Shared Prosperity, and, most recently, the Patriotic Millionaires. The Patriotic Millionaires have focused in on three policy priorities: support for progressive taxation and increased minimum wages, along with campaign finance reform to reduce the influence of money and politics.

These networks have played an important role validating public policies that will reduce inequality. For example, enlisting over a thousand multi-millionaires and billionaires to defend the federal estate tax, as described in chapter 5, had a hugely positive role in changing the debate. Wealthy people saying "tax me" is the proverbial "man bites dog" story that makes something newsworthy.

Some of this work takes place in these organizations and networks. For example, members of the Patriotic Millionaires regularly demystify the process of wealth creation. "Rich people don't create jobs," says venture capitalist Nick Hanauer. "What does lead to more employment is a circle-of-life-like feedback loop between customers and businesses. And only consumers can set in motion this virtuous cycle of increasing demand and hiring. In this sense, an ordinary middle-class consumer is far more of a job creator than a capitalist like me." Public investments in education and infrastructure will do more to boost the middle class, Hanauer argues.[11]

So wealthy people can be effective messengers, telling true stories about public investments that have made wealth possible, and helping puncture the mythologies of deservedness.

The Patriotic Millionaires attract a huge amount of attention. Ironically, none of the two-hundred-plus members are thrilled about being identified as patriotic millionaires. "It seems boastful and unseemly," one member told me. "But I'm willing to endure the embarrassment for the cause. If it helps change the political narrative, let me be a foot soldier."

State initiatives to raise taxes on millionaires are advancing in many states. In my home state of Massachusetts, I've been part of a coalition to amend our state constitution, which allows only one tax bracket, to add a rate on incomes over $1 million. The levels of inequality in Massachusetts lead the nation, yet we have one of the most regressive state tax systems in the country. The lowest-income fifth of taxpayers, those with incomes under $22,000, pay 10.4 percent of their income in state and local taxes. The top 1 percent of taxpayers with incomes over $860,000 pay only 6.4 percent of their income.[12]

The question will go to the ballot in 2018. Members of the Patriotic Millionaires and the Alliance for Business Leadership are outspoken in favor of the tax hike.

"It's time for us to return to where we once had been before taxes were demonized and government was demonized," says Arnold Hiatt, former chief executive of the shoe company Stride Rite. Hiatt is a Patriotic Millionaire and one of the lead signers on the Massachusetts initiative. He remembers when people who earned more than $150,000 in the United States paid as high as 70 percent in taxes. "I was delighted. I felt privileged to be in a position to pay."

— CHAPTER 19 —

All Hands on Deck

It is a strategic and personal waste of energy to stay in a place of hatred, rage and resentment. There are allies in this room you don't know about.

FELICE YESKEL

I am surrounded by a sea of red shirts, marching through the streets of Washington, DC. It is an unusually warm November day — and the trees have long since shed their leaves.

An estimated six thousand people are marching in favor of a tax on Wall Street financial transactions. It is thrilling for me to be at such a large demonstration in favor of a great nerdy progressive tax idea.

I've attended hearings, press conferences, and endless meetings about good tax ideas, but never a demonstration of thousands. A year earlier, the total number of people proposing a financial transaction tax could have fit into a church basement. Until now.

The game changer is that National Nurses United has adopted the Wall Street tax as a centerpiece of their policy agenda. Five thousand of these marchers are nurses and they are all wearing red shirts.

As I walk along, I start chatting with a nurse who is walking beside me. I ask her where she is from. "Taunton," she replies with an Eastern Massachusetts accent.

"Taunton!" I exclaim. "I know lots of people in Taunton." She tells me her name is Eleanor and she works at the emergency room at Morton Hospital.

"So Eleanor," I ask her. "Why are you here?"

"Well, I got off my shift last night at seven o'clock, and I got on the bus with the rest of my sisters from the union."

I look more closely at Eleanor. She's a white woman, about fifty years old, with short hair and small silver earrings. Like the others, she is wearing a red shirt with her union logo. On the back it says, "If you save a life, you're a hero. If you save one hundred lives, you're a nurse."

Eleanor is carrying a placard that says, "Heal America: Tax Wall Street." Who better to talk about "healing America" than our nation's nurses?

"We rode all night. I didn't sleep much," she laughs. "We were so hyped up. We're marching and then we have meetings with our congressmen. After that we have two hours of free time to look around before getting back on the bus back to Taunton. I'm going to the Smithsonian."

Eleanor looks wide-eyed at the white stone federal office buildings and a sparkling fountain along Pennsylvania Avenue. "I've never been to Washington, DC, before." She grins. "Pretty nice town."

"Wow," I say, appreciative of her overnight bus travel feats. "But Eleanor, *why* are you here?"

"Oh, that's simple," she says, fixing her brown eyes on mine. "I've been watching the unequal economy come into the hospital on the bodies of my patients. People are hurting themselves, hurting loved ones. I've seen people injured because they're working two or three jobs and exhausted. I've seen folks with stress-related illnesses, freaking out because of the economy."

Eleanor stands still for a moment and I stop with her. A flow of marchers stream around us, as if we are a boulder in the middle of the roaring river.

"The clincher for me was a couple weeks ago," she says, looking at me with a surprising intensity. "An older guy comes into the emergency room present-ing with a cardiac arrest. I've got him lying on the gurney, taking his blood pressure and filling out forms. I ask him, 'Mr. Thomas, what is your address?'"

Eleanor's eyes begin to well up with tears. "He clutches his chest and says, almost in a whisper, 'I just lost my house. Bank took it. After 35 years . . .'"

Her voice cracks.

"'. . . that's why I got this chest pain.'" She clutches her own chest.

Eleanor shakes her head and her eyes look skyward. "You know, you see enough broken people, you think, 'Damn, I gotta do something about the greed that is wrecking this country and hurting all these people.' It's not enough to just go to work. I gotta get on the bus and raise my voice."

The way Eleanor says "get on the bus" is full-voiced and passionate. She smiles and we start walking quickly again, rejoining the pace of the march.

I'm speechless and Eleanor seems slightly embarrassed by the intensity of her words.

"Hey, you know about this Wall Street tax?" The tone of her voice is now chipper. "If we tax financial transactions a penny on every four bucks it would raise over $300 billion a year. We could make sure everyone had decent health care and stop all those foreclosures."

"I've heard about it," I say, thinking of all the papers, articles, and conference calls. "But tell me more about it."

"It's really simple," she says, picking up her stride and looking up the road toward the US Capitol Building, our destination. "Too many financial shenanigans don't create anything real. We should tax them and use the money for something good." We keep walking and talking, the midday sun shining down on a procession of bobbing red shirts.

The Movement to Reverse Extreme Inequality

Throughout the day I kept happily ruminating, "Eleanor got on the bus." This is what a movement looks like, when people get fed up enough to interrupt their weekend plans and take to the streets in protest.

The emerging movements against inequality will look like nurses marching to "Heal America: Tax Wall Street." It will be students pressing politicians to do something about the student debt crisis and fast-food workers demanding a higher minimum wage. The engine of mobilization will be sparked by those most deeply affected, leaders from working-class and marginalized communities that decide they've had enough, that the rules of the economy should enable everyone to have a good life.

Will wealthy people be barriers or allies to these movements? I'm reminded again of what my friend Les Leopold wrote in his book *Runaway Inequality*: "Economic elites will only give up power and wealth when they're forced to do so by a powerful social movement."

But is this true? For meaningful change, will the privileged need to be forced? This may be true if "economic elites" are defined as a few thousand billionaires and CEOs of transnational companies. They are not sitting around reflecting on their "unearned privilege." But if we are talking about all the residents of Richistan, including Affluentville, then there may be many potential allies.

There are abundant examples from history of privileged people standing up against oppressive institutions, such as slavery, human trafficking, and child labor. The historian Adam Hochschild has chronicled the British antislavery movement and the first human rights campaigns against slave labor in the Belgian Congo. The 1902 campaign against King Leopold was an example of solidarity between people in Britain and the Congolese people who were subjects of the king's forced labor practices.[1]

Don't these movements to resist oppression benefit from allies in the privileged classes? A century ago, a powerful movement of rural populist farmers and urban workers pushed back against the extreme inequalities of the first Gilded Age. But they were aided, in part, by privileged progressives and even a few plutocrats in their program to end child labor and corporate consolidation, and to establish public banks, corporate regulations, and social welfare. That's why industrialist Andrew Carnegie and President Theodore Roosevelt were vocal advocates of taxing the wealthy.

Throughout US history, wealthy radicals and prosperous progressives have donated money to fundamental social change. A group of privileged women, dubbed the "mink brigade," funded organizing of women's trade union workers and joined their picket lines. One "mink brigader" was Anne Morgan, the daughter of Wall Street financier J. P. Morgan. Days after the Triangle Shirtwaist fire that killed 146 women workers in March 1911, Morgan rented the Metropolitan Opera House for a meeting to honor the victims and mobilize the city's wealthy to pass successful landmark labor laws in New York State.[2]

The rights movements, including civil rights and women's rights, have strategic allies among the "oppressor groups." And there are abundant examples throughout history of privileged sectors being divided, creating political space for unrepressed social movements to flourish.

The idea that *Only the Super-Rich Can Save Us* — the title of Ralph Nader's novel — is wrong. But it may be accurate to say, "Only We Can Save Ourselves, But It Will Happen Faster (and Less Violently) If We Have Some Super-Rich Allies."

There Are Allies in the Room

Most of what I've learned about privilege has been from accompanying working-class activists, like my close collaborator Felice Yeskel. She never hesitated to tell me when I was out of line. But mostly she loved me as a friend and colleague, and we laughed at how our different socializations trained us see the world.

Because of Yeskel's interest in talking to people about class, she heard many personal stories about the inner wounds and outer violence caused by our unequal economic system. She found it amusing when commentators would dismiss our work on inequality as fomenting class war against the affluent. "I'd like to take them on a personal reality tour," she quipped. "And introduce them to the real casualties of our global class war and poverty. I'll take them to the emergency rooms, the unemployment offices, and the desperate kitchen tables."

I was struck by how little rage and resentment Yeskel felt toward the rich. She was curious, in an anthropological sense, about the lives people led. And sometimes she was exasperated with the way that class privilege seemed to confound and confuse people. But she didn't hate the rich as a class or as individuals.

When we cofounded United for a Fair Economy in 1995, we frequently led programs together about class and growing inequality. We would often encounter people with bitter antirich anger and resentment. Yeskel had a remarkable way of welcoming all emotions into the room, honoring the wounds and the rage. It was harder for me, as I would take it personally, and sometimes the attacks were personal. One person said outright, "I hate you and I'll never like you because you were born rich."

Yeskel would coach me: "Allow yourself to be a target. Let people voice their emotions. Listen attentively and learn something. Don't take it personally. It is a necessary part of the healing work that has to be done."

She was right, of course. I can't say I enjoyed being a target, but I am now less fearful of upheaval. And I learned to trust that it isn't always about me or my behavior.

"Beware of people who judge you for the circumstances of your birth," Yeskel would say. "If someone doesn't like you for something outside of your control, that's prejudice. Just like if you didn't like me because I was born in public housing or Jewish. It's what we do with our lives that counts — and what we should all be held accountable for."

Once, at a workshop program at a university, a self-proclaimed radical attacked us for our approach to inequality. "You are defusing the hatred toward the rich by talking about building alliances. We should be mobilizing for class war, to fight back against the rich. They are evil and unreachable."

"So how's that working for you?" Yeskel asked calmly.

"It doesn't matter. We have to fight fire with fire," the woman replied, her fuse igniting. She vented for another few minutes until Yeskel held up her hand.

"Some people would rather stay angry than be effective," Yeskel observed. "That's your right. Personally, I want to transform the system. I think it is a strategic and personal waste of energy to stay in a place of hatred, rage, and resentment. It will physically make you sick. You'll burn yourself out and die a bitter person. It's also not accurate. People are more complicated. There are allies in this room you don't know about. And your anger is keeping you from being strategic and forming alliances."

The woman looked around the room and sat down.

Yeskel and I had a regular debate. "If wealthy people really want to reduce inequality," I would ask, "shouldn't they just become less wealthy? Doesn't that mean giving up material privilege, wealth, and the justification for it?"

"Hmmm," Yeskel would ponder out loud. "It's too easy to tell someone else what they should do. But what does it concretely mean to give up privilege? I'm trying to think if I've given up any white privilege lately and what that looks like." With her profound sense of empathy, Yeskel wouldn't prescribe a course of action for someone else that she hadn't contemplated for herself.

"But there something unique about wealth and class, where the great assets and power inequities are inherently oppressive," I would argue. "Isn't it the wound that keeps wounding?"

"Yes, I think it's different," she would say. "We can't fix the system unless the wealth and power are redistributed. It's the intersection of personal change and system rewiring."

Inviting the Wealthy Home

"How should the 99 percent view the 1 percent?" asked my friend Charlie Derber, a sociology professor at Boston College. Derber is the best teacher I've ever seen in action, holding undergraduate students riveted for hours of interactive seminar discussions. "What would you say to people in the 99 percent? What is your view on the actions they should take?"

For most of this book, I've personally addressed my people in the wealthiest 1 percent. Now I would like to speak as someone who has spent the last thirty years organizing social movements to reduce inequality and ecological destruction and increase the power of the 99 percent. I urge my friends in the 99 percent to:

- Organize our communities to defend ourselves against the worst excesses of predatory and extractive capitalism — to build racial and economic equity and resilience.
- Recognize the 1 percent that lives in all of us — the ways in which we have privileges and advantages compared with others around the world. Allow this to inform our strategy. Proceed with empathy.
- Reach out to the isolated and disconnected members of the 1 percent and build real connections with them, founded on respect and empathy.
- Create opportunities to invite the wealthy home — to bring to a locality their investment capital, charitable giving, social networks, and deep personal stake in their own liberation and well-being.

Defend Our Communities

Our current economic system may have inflicted violence on you, the people you love, and others around the world. There is no way to properly apologize for this, just as it is impossible to fully respond to the legacy of slavery or genocide.

Extractive capitalism is trying to squeeze you in a variety of ways to take your money and get you to work longer hours for less pay. It is nickel-and-diming you with fees at every turn, making everything into commodities, including what was once sacred and private.

If you've flown on a commercial airline flight in the last couple of years, we have a metaphor for predatory capitalism. The airlines are squeezing us, physically and financially. They can't add more perks to first class, so they now take away things from coach passengers that used to be free — legroom, snacks, movies, checked luggage — and charge us to get them back. The passengers in coach are pitted against each other, jostling one another for room, resenting one another, occasionally erupting into air rage.

Predatory capitalism is trying to take things that are your birthright — access to clean water, for example — and sell it back to you for a profit. There are global corporations whose business model is to shift their costs to you and the planet. They want you to pay more, so they can pay less. They want you as a taxpayer to cover the emergency room expenses of their low-paid workers, so they don't have to pay them adequately or provide benefits. They want you to spend your time standing in line, filling out forms, waiting on hold, so they can cut costs. They want to dump their pollution and other externalities into our common yard, so they don't have to pay the fees.

We must organize social movements to defend our communities against the worst excesses of predatory and extractive capitalism, building alliances across class and race to resist corporate encroachment.

The 1 Percent That Lives Inside Us

In order to build these alliances, we must recognize the 1 percent that lives in all of us — the ways in which most of us in the United States have privileges and advantages compared with others around the world. This requires us to both see the atrocities and hold the complexity of our own role and cooperation with these systems.

When was the last time you thought about the plight of a Bangladeshi farmer who lost his arable land to climate change and rising sea levels? When did you last think about his children, who will become climate refugees thanks to your lifetime of burning fossil fuels? For most of us, out of sight, out of mind would be true. In the eyes of Bangladeshi farmers, most of us are in the global elite, the powerful actors who have consumed more than our fair share of the world's natural capital and in so doing have taken a dramatic toll on their everyday lives.

All the judgments we make toward the 1 percent in the United States are relevant to most of us in the United States. Is it true that you will never give up the privileges of living in an affluent industrial society, unless you are forced? Or might you change, depending on who engaged with you and how they engaged with you? Most of us believe if we fully understood the chain of relationships, we would make different choices.

Proceed with Empathy

It is hard to see and respect the wounds that the wealthy carry because we are surrounded by so many perks, privileges, and comforts. But they are there, sometimes in the shadows. There are families with painful deep disconnections and distances, many of them connected to the relentless pursuit of status and money.

Michael Thomas, a novelist and former investment banker, told the *New York Times* that if he were to ever write a book about his own privileged upbringing, he would title it, *Orphans with Parents* — meaning, he said, "that despite the private clubs, the best schools and all the many things that money can buy, there has always been for those born into this world a sense of acute loneliness that can strain ties with parents and mark a child forever."[3]

New York wealthy society was shocked in early January 2015, when Thomas Strong Gilbert Jr., age 30, walked into the office of his hedge fund manager father, with the same name, and murdered him, apparently after having had his allowance reduced.

Laid bare, this is a story of the stresses of downward mobility and status disruption within the 1 percent. At age 70, Thomas Sr. was working twelve-hour days and weekends to launch a new hedge fund that was growing but still a minnow in the world of New York City finance. The family had just downsized to a smaller house — and Thomas Jr., ill prepared for the world of work, lashed out in anger. All the best lawyers and medical help couldn't put Thomas Jr. back together again.

Wealthy parents fear that their children will suffer a decline in status — and that their children's lack of success will reflect back upon them. In affluent neighborhoods and private schools, the pursuit of the "right schools" and college preparation becomes the dominant topic for students and parents in high school.

The pressure is extraordinary. A friend of mine who works as a guidance counselor at a private girls' school tells me stories about girls who are under extraordinary family pressure to perform academically and distinguish themselves in other ways, to make themselves more attractive to elite colleges. As a result, they are overmedicated, suicidal, and physically and emotionally depressed.

Consider us members of a long-lost branch of your own extended family. Envision us as children, whisked away from stable and connected working-class communities that would have nurtured us quite differently and taught us useful life skills. Envision us as children, relocated to a world of pretention, disconnection, and status shows. Raised on a diet of rich food and myths of self-importance and deservedness, we are told that our personal worth is tied to our financial net worth and that great things are expected.

As children, when we asked the adults around us about poverty and difference, we were often told stereotypes, myths, and outright lies about the undeservedness of other people. Those people "don't work hard . . . have too many children . . . have addictions . . . lack ambition . . . made bad decisions and choices . . . can't delay gratification." These were justifications for our having so much more than others, without guilt.

As children, we were told implicitly or explicitly to fear and distrust the rest of the world. We were warned about hustlers and robbers and people out to take our money. We were told to be wary of the motivations of the people closest to us.

As a result, as we grow older there is an armoring of the heart. The distance grows between us and people of different circumstances. There comes greater physical separation and disconnection, as wealthy people seek out social and residential enclaves, minimizing our authentic contact with nonwealthy people.

Fear festers. The world is an insecure place, even for the most privileged. Some wealthy become like hoarders, filling up their accounts with more money than they could ever use. If we are parents, we build walls around our children, protecting them but also disconnecting them from the world's suffering, toil, vagaries. We also cut them off from the rich tapestries of our blended communities, from joy, celebration, and sources of community resilience. The cycle of disconnection and fear continues.

It is hard to hate someone when you know their story. In the spirit of reciprocity, it is important that you share your own story, but also listen to the stories behind the mask. Here are several other parts of the invitation:

Build Connections with the Wealthy. Reach out to the isolated and disconnected members of the 1 percent and build real connections with them, founded on respect and empathy. This may be hard, as the wealthy and powerful have purposely distanced themselves from the rest of humanity.

This is why we must all encourage the 1 percent to organize within their own ranks.

Engagement. Don't dismiss the power of fearless and direct engagement and conversation with those with wealth and power. When you have an opportunity — whether on a street, at a shareholder meeting, in an elevator, or in any other circumstance that comes your way — engage with people in the 1 percent that own and control global corporations. Reach within to do so with respect and empathy, while holding them accountable for the power they possess.

Transformative Pressure. The wealthy and powerful have disproportionate power and responsibility to shift this system. But they will need *transformative pressure* to move out of their comfortable privileged places and rejoin humanity's wider struggle. The way we approach this — whether from hate or love or compassion — will make all the difference. It will be challenging and require enormous creativity and courage.

You may also find wealthy people feel powerless to change the system. They may need to be reminded that they have more power than 99 percent of the population, including the capacity to take risks that others cannot.

In order to reverse extreme inequality and avert climate catastrophe, we need to try some different strategies. We will transform our system faster — and the 99 percent will get a better "payoff," if you will — if we try approaches that recognize the full humanity of the people at the top of the pyramid.

"What if we did a hunger strike at Alice Walton's house in New York City?" Felice once asked out loud. "What if we just stood there with a sign saying 'Share the Wealth.'

"Or maybe we should show up with gifts — jams that we made or crafts, nothing store-bought." She chuckled. "Give a gift, not ask for anything in return. Instead of 'eat the rich,' we should invite the wealthy to lunch and ask them to bring their capital and skills toward fixing all our shared problems."

— CONCLUSION —

I'm from Bloomfield Hills

Any real change implies the breakup of the world as one has always known it, the loss of all that gave one an identity, the end of safety. And at such a moment, unable to see and not daring to imagine what the future will now bring forth, one clings to what one knew, or dreamed that one possessed. It is only when a man is able, without bitterness or self-pity, to surrender a dream he has long cherished or a privilege he has long possessed that he is set free — he has set himself free — for higher dreams, for greater privileges.

JAMES BALDWIN

"**Y**ou are making us proud," says Ron Frederick, a man who I've known since I was a toddler. "Over my lifetime, I didn't do much to change the system of unequal wealth. But it's not too late. You've inspired me."

Ron is in his mid-80s, and I have not seen him in more than four decades. But he has the same munificent smile and warm embrace that I remember from my teenage years. Every Sunday, our families attended church together, and afterward we all went to Arby's. We went on vacations together, including adventures to Puerto Rico.

I've come home. Not to my neighborhood in Boston, where I've lived since 1990. But to the home where I grew up, Bloomfield Hills, Michigan. I've been invited to speak at a local church about "Escalating Inequality."

Bloomfield Hills. God, I've been ashamed that this is where I'm from. When people ask me where I grew up, I usually say, "the Detroit area." If they insist on more details, I say, "Royal Oak" or "Birmingham." I cannot find my way to mouth the words "Bloomfield Hills."

Bloomfield Hills is solidly one of the most affluent communities in the northern Midwest. Zip code 48304 is home to Motor City auto barons and the CEOs that I carried golf clubs for as a caddy at the Bloomfield Hills Country Club. Racial diversity is limited to the also wealthy, like singer Aretha Franklin or former Detroit Piston Isiah Thomas, and to the servants who work by day to care for people and property, but depart by nightfall.

In Michigan, Bloomfield Hills is the rhetorical proxy for "rich." In an exposé on the contaminated water debacle in Flint, Michigan, journalists criticized the environmental racism that state officials exhibited toward the mostly brown, black, and poor residents of Flint. One elected state representative decried, "If Bloomfield Hills had had a water crisis, the state would not have taken so long to react."

So here I am, in the home of my discontent, the object of my own shame and derision. I'm sitting near the podium and over 160 people are filing into the event. Additional chairs are being set up.

Sitting a few rows back is Rob Hendrickson, my best friend at the age of 5, whom I had so many adventures with — exploring the neighborhood woods, organizing a fair, and riding our Sting-Ray bikes everywhere. Rob's big sister Kim once cornered us out in a field and said, "Hey boys, want to smoke a cigarette? It's really cool. Here's how you do it." She lit up two cigarettes and instructed us to breathe in as hard as we could. We followed her lead, pulling full inhalation on our first taste of a cigarette. We both immediately choked, turned green, and at least one of us vomited. Rob's evil big sister's plan worked. Neither of us touched a cigarette again for the rest of our lives.

There is Carol, who I remember from third grade. I flash back to her warmth and friendliness on the first day, welcoming me as the new kid at Brookside elementary school. She is the granddaughter of one of one of Detroit's beloved department store founders. She still lives in the area and is closely connected to many of our high school friends.

There is Mrs. Clark, my sixth-grade English teacher who had us keep journals for our reflections, ideas, and stories. On special days she read aloud to us from Eudora Welty, John Steinbeck, Italo Calvino. She held us to high standards and exhorted us, "You must read, read, read!" Mrs. Clark took us Brookside suburban kids on field trips to Upland Hills Farm to milk cows and contemplate where our food came from. She was one of several of the remarkable teachers who opened up our horizons.

Into the church hall come more old classmates, former teachers, friends of my parents, people from the Stillmeadow subdivision where I lived. They are filling up chairs on a snowy cold January night for my talk about wealth inequality.

I start my remarks with my Bloomfield Hills roots. "I suspect some of you might be worried that I'll stir up feelings of guilt and class war." The audience laughs nervously. "And some of you might be disappointed if I don't."

I talk about the moment we are in, the challenges of extreme inequality and climate change. I tell stories I've recounted in this book. I borrow the warning words of Gar Alperovitz, that we may be facing a "nasty brew" of social forces. As the society enters a new phase of economic and ecological precariousness and instability, we can expect social and political upheavals in its wake. Donald Trump is leading in the polls and I talk about how a polarized economy gives rise to a polarized politics, as people feel their standards of living collapse and look for scapegoats. Excessive wealth inequality will make our already volatile economy even more unstable.

In the discussion after my talk, dozens of people line up to offer thoughtful questions and comments. One man asks, "Don't people in the 1 percent see how these trends undermine their lives, that they won't be able to escape? How do we get them to see it?"

"Yes, these conditions of wealth inequality and climate instability are bad for everybody," I reply, repeating the themes from the beginning of this book. "It is a delusional fantasy that the rich will decamp to another planet or luxury satellite or mountain or island getaway. There is only one planet, and even if you get to ride out the worst of repercussions, what kind of world are we leaving to the next generation, including your own children and grandchildren, nieces and nephews?"

One man describes his excitement about the possibilities of expanding worker ownership as a path to reduce wealth disparities. In response, I tell the story of the CERO cooperative in Boston and the growing movement to shift capital out of the globalized speculative economy and into local enterprises, including expanded worker ownership. People are animated by the idea of "bringing wealth home," investing in these new economy possibilities.

"Why is it young people are so enamored with a 74-year old curmudgeon from Vermont?" asks one woman, referring to the Bernie Sanders campaign for president. I've known Senator Bernie since he was mayor of

Burlington, Vermont, in the 1980s. He's been saying the same thing for decades, but young people find he's telling the truth! I am heartened by how Bernie's message about inequality is changing the conversation in the presidential campaign.

People are hungry to hear signs of possibility and hope. I share what I see — that the next decade will be a time of upheaval and instability, but also tremendous possibility.

The good news is there are people waking up — from students to low-wage workers to people in the 1 percent. There are people organizing to prevent new fossil fuel infrastructure from being built. There are billions shifting out of the investments in the dying economy and into the life-giving thriving new economy.

While Congress and national politics have been captured by the "rule riggers" in the 1 percent and a couple thousand transnational corporations, among the wider public there is a fundamental realignment of perspectives. The angry voices are loud, but quietly below the surface, the localist revolution is taking hold, like seeds sprouting after a spring rain.

One older woman, standing in a foot cast with crutches, approaches the microphone. "I'm in assisted living now," she tells the assembled. "There are a lot of very wealthy people in our community. It seems like there are two groups — the people who still feel like they don't have enough, even though they have millions and a big lake house up north, and the people who feel incredible gratitude for their lives. As best I can tell, this difference has nothing to do with how much money they have."

She leans forward on her crutches, her white hair neatly fixed in place. "Why is it that some people feel gratitude and others hold on so tightly?"

This question is a piece of the human puzzle and I don't have an answer. I suspect that the people who feel gratitude "see the commonwealth." They look out and see the matrix of gifts, supports, nature, public goods, love, and the commons around us that make our lives possible. And it stirs in them a feeling of gratitude. I mention a quote from Brené Brown, "What separates privilege from entitlement is gratitude."

When we see the web, we have no choice but become allies to everyone, in their struggles for decent lives. To do this, we have to connect across difference, make friends with people who have very diverse sensibilities. We have to emerge from the gated communities and gated hearts.

"There are days when I don't know what to do, the problems seem so big," she confesses, having more to say. "But then I learn about a group of fast-food workers who are having a protest to raise their minimum wage. So I go to their demonstration and I stand there with my crutches and a sign that says, "Pay a Living Wage." I introduce myself, "Hi, I'm Dorothy from Bloomfield Hills." These workers look at me funny for a moment, but then they say, "Hey, thanks, Dorothy, for standing here with us." And I get to know them and we talk about our kids. And I sometimes give $50 to the organizing fund, but that's not the important thing. It's just important that I'm there, *accompanying* them in their struggle for dignity.

"I really wish there was a way I could stand with all these younger people who are feeling the brunt of these inequalities, who are fighting for a debt-free college education," Dorothy says. "But as you can see, it's not that easy for me to stand." Everyone in the room laughs with Dorothy. "But I figure we'll have that opportunity pretty soon, right?"

I did not anticipate that I would have strong emotions standing with these people who raised me. I feel a rush of gratitude, embarrassment, and affection, all mashed into one. Gratitude for the generosity people showed me — and how supremely lucky I am to have these people in my life.

But also I feel shame and embarrassment for how I have slandered them, unfairly made assumptions about them, and given up on them as potential allies for change. I drew caricatures of them in my mind and didn't let them speak for themselves. I have libeled the people who I grew up with, out of my own humiliation and confusion about class, race, and the blowback of a grossly unequal society.

Not only that, I unconsciously rejected people. I disconnected from friends, teachers, neighbors, and classmates. I lost touch, failed to visit, skipped reunions, missed funerals, got busy, and led a different life.

I did not expect to have my heart cracked open in Bloomfield Hills.

In this moment, standing in a church, I pledge to reconnect with my people, rekindle these relationships, and remember that "coming home" isn't just about putting roots down in a new place; it is about staying connected to the community that raised me. I wonder: Is it too late? But then I realize, no, it's never too late.

I need to stand, like Dorothy, alongside people in their fight for dignity. I want to be more like Abe Lateiner, and join the struggle for racial economic justice while being my complete and honest self. Sometimes this means I will simply accompany others. But I don't need to pretend to be someone I'm not or from a different town.

Each of us can use our gifts to turn everything that has been upside down to right-side up. But it starts with connections, with people around us, with people who are completely different, but also with the people who are most like us.

We may not always know what to do. But if we do what cracks open our hearts, I believe the next step will reveal itself to us.

—◇—

What an exciting time to be alive.

In a 2015 song, Jackson Browne sings, "If I could be anywhere; If I could be anywhere in time; If I could be anywhere and change the outcome, it would have to be now."

I'm confident that it is not a cliché at this particular moment to say we live in extraordinary times.

Our job is to serve as hospice workers for the old world, the old story, as it sputters to its predictable demise. And we must serve as midwives to the new world, the new story as it is born and comes into being. There will be loss, farewells, and the end of comfortable and predictable futures. There will be passings, memorials, tributes, and unwindings of familiar institutions and practices.

And there will be a birth of community, connection, and a flourishing of face-to-face culture. We will have to depend on one another in ways we haven't before. We will be called to act in ways we have not been called before. As Rebecca Solnit reminds us in *A Paradise Built in Hell*, we have tremendous inner capacities to respond to challenges. We have latent generosity and powers of mutuality that are waiting to emerge.

Those of us who hold and control the wealth of the commons will either withdrawal to illusory private paradises — or rejoin humanity, warts and all. Here's my wish: Don't withdraw or disconnect. Come home.

Acknowledgments

I had a village of helpers with this book, including readers, mentors, family, friends, and neighbors. My apologies for any debts I have forgotten to acknowledge.

Thanks to Jenny Ladd and Felice Yeskel — I know you're not far away — for helping frame this book and melting the confusion with compassion.

Thanks to all my colleagues at the Institute for Policy Studies, Patriotic Millionaires, and Class Action, who are my community of ideas, practice, and action. With extra gratitude to Josh Hoxie, Sarah Byrnes, Anne Phillips, Annie Hamilton, Tracy Bindel, Betsy Leondar-Wright, Joanie Parker, Erica Payne, Morris Pearl, Justin Strekal, John Cavanagh, Scott Klinger, Sam Pizzigati, Sarah Anderson, Marc Bayard, Karen Dolan, Bob Lord, Jodie Evans, E. Ethelbert Miller, and Julia Ravel.

This book draws on the experience of a wider community and neighborhood of thinkers and doers, including those from the Jamaica Plain New Economy Transition, First Church Jamaica Plain Unitarian Universalist, and our local crew of pipeline resisters. These people include Orion Kriegman, Hannah Thomas, Andrée Zaleska, Rhea Becker, Kannan Thiruvengadam, Dakota Butterfield, Jom Michel, Carlos Espinoza-Toro, Jenny Jones, Samantha Wechsler, Cathy Hoffman, Anne Bancroft, Martha Niebanck, Marla Marcum, and Marisa Shea.

I am indebted to the community thinking about the intersection of inequality and ecological change and the commons. Novenas to Fran Korten, Kat Gjovik, Sarah van Gelder, Rob Hopkins, Peter Lipman, Asher Miller, Janet Redman, Richard Heinberg, Julie Schor, Vicki Robin, Peter Barnes, Marjorie Kelly, Gus Speth, Gar Alperovitz, David Korten, Julie Ristau, Harriet Barlow, Jay Walljasper, Ana Micka, Daniel Moss, Alexa Bradley, Ellen Dorsey, Jenna Nichols, and Ruairi McKiernan.

Thanks to all the people who helped shed light on the nature of power and privilege, including Bill Gates Sr., Alison Goldberg, Peter Buffett, Jeannette Huezo, Mike Lapham, Christopher Ellinger, Jo Saunders, Ralph Nader, Dean

Baker, Cecelia Kingman, Alan Preston, Martin Rothenberg, Felicia Mednick, Kathy Power, Anne Ellinger, Charles Eisenstein, and Fran Benson.

Bless the storytellers Norah Dooley, Andrea Lovett, Robin Maxfield, Andy Davis, Cheryl Hamilton, Mary Wallace, and the MassMouth community.

Deep gratitude to my readers at different stages, including Shane Lloyd, Bill Creighton, Jess Specter, Mike Markovitz, Betsy Leondar-Wright, Sister Margaret Leonard, Tom Burgess, Abe Lateiner, Will Meyer, Charlie Derber, Alan Preston, Mary Wallace, Rivera Sun, Jen Wade, Nora Collins, and Dariel Garner. Thanks for your feedback, suggestions, and encouragement.

Thanks to those who shared their stories, including Dariel Garner, Deborah Frieze, Arthur Cornfeld, Lisa Renstrom, Abe Lateiner, and Jenny Ladd. And those that allowed me to quote from them anonymously. In addition to people interviewed in this book, I had very helpful conversations with Marion Moore, Karen Pittleman, George Pillsbury, Artemis Joukowsky, Dedrick Muhammad, Thomas Shapiro, Darshan Brach, and Ray Madoff. Thanks to my "mutuality sisters" who taught me so much about the brain science of mutuality, including Judy Jordan, Sister Margaret Leonard, Christine Dixon, and Karen Hunter.

Kimberly French was a huge help with several chapters and coached me on narrative writing over a decade ago. A special thanks to Bob Kuttner who encouraged me to write an article for *The American Prospect* that is the foundation for the chapter Unequal Opportunity.

Mountains of thanks to Joni Praded at Chelsea Green, who has been a terrific partner and editor throughout this process. Thanks to the whole Chelsea Green team and the practical and transformative books that you that publish.

Thanks to my family, Mary, Sam, Nora, and Caleb, for the joy that makes all things possible. And thanks to my parents, Anne, Ed, and Barbara Collins for your acceptance and humor. I love you all and hold you blameless for my transgressions.

My partner, Mary, was totally game for the journey, from visits to mobile home parks to attending events like "Step into the Roaring Twenties." She's in almost all of the groups mentioned above. You're my spark.

Resources

Chuck Collins Affiliate Organizations

Class Action. Inspiring action to end classism and class biases. www.classism.org

Inequality.org. A portal for data, analysis, and commentary about wealth and income inequality; a program of the Institute for Policy Studies. www.inequality.org

Institute for Policy Studies. Public scholars and organizers working with social movements to promote democracy and challenge concentrated wealth, corporate influence, and military power. www.ips-dc.org

Jamaica Plain New Economy Transition (JP NET). Building community resilience in the Boston neighborhood of Jamaica Plain. www.jptransition.org

Patriotic Millionaires/Wealth for the Common Good. A network of high-net-worth individuals pressing for tax fairness, fair wages, and reducing the influence of big money in our democracy. www.patrioticmillionaires.org

Income and Wealth Inequality

Center for Economic Policy Research. Accessible economic and policy research addressing global and US inequalities. www.cepr.net

Demos. Research and advocacy for a more equitable economy with widely shared prosperity and opportunity. www.demos.org

Equality Trust. A U.K.-based project aimed at reducing inequality through education and policy campaigns. www.equalitytrust.org.uk

Inequality.org. A portal for data, analysis, and commentary about wealth and income inequality. www.inequality.org

Luxembourg Income Study. International data on comparative inequality and commentary. www.lisproject.org

Other 98 Percent. A grassroots network working to retake our democracy and economy from the power of wealth. www.other98.com

Population Health Forum. Looking at the interaction between inequality and health indicators. www.depts.washington.edu/eqhlth

United for a Fair Economy. Popular education on the inequality problem. www.faireconomy.org

Class and Privilege

Class Action. Inspiring action to end classism and class biases. www.classism.org

Resource Generation. Programs for young people with wealth to explore how to leverage their financial resources for social justice. www.resourcegeneration.org

White Privilege Conference. An annual gathering and resource exploring white privilege. www.whiteprivilegeconference.com

Racial Equality and Opportunity

Institute of the Black World. Research, policy, and advocacy around black liberation and reparations. www.ibw21.org

Institute on Assets and Social Policy. Research on racial wealth disparities and solutions. www.iasp.brandeis.edu

Leadership Conference on Civil Rights. The nation's premier civil rights coalition of over 180 organizations. www.civilrights.org

National Association for the Advancement of Colored People. The nation's oldest existing civil rights organization. www.naacp.org

National Council of La Raza. The largest Hispanic organization working to improve life opportunities for Hispanic Americans. www.nclr.org

Racial Wealth Divide Project of the Corporation for Enterprise Development. Research and policy solutions to reduce racial wealth disparities. www.cfed.org

Tax Fairness and Tax Havens

Americans for Tax Fairness. A coalition of 425 national and regional organizations working on tax fairness. www.americansfortaxfairness.org

Citizens for Tax Justice. Research on individual and corporate taxation. www.ctj.org

Financial Accountability and Corporate Transparency (FACT) Coalition. A US coalition addressing tax haven abuse and corporate chicanery. www.thefactcoalition.org

Global Financial Integrity. Tracking global illicit financial flows, producing research, and advising governments. www.gfintegrity.org

Tax Justice Network. An international network focused on tax haven abuses. www.taxjustice.net

About the Climate Crisis

350.org. A global advocacy network on climate change. www.350.org

Climate Justice Alliance. Bringing communities together to ensure a just transition. www.ourpowercampaign.org

Post Carbon Institute. Addressing the challenges of our energy future. www.postcarbon.org

Building Resilience as Communities Transition to a New Economy

On the Commons. An organization and web portal that provides an introduction of commons thinking and movements. www.onthecommons.org

Resident Owned Communities (ROC-USA). Supporting the creation of resident-owned manufactured housing communities. www.rocusa.org

Resilience Circles. A resource for communities wanting to start Resilience Circles. www.localcircles.org

Transition United States. Providing support and inspiration to transition efforts in the United States. www.transitionus.org

Transition Network. A global resource for transition communities. www.transition network.org

Giving and Philanthropy

Bolder Giving. Working to inspire and support deeper giving at full lifetime potential. www.boldergiving.org

Inside Philanthropy. Monitoring news and insights about foundations and individual giving. www.insidephilanthropy.com

National Committee for Responsive Philanthropy. Working to make organized philanthropy more responsive to socially, economically, and politically disenfranchised people. www.ncrp.org

Solidaire Network. Promoting funding for social change movements. www.solidaire network.org

Investing

CDFI Coalition. A national association of community development financial institutions (CDFI) encouraging fair access to financial capital for underserved people and communities. www.cdfi.org

Divest-Invest. A movement to divest from the fossil fuel sector and redirect capital to a new energy economy. www.divestinvest.org

Forum for Sustainable and Responsible Investment. A hub for the sustainable, responsible, and impact investment sector in United States. www.ussif.org

Play BIG/Renewal Partners. A network of wealthy individuals leveraging grant making and investments for social transformation. www.renewalpartners.com/collaborations /conferences/playbig

RSF Social Finance. A nonprofit financial services organization offering investing, lending, and philanthropic services to individuals and enterprises. www.rsfsocialfinance.org

Policy Research and Advocacy

Campaign for America's Future. A center for ideas and action that works to build an enduring majority for progressive change. www.ourfuture.org

Center for Community Change. Empowering low-income people to make change that improves their communities. www.communitychange.org

Hedgeclippers. A campaign exposing the oversized influence of hedge funds and billionaires on our government and politics. www.hedgeclippers.org

Institute for Policy Studies. Public scholars and organizers working with social movements to promote democracy and challenge concentrated wealth, corporate influence, and military power. www.ips-dc.org

Institute for Women's Policy Research. Exploring how poverty and inequality affect women. www.iwpr.org

Jobs with Justice. A national organization leading the fight for workers' rights and an economy that benefits everyone. www.jwj.org

National Domestic Workers Alliance and **Caring Across Generations.** A national coalition that aims to achieve respect, recognition, and inclusion in labor protections for domestic workers. www.domesticworkers.org

National People's Action. A network of grassroots organizations that work to advance a national economic and racial justice agenda. www.npa-us.org

Patriotic Millionaires/Wealth for the Common Good. A network of high-net-worth individuals pressing for tax fairness, fair wages, and reducing the influence of big money in our democracy. www.patrioticmillionaires.org

Public Citizen. A consumer rights advocacy group and think tank that works to ensure that all citizens are represented in the halls of power. www.citizen.org

Restaurant Opportunities Centers United. A national coalition that seeks to improve the wages and working conditions for the nation's restaurant workforce. www.rocunited.org

RESULTS. Education, civic engagement, and advocacy on issues related to hunger and poverty. www.results.org

United Workers Congress. An alliance of workers that are either by law or by practice excluded from the right to organize. www.unitedworkerscongress.org

US Action. A grassroots coalition of twenty-two state affiliates organizing for power, for democracy, and for change. www.usaction.org

Transition to a New Economy

Capital Institute. Focused on transforming finance to aid the economic transition to a more just, regenerative, and sustainable way of life. www.capitalinstitute.org

The Democracy Collaborative. Research and field activities focused on expanding community wealth. www.democracycollaborative.org

New Economy Coalition. An association of organizations working to transform the economy and politics to be more sustainable and equitable. www.neweconomy.net

Next System Project. Thinking boldly about systemic challenges to US society. www.thenextsystem.org

Resilience.org. A news portal for the community resilience movement. www.resilience.org

Notes

Introduction: Time to Come Home

1. Nicholas Confessore, Sarah Cohen, and Karen Yourish, "The Families Funding the 2016 Presidential Election," *New York Times*, October 10, 2015, http://www.nytimes .com/interactive/2015/10/11/us/politics/2016-presidential-election-super-pac -donors.html. The *New York Times* observes that "nearly half," as, "The 158 families each contributed $250,000 or more in the campaign through June 30, according to the most recent available Federal Election Commission filings and other data, while an additional 200 families gave more than $100,000. Together, the two groups contributed well over half the money in the presidential election — the vast majority of it supporting Republicans."
2. Thom Hartmann, "President Jimmy Carter: The United States Is an Oligarchy," Thom Hartman Program, July 28, 2015, http://www.thomhartmann.com/bigpicture /president-jimmy-carter-united-states-oligarchy.

Chapter 1: I Heart the 1 Percent

1. Paresh Dave, "Critics Say Mark Zuckerberg Isn't Quite 'Giving' Away His Wealth," *Los Angeles Times*, December 4, 2015, http://www.latimes.com/business/technology /la-fi-tn-mark-zuckerberg-llc-charity-20151204-story.html. I am skeptical myself, as I wrote here: Chuck Collins, "Commentary: Is Zuckerberg Another Billionaire Tax Dodger," *Palm Beach Post*, January 16, 2016, http://www.palmbeachpost.com/news /news/opinion/commentary-is-zuckerberg-another-billionaire-tax-d/np3wn.
2. I double-checked this and calculated that $500,000 invested in the S&P in 1986 — with the dividends reinvested — would have grown 1,554.3 percent, the equivalent of $7.75 million in December 2015. Of course, most managed wealth accounts beat the S&P.
3. Christopher Mogil and Anne Slepian with Peter Woodrow, *We Gave Away a Fortune: Stories of People Who Have Devoted Themselves and Their Wealth to Peace, Justice and the Environment* (New Society Publishers, 1992).

Chapter 2: Proceed with Empathy

1. Les Leopold, *Runaway Inequality: An Activist's Guide to Economic Justice* (New York: Labor Institute Press, 2015).
2. In 2014 the median income was just under $54,000. A person earning this amount would be in the top 1.1 to 1.8 percent of global income earners according to two calculators: See "How Rich Am I?," Giving What We Can, accessed April 9, 2016, https://www.givingwhatwecan.org/get-involved/how-rich-am-i; also see "World Wealth Calculator," World Wealth Calculator, accessed April 9, 2016, http://www .worldwealthcalculator.org.

3. Robert Frank, *Richistan: A Journey Through the American Wealth Boom and the Lives of the New Rich* (New York: Crown Publishers, 2007), 6–12.

4. Emmanuel Saez and Gabriel Zucman, "Wealth Inequality in the United States Since 1913," National Bureau of Economic Research, October 2014, http://gabriel-zucman .eu/files/SaezZucman2014Slides.pdf. Figures adapted to 2015 dollar values.

5. These wealth figures are adjusted to 2015 figures from analysis of the 2013 Federal Reserve Survey of Consumer Finance. Average wealth of the third percentile is $3 million; average wealth of the 1 percent is $7.8 million. Author analysis with assistance from Josh Hoxie and Salvatore Babones.

6. See Thomas J. Stanley and William D. Danko, *Millionaire Next Door: The Surprising Secrets of America's Wealthy* (New York: Pocket Books, 1996).

7. Saez and Zucman, "Wealth Inequality in the United States Since 1913." Figures adapted to 2015 dollar values.

8. Credit Suisse does an annual Global Wealth Report that tracks the movements of "High Net Worth Individuals (HNWI)," four million individuals with assets ranging between $1 million and $5 million, and a combined wealth of $13.9 trillion. Credit Suisse considers those with over $30 million assets as "Ultra High Net Worth Individuals" (UHNWI). See "The United States Wealth Report," Capgemini, accessed April 27, 2016, https://www.worldwealthreport.com/uswr. The definition of "Ultra High Net Worth Individuals" also includes over $20 million in investable assets. See also Chrystia Freeland, *Plutocrats: The Rise of the New Global Super-Rich and the Fall of Everyone Else* (Penguin, 2012), 58–60.

9. Frank, *Richistan*, 11.

10. "Forbes 400," *Forbes*, September 29, 2015, http://www.forbes.com/forbes-400.

11. Ralph Nader, *Only the Super-Rich Can Save Us!* (New York: Seven Stories Press, 2009), 11–13.

12. There's a good chance Fitzgerald may have never said this. See Eddy Dow, "The Rich Are Different," *New York Times*, November 13, 1988, http://www.nytimes.com /1988/11/13/books/l-the-rich-are-different-907188.html.

Chapter 3: Cracking Hearts Open

1. Scott Klinger, "Boeing, Second Largest Federal Contractor, Pays No Federal Income Tax in 2013," Center for Effective Government, February 19, 2014, http://www .foreffectivegov.org/blog/boeing-second-largest-federal-contractor-pays-no-federal -income-tax-2013; see also Dylan Matthews, "Donald Trump Isn't Rich Because He's a Great Investor. He's Rich Because His Dad Was Rich," *Vox*, last updated March 30, 2016, http://www.vox.com/2015/9/2/9248963/donald-trump-index-fund.

Chapter 4: I Didn't Do It Alone

1. Lieber quoted in John Sproat, *The Best Men: Liberal Reformers in the Gilded Age* (New York: Oxford University Press, 1968), 105.

2. Malcolm Gladwell, *Outliers: The Story of Success* (New York: Little, Brown and Company, 2008), 33 and 268.

3. Eugene Kiely, "'You Didn't Build That,' Uncut and Unedited," FactCheck, last updated July 24, 2012, http://www.factcheck.org/2012/07/you-didnt-build-that-uncut-and -unedited.

4. A good chronicle of this tendency is Brian Miller and Mike Lapham, *The Self-Made Myth: And the Truth About How Government Helps Individuals and Businesses Succeed* (San Francisco: Berrett-Koehler, 2012). This was based on an earlier monograph that I co-authored: Chuck Collins, Mike Lapham, and Scott Klinger, "I Didn't Do It Alone: Society's Contribution to Individual Wealth and Success" (Boston: United for a Fair Economy, 2004).

5. Brooks Jackson, "Bush as Businessman: How the Texas Governor Made His Millions," CNN, May 13, 1999, http://www.cnn.com/ALLPOLITICS/stories/1999/05/13 /president.2000/jackson.bush.

6. David Corn, "Secret Video: Romney Tells Millionaire Donors What He REALLY Thinks of Obama Voters," *Mother Jones*, September 17, 2012, http://www.mother jones.com/politics/2012/09/secret-video-romney-private-fundraiser. See the full transcript at MoJo News Team, "Full Transcript of the Mitt Romney Secret Video," *Mother Jones*, September 19, 2012, http://www.motherjones.com/politics/2012/09 /full-transcript-mitt-romney-secret-video.

7. Michael Orr, "In 1994, Ann Romney Described Her Life as Financially 'Struggling' College Student," MSNBC, last updated September 6, 2013, http://www.msnbc.com /the-ed-show/1994-ann-romney-described-her-life?lite.

8. In light of Trump's 2016 presidential run, others have dug into the question of Trump's inheritance. For a good overview, see Dylan Matthews, "Donald Trump Isn't Rich Because He's a Great Investor. He's Rich Because His Dad Was Rich," *Vox*, March 30, 2016, http://www.vox.com/2015/9/2/9248963/donald-trump-index-fund. Also see "Donald Trump Profile," *Forbes*, May 2011, http://www.forbes.com/profile /donald-trump.

9. Gwendolyn Parker, "George W. Bush's Secret of Success," *New York Times*, May 28, 1999. Her memoir is *Trespassing: My Sojourn in the Halls of Privilege* (Houghton Mifflin, 1997).

10. Corn, "Secret Video."

11. Ezra Klein, "Romney's Theory of the 'Taker Class,' and Why It Matters," *Washington Post*, September 17, 2012, http://www.washingtonpost.com/blogs/wonkblog/ wp/2012/09/17/romneys-theory-of-the-taker-class-and-why-it-matters.

12. See Chuck Marr and Chye-Ching Huang, "Misconceptions and Realities About Who Pays Taxes," Center on Budget and Policy Priorities, September 12, 2012, http://www .cbpp.org/research/misconceptions-and-realities-about-who-pays-taxes.

13. Paul Ryan, "A Better Way Up from Poverty," *Wall Street Journal*, August 15, 2014, http://www.wsj.com/articles/paul-ryan-a-better-way-up-from-poverty-1408141154 ?cb=logged0.4920838379766792&cb=logged0.21771539538167417.

   Many of Ryan's earlier sentiments are captured in Brett Brownell and Nick Baumann, "VIDEO: Paul Ryan's Version of '47 Percent' — the 'Takers' vs. the 'Makers,'" *Mother Jones*, October 5, 2012, http://www.motherjones.com/politics/2012 /10/paul-ryans-47-percent-takers-vs-makers-video.

Chapter 6: The Privilege Drug

1. Ampersand, "Privilege Is Driving a Smooth Road and Not Even Knowing It," *Alas! A Blog*, December 2, 2005, http://amptoons.com/blog/?p=1988.
2. Andrew Sum, Ishwar Khatiwada, Mykhaylo Trubskyy, and Martha Ross, with Walter McHugh and Sheila Palma, "The Plummeting Labor Market Fortunes of Teens and Young Adults," Brookings Institution, March 2014, http://www.brookings.edu /~/media/Research/Files/Reports/2014/03/14%20youth%20workforce/BMPP _Youth_March10EMBARGO.pdf.

Chapter 7: The Greatest Subsidized Generation

1. Michael J. Barga, "The 'Bonus March' (1932): The Unmet Demands and Needs of WWI Heroes," The Social Welfare History Project, accessed April 30, 2016, http://www.socialwelfarehistory.com/eras/great-depression/bonus-march. Also see Roger Daniels, *The Bonus March: An Episode of the Great Depression* (Connecticut: Greenwood Press, 1971).
2. See *No End in Sight*, documentary, directed by Charles Ferguson (2007; Magnolia Pictures), and this more recent article, Neil Swidey, "Where Did ISIS Come from? The Story Starts Here," *Boston Globe Magazine*, March 10, 2016, https://www.bostonglobe .com/magazine/2016/03/10/where-did-isis-come-from-the-story-starts-here/eOHwJ QgnZPNj8SE91Vw5hK/story.html.
3. Harvard President James Conant wrote in a report to the Harvard trustees, "Unless high standards of performance can be maintained in spite of sentimental pressures and financial temptation, we may find the least capable among the war generation, instead of the most capable, flooding the facilities for advanced education in the United States." "Conant Suggests GI Bill Revision," *Harvard Crimson*, January 23, 1945, http://www.thecrimson.com/article/1945/1/23/conant-suggests-gi-bill-revision -pentering.
4. Robert Hutchins, "The Threat to American Education," *Collier's Weekly* 114 (December 30, 1944): 20–21.
5. Two point two million veterans attended college or graduate school and 5.6 million took advantage of vocational education. Suzanne Mettler, *Soldiers to Citizens: The G.I. Bill and the Making of the Greatest Generation* (Oxford: Oxford University Press, 2005).
6. FHA mortgage insurance made it possible for eleven million families to purchase their own homes and another twenty-two million to improve their properties. The housing programs had the dual impact of stimulating construction trades and enabling people to purchase homes. See Mettler, *Soldiers to Citizens*.
7. Daniel K. Fetter, "The Twentieth Century Increase in US Home Ownership: Facts and Hypotheses," in *Housing and Mortgage Markets in Historical Perspective*, ed. Eugene White, Kenneth Snowden, and Price Fishback (Chicago: University of Chicago Press, 2014), 329–350. To learn more about the postwar process of suburbanization see Kenneth T. Jackson, *Crabgrass Frontier: The Suburbanization of the United States* (Oxford, UK: Oxford University Press, 1985).

8. Wesley K. Clark and Jon Soltz, "McCain Must Lead the Charge," *Los Angeles Times*, April 10, 2008, accessed May 2, 2016, http://articles.latimes.com/2008/apr/10/opinion/oe-clark10.

9. David M. Gosoroski, "World War II's 'Silent Army' Produced 'Silent Revolution,'" VFW, October 1997, p. 7, http://www.ww2hc.org/articles/silentrevolution.pdf. See Mettler, *Soldiers to Citizens*.

10. Aaron Glantz, "Forgotten Promises of the GI Bill," *CBS News*, November 29, 2007, accessed May 2, 2016, http://www.cbsnews.com/news/forgotten-promises-of-the-gi-bill.

11. W. L. Mertz and Joyce Ritter, "Building the Interstate," US Department of Transportation, accessed April 10, 2016, https://www.fhwa.dot.gov/infrastructure/build.pdf; also see Felix G. Rohatyn, *Bold Endeavors: How Our Government Built America, and Why It Must Rebuild Now* (New York: Simon and Schuster, 2009).

12. Stephanie Coontz, *The Way We Never Were: American Families and the Nostalgia Trap* (New York: Basic Books, 2000), 76.

13. "SOI Tax Stats — Historical Table 23," Internal Revenue Service, updated May 1, 2013, accessed April 3, 2016, https://www.irs.gov/uac/SOI-Tax-Stats-Historical-Table-23; also see "CPI Inflation Calculator," US Department of Labor Bureau of Labor Statistics, http://data.bls.gov/cgi-bin/cpicalc.pl.

14. "SOI Tax Stats — Historical Table 24," Internal Revenue Service, updated May 9, 2014, accessed April 3, 2016, https://www.irs.gov/uac/SOI-Tax-Stats-Historical-Table-24; data on effective corporate tax rates from "The Sorry State of Corporate Taxes," Citizens for Tax Justice, February 2014, http://www.ctj.org/corporatetaxdodgers.

15. Sarah E. Turner and John Bound, "Closing the Gap or Widening the Divide: The Effects of the G.I. Bill and World War II on the Educational Outcomes of Black Americans," National Bureau of Economic Research, July 2002, http://www.nber.org/papers/w9044.

16. Robert R. Callis and Mellisa Kresin, "Residential Vacancies and Homeownership in the Third Quarter 2014," US Census Bureau, October 28, 2014, http://www.census.gov/housing/hvs/files/qtr314/q314press.pdf.

17. "Farm Programs," US Government Accountability Office, http://www.gao.gov/key_issues/farm_programs/issue_summary.

18. John Tierney, "Which States Are Givers and Which Are Takers," *The Atlantic*, May 5, 2014, http://www.theatlantic.com/business/archive/2014/05/which-states-are-givers-and-which-are-takers/361668.

19. Average annual tuition at a four-year private liberal arts college is $31,000. "College Costs: FAQs," The College Board, accessed April 3, 2016, https://bigfuture.collegeboard.org/pay-for-college/college-costs/college-costs-faqs; average student debt is roughly $35,000. Over forty million households are holding student debt. Jeffrey Sparshott, "Congratulations, Class of 2015. You're the Most Indebted Ever (for Now)", *Wall Street Journal*, May 8, 2015, http://blogs.wsj.com/economics/2015/05/08/congratulations-class-of-2015-youre-the-most-indebted-ever-for-now.

Chapter 8: Black Wealth, Brown Wealth, White Wealth

1. "Jobs and the Economy," The State of Young America, November 2011, http://www
   .demos.org/sites/default/files/imce/SOYA_JobsandtheEconomy_0.pdf; Catherine
   Ruetschlin and Tamara Draut, "Stuck: Young America's Persistent Job Crisis," Demos,
   April 4, 2013, http://www.demos.org/publication/stuck-young-americas-persistent
   -jobs-crisis; and "New Report Shows Staggering Youth Unemployment Rates,"
   Demos, April 4, 2013, http://www.demos.org/press-release/new-report-shows
   -staggering-youth-unemployment-rates.
2. Rakesh Kochhar and Richard Fry, "Wealth Inequality Has Widened Along Racial,
   Ethnic Lines Since End of Great Recession," Pew Research Center, December 12, 2014,
   http://www.pewresearch.org/fact-tank/2014/12/12/racial-wealth-gaps-great-recession.
3. Ibid.
4. Martin Luther King Jr., *Where Do We Go from Here: Chaos or Community?* (Boston:
   Beacon Press, King Legacy Edition, 2010), section III.
5. Ta-Nehisi Coates, "The Case for Reparations," *The Atlantic*, June 2014, http://www
   .theatlantic.com/magazine/archive/2014/06/the-case-for-reparations/361631.
6. "Residential Vacancies and Homeownership in the Fourth Quarter 2015," US Census
   Bureau, January 28, 2016, accessed April 10, 2016, http://www.census.gov/housing
   /hvs/files/currenthvspress.pdf.
7. James S. Hirsch, *Riot and Remembrance: The Tulsa Race War and Its Legacy* (New York:
   Houghton Mifflin Company, 2002), 119.
8. "Ceremony to Mark 81st Anniversary of Rosewood Massacre," *Florida Times-Union*,
   last updated December 31, 2003, http://jacksonville.com/apnews/stories/123103
   /D7VPIOTG1.shtml.
9. Coates, "The Case for Reparations."

Chapter 9: Unequal Opportunity

1. This chapter is based on a piece I wrote for *The American Prospect*. See Chuck Collins,
   "The Wealthy Kids Are All Right," *The American Prospect*, May 28, 2013, http://
   prospect.org/article/wealthy-kids-are-all-right.
2. David Leonhardt, "A Simple Way to Send Poor Kids to Top Colleges," *New York Times*,
   March 31, 2013, http://www.nytimes.com/2013/03/31/opinion/sunday/a
   -simple-way-to-send-poor-kids-to-top-colleges.html?pagewanted=all&_r=0.
3. On rising disability claims in rural areas, see: Chana Joffe-Walt, "Unfit for Work: The
   Startling Rise in Disability in America," National Public Radio, March 25–26, 2013,
   http://apps.npr.org/unfit-for-work; 44 percent of military recruits come from rural
   areas. See Ann Scott Tyson, "Youths in Rural US Are Drawn to Military," *Washington
   Post*, November 4, 2005, http://www.washingtonpost.com/wp-dyn/content/article
   /2005/11/03/AR2005110302528.html.
4. Two primary sources for this chapter are two volumes of academic articles from
   the Russell Sage Foundation, both connected with the Cross-National Research on
   the Intergenerational Transmission of Advantage (CRITA): John Ermisch, Markus
   Jäntti, and Timothy Smeeding, eds., *From Parents to Children: The Intergenerational*

Transmission of Advantage (New York: Russell Sage Foundation, 2012); and Timothy M. Smeeding, Robert Erikson, and Markus Jäntti, eds., *Persistence, Privilege, and Parenting: The Comparative Study of Intergenerational Mobility* (New York: Russell Sage Foundation, September 2011).

5. See page 4 of "Does America Promote Mobility as Well as Other Nations?," Pew Charitable Trusts, Economic Mobility Project, November 2011, http://www.pew trusts.org/~/media/legacy/uploadedfiles/pcs_assets/2011/critafinal1pdf.pdf.

6. The Survey of Economically Successful Americans has been looking at the gap between the priorities of the rich and everyone else. See Benjamin I. Page and Larry M. Bartels, "The 1% Aren't Like the Rest of Us," *Los Angeles Times*, March 22, 2013, http://articles.latimes.com/2013/mar/22/opinion/la-oe-page-wealth-and-politics -20130322.

7. Jane Mayer, *Dark Money: The Hidden History of the Billionaires Behind the Rise of the Radical Right* (New York: Doubleday, 2016).

8. Michael Mitchell and Michael Leachman, "Years of Cuts Threaten to Put College Out of Reach for More Students," Center on Budget and Policy Priorities, May 13, 2015, http://www.cbpp.org/research/state-budget-and-tax/years-of-cuts-threaten-to-put -college-out-of-reach-for-more-students; also see: Robert Hiltonsmith and Tamara Draut, "The Great Cost Shift Continues: State Higher Education Funding After the Recession," Demos, March 14, 2014, http://www.demos.org/publication/great -cost-shift-continues-state-higher-education-funding-after-recession.

9. Calculated from table 2 of "Trends in College Pricing 2014," College Board, 2014, https://secure-media.collegeboard.org/digitalServices/misc/trends/2014-trends -college-pricing-report-final.pdf; and Carmen DeNavas-Walt and Bernadette D. Proctor, "Income and Poverty in the United States: 2013," US Census Bureau, September 2014, http://www.census.gov/content/dam/Census/library /publications/2014/demo/p60-249.pdf. Tuition, room, and board in 1994 was $10,267 and had grown to $18,781 in 2014, a change of $8,514 or 45 percent. Private school costs went from $26,532 to $42,517, an increase of $15,985 in 2015 dollars, or 37.59 percent. The median income in 1995 was $52,604 and had increased to $54,657 in constant dollars, a change of 1.9 percent. See Phil Oliff, Vincent Palacios, Ingrid Johnson, and Michael Leachman, "Recent Deep State Higher Education Cuts May Harm Students and the Economy for Years to Come," Center on Budget and Policy Priorities, March 19, 2013, http://www.cbpp.org/cms/index.cfm?fa=view&id =3927.

10. Miles Corak, Lori J. Curtis, and Shelley Phipps, "Economic Mobility, Family Background, and the Well-Being of Children in the United States and Canada," in *Persistence, Privilege, and Parenting*, ed. Smeeding, Erikson, and Jäntti. For a summary of the book, with this statistic on Canada, see "Persistence, Privilege, and Parenting," Russell Sage Foundation, https://www.russellsage.org/publications/persistence-privilege-and-parenting; and Rohan Mascarenhas, "Comparing Economic Mobility in Canada and America: An Interview with Miles Corak," Russell Sage Foundation, May 18, 2012, http://www.russellsage.org/blog/comparing-economic-mobility -canada-and-america-interview-miles-corak.

11. Rohan Mascarenhas, "Early Childhood and Mobility: An Interview with Jane Waldfogel," Russell Sage Foundation, May 21, 2012, http://www.russellsage.org/blog /early-childhood-and-mobility-interview-jane-waldfogel.

12. Meredith Phillip, "Parenting, Time Use, and Disparities in Academic Outcomes," in *Whither Opportunity?: Rising Inequality, Schools, and Children's Life Chances*, ed. Greg J. Duncan and Richard J. Murnane (New York: Russell Sage Foundation, 2012), 2017–228. Summary at "Whither Opportunity?," Russell Sage Foundation, https:// www.russellsage.org/publications/whither-opportunity.

13. Robert D. Putnam, Carl B. Frederick, and Kaisa Snellman, "Growing Class Gaps in Social Connectedness Among American Youth, 1975–2009," Harvard Kennedy School of Government, July 12, 2012, http://www.hks.harvard.edu/saguaro/pdfs /SaguaroReport_DivergingSocialConnectedness.pdf.

14. Ibid.

15. Mascarenhas, "Early Childhood and Mobility."

16. Sean F. Reardon, "The Widening Academic Gap Between the Rich and the Poor: New Evidence and Possible Explanations," in *Whither Opportunity?*, 91–116.

17. Research by Caroline M. Hoxby of Stanford and Christopher Avery of Harvard, as cited in David Leonhardt, "Better Colleges Failing to Lure Poor," *New York Times*, March 16, 2013, http://www.nytimes.com/2013/03/17/education/scholarly-poor -often-overlook-better-colleges.html?hp&_r=0.

18. The income achievement gap is now twice as large as the black–white achievement gap, compared with 1971, when the black–white gap was 1.5 to 2 times greater than the income gap. Reardon, "The Widening Academic Gap."

19. "Jobs and the Economy."

20. Jaison R. Abel and Richard Deitz, "Do the Benefits of College Still Outweigh the Costs?," *Current Issues in Economics and Finance* 20, no. 3 (2014), https://www.newyork fed.org/medialibrary/media/research/current_issues/ci20-3.pdf.

21. Martha J. Bailey and Susan M. Dynarski, "Gains and Gaps: Changing Inequality in US College Entry and Completion," National Bureau of Economic Research, December 2011, http://www.nber.org/papers/w17633.pdf; also see Suzanne Mettler, *Degrees of Inequality: How the Politics of Higher Education Sabotaged the American Dream* (New York: Basic Books, 2014).

22. Bailey and Dynarski, "Gains and Gaps."

23. Jere R. Behrman, Olivia S. Mitchell, Cindy K. Soo, and David Bravo, "How Financial Literacy Affects Household Wealth Accumulation," AER Papers, January 6, 2012, 8, https://www.aeaweb.org/articles?id=10.1257/aer.102.3.300.

24. Sally Koslaw, *Slouching Toward Adulthood: Observations from the Not-So-Empty Nest* (New York: Viking Press, 2012). The "middle class trust fund" cited in Ron Lieber, "From Parents, a Living Inheritance," *New York Times*, September 21, 2012, http:// www.nytimes.com/2012/09/22/your-money/the-hidden-inheritance-many-parents -already-provide.html?pagewanted=all&_r=1&.

25. Research by Caroline M. Hoxby of Stanford and Christopher Avery of Harvard, as cited in Leonhardt, "Better Colleges Failing to Lure Poor."

26. "Jobs and the Economy"; also see Leonhardt, "Better Colleges Failing to Lure Poor."

27. David Leonhardt, "A Simple Way to Send Poor Kids to Top Colleges."

28. I did extensive research on the GI Bill and PELL grants for my book, co-authored with Bill Gates Sr., *Wealth and Our Commonwealth: Why America Should Tax Accumulated Fortunes* (Boston: Beacon Press, 2013); and op-eds such as Bill Gates Sr. and Chuck Collins, "It's Time for a GI Bill for the Next Generation," *Chron*, June 22, 2004, http://www.chron.com/opinion/outlook/article/It-s-time-for-a-GI-Bill-for-the-next -generation-1504916.php.

29. Jillian Berman, "America's Growing Student-Loan Debt Crisis," MarketWatch, January 19, 2016, http://www.marketwatch.com/story/americas-growing-student -loan-debt-crisis-2016-01-15; see projected growth at Mark Huelsman, "Reflecting on $1 Trillion in Student Debt, and Why We're Headed for $2 Trillion," Demos, April 24, 2014, http://www.demos.org/blog/4/24/14/reflecting-1-trillion-student-debt-and -why-were-headed-2-trillion.

30. Richard Fry, "A Record One-in-Five Households Now Owe Student Loan Debt," Pew Research Center, September 26, 2012, http://www.pewsocialtrends.org/2012/09/26 /a-record-one-in-five-households-now-owe-student-loan-debt; see also "Household Debt Continues Upward Climb While Student Loan Delinquencies Worsen," Federal Reserve Bank of New York, February 17, 2015, http://www.newyorkfed.org/newsevents /news/research/2015/rp150217.html.

31. Mark Huelsman, "The Federal Reserve Just Released a Boatload of Information on Student Debt. Here's What It's Telling Us," Demos, February 20, 2015, http://www .demos.org/blog/2/20/15/federal-reserve-just-released-boatload-information-student -debt-here's-what-it's-tellin.

32. Richard Fry, "Young Adults, Student Debt and Economic Well-Being," Pew Research Center, May 14, 2014, http://www.pewsocialtrends.org/2014/05/14/young-adults -student-debt-and-economic-well-being.

33. Ross Eisenbrey, "Unpaid Internships Hurt Mobility," Economic Policy Institute, January 5, 2012, http://www.epi.org/blog/unpaid-internships-economic-mobility.

34. Michael Laracy, "Internships: Gateway to Opportunity or an Obstacle for Low-Income Students?," *Huffington Post*, November 3, 2010, http://www.huffingtonpost .com/mike-laracy/internships-gateway-to-op_b_777951.html.

35. Sociologist Heather Beth Johnson has analyzed the dozens of intergenerational wealth transfers — some modest amounts under $1,000 — that help young adults stay afloat or have more choices. Heather Beth Johnson, *The American Dream and the Power of Wealth: Choosing Schools and Inheriting Inequality in the Land of Opportunity* (London: Routledge, 2006).

36. Reihan Salam, "Should We Care About Relative Mobility?" National Review Online, November 29, 2011, accessed March 30, 2016, http://www.nationalreview.com /agenda/284379/should-we-care-about-relative-mobility-reihan-salam.

37. Ermisch, Jäntti, and Smeeding, *From Parents to Children*; also see, "Does America Promote Mobility as Well as Other Nations?"

38. Oliff, Palacios, Johnson, and Leachman, "Recent Deep State Higher Education Cuts."

39. J. Maureen Henderson, "Are Creative Careers Now Reserved Exclusively for the Privileged?," *Forbes*, August 31, 2012, http://www.forbes.com/sites/jmaureen henderson/2012/08/31/are-creative-careers-now-reserved-exclusively-for-the -privileged; much was stirred up by Canadian writer Alexandra Kimball's column that chronicles her attempt to break into journalism. See Alexandra Kimball, "How to Succeed in Journalism When You Can't Afford an Internship," Hazlitt, August 23, 2012, http://www.randomhouse.ca/hazlitt/feature/how-succeed-journalism-when -you-cant-afford-internship.

40. Chuck Collins, "Tax Wealth to Broaden Wealth," *The American Prospect*, April 16, 2003, http://prospect.org/article/tax-wealth-broaden-wealth.

Chapter 10: Miro in the Bathroom: Encounters with the Charitable Industrial Compex

1. Table 2 from Emmanuel Saez, "Striking It Richer: The Evolution of Top Incomes in the United States," University of California–Berkeley, June 25, 2015, http://eml .berkeley.edu/~saez/saez-UStopincomes-2014.pdf.

2. Foundation breakout data is from 2012. "Key Facts on US Foundations," Foundation Center, http://foundationcenter.org/gainknowledge/research/keyfacts2014; find charitable-giving information at the following links: "Charitable Giving Statistics," National Philanthropic Trust, http://www.nptrust.org/philanthropic-resources /charitable-giving-statistics; "Foundation Stats," Foundation Center, http://data .foundationcenter.org/#/foundations/all/nationwide/total/list/2013; and Melissa Ludlum, "Domestic Private Foundations, Tax Years 1993–2002," Internal Revenue Service, http://www.irs.gov/pub/irs-soi/02eopf.pdf.

3. "Giving USA: Americans Donated an Estimated $358.38 Billion to Charity in 2014; Highest Total in Report's 60-Year History," Giving USA, June 29, 2015, http://givingusa .org/giving-usa-2015-press-release-giving-usa-americans-donated-an-estimated-358-38 -billion-to-charity-in-2014-highest-total-in-reports-60-year-history.

4. For breakout statistics on charitable giving, using Giving USA 2015 data, see "Giving Statistics," Charity Navigator, http://www.charitynavigator.org/index.cfm/bay /content.view/cpid/42#.VP3FyFpDbKA.

   Historically, as we saw in 2014, donations from individuals account for roughly 75 percent of all donations. If you add in gifts from bequests and family foundations, which are essentially gifts from individuals, then the category accounts for nearly 90 percent of all giving. In other words, the donating public, not big foundations or corporations, is responsible for the vast majority of annual donations.

5. Foundation breakout data is from 2012. "Key Facts on US Foundations," Foundation Center, http://foundationcenter.org/gainknowledge/research/keyfacts2014.

6. One study examining the funding priorities of the nation's wealthiest donors found that very little money flowed to organizations helping the poor and needy. The main recipients of funds by wealthy donors are universities and colleges, medical organizations, and arts and cultural institutions. Both studies cited in Pablo Eisenberg, "What's Wrong with Charitable Giving — and How to Fix It," *Wall Street Journal*,

November 9, 2009, http://www.wsj.com/articles/SB10001424052748704500604574481773446591750.

7. Ray Madoff, "A Better Way to Encourage Charity," *New York Times*, October 5, 2014, http://www.nytimes.com/2014/10/06/opinion/a-better-way-to-encourage-charity.html?_r=1.

8. "America's 50 Top Givers," *Forbes*, 2013, http://www.forbes.com/special-report/2013/philanthropy/top-givers.html.

9. Daniel Golden, *The Price of Admission: How America's Ruling Class Buys Its Way into Elite Colleges — and Who Gets Left Outside the Gates* (New York: Broadway Books, 2007).

10. Some background on charitable giving and artwork can be found in Joy Gibney Berus, "The Art of Donating Art: The Charitable Contribution of Art, Antiques and Collectibles," Planned Giving Design Center, October 21, 2008, http://www.pgdc.com/pgdc/art-donating-art-charitable-contribution-art-antiques-and-collectibles.

11. Globe Staff, "Some Officers of Charities Steer Assets to Selves," *Boston Globe*, October 9, 2003, http://archive.boston.com/news/nation/articles/2003/10/09/some_officers_of_charities_steer_assets_to_selves/?page=full.

12. Chronicle of Philanthropy survey, as cited in Pablo Eisenberg, "Foundation Trustees Shouldn't Be Paid Millions of Dollars," *Huffington Post*, July 24, 2014, http://www.huffingtonpost.com/pablo-eisenberg/foundation-trustees-shoul_b_5618667.html.

13. Globe Staff, "Some Officers of Charities."

14. The IRS has not released reliable data on enforcement actions in several years. I consulted with experts Aaron Dorfman and Marc Owens on April 30, 2016, who from surveying IRS Data Book, Table 13, estimate no more than 119 cases have been closed in the last few years. Also see, "Tax-Exempt Organizations: Better Compliance Indicators and Data, and More Collaboration with State Regulators Would Strengthen Oversight of Charitable Organizations," United States Government Accountability Office, December 2014, http://www.gao.gov/assets/670/667595.pdf.

Chapter 11: When Charity Disrupts Justice

1. Eisenberg, "What's Wrong with Charitable Giving."

2. Rob Reich, "Not Very Giving," *New York Times*, September 4, 2013, http://www.nytimes.com/2013/09/05/opinion/not-very-giving.html?_r=0; also see Rob Reich, "A Failure of Philanthropy: American Charity Shortchanges the Poor, and Public Policy Is Partly to Blame," *Stanford Social Innovation Review* (Winter 2005), http://ssir.org/articles/entry/a_failure_of_philanthropy.

3. Ray Madoff, "Dog Eat Your Taxes?," *New York Times*, July 9, 2008, http://www.nytimes.com/2008/07/09/opinion/09madoff.html.

4. The percentage of tax filers who itemize increases as we move up the income scale. Andrew Lundeen and Scott A. Hodge, "Higher Income Taxpayers Are Most Likely to Claim Itemized Deductions," Tax Foundation, November 7, 2013, http://taxfoundation.org/blog/higher-income-taxpayers-are-most-likely-claim-itemized-deductions. In theory, the standard deduction utilized by nonitemizers factors in a certain amount of charitable giving.

5. Zachary Mider, "The $13 Billion Mystery Angels: Who Is Funding the Fourth-Largest Charity in the US?," *Bloomberg Business*, May 8, 2014, http://www.bloomberg.com /bw/articles/2014-05-08/three-mysterious-philanthropists-fund-fourth-largest-u-dot -s-dot-charity#p2.

6. Some might even ask the more fundamental philosophical question of "What is money?" and "Where does it come from?" This is beyond the scope of this work, but it is a very worthwhile discussion. See David Graeber, *Debt: The First 5,000 Years* (London: Melville House Publishing, 2011).

7. This is the reality for many low- and middle-income donors who don't itemize but give generously to charities.

8. James Aloisi, "A Short and Long-Term Plan," *CommonWealth Magazine*, February 23, 2015, http://commonwealthmagazine.org/transportation/short-long-term-plan.

9. Louis Uchitelle, "Private Cash Sets Agenda for Urban Infrastructure," *New York Times*, June 6, 2008, http://www.nytimes.com/2008/01/06/business/06haven.html?page wanted=all&_r.

10. Charitable giving as percent of GDP from Uchitelle, "Private Cash Sets Agenda." Updated statistic on infrastructure from "An Economic Analysis of Transportation Infrastructure Investment," The White House, July 2014, 18, https://www.white house.gov/sites/default/files/docs/economic_analysis_of_transportation _investments.pdf.

11. "2013 Report Card for America's Infrastructure," American Society of Civil Engineers, 2013, http://www.infrastructurereportcard.org.

12. "SNAP/Food Stamp Participation Data," Food Research & Action Center, 2015, http://frac.org/reports-and-resources/snapfood-stamp-monthly-participation-data.

13. "Policy Basics: Introduction to the Supplemental Nutritional Assistance Program (SNAP)," Center on Budget and Policy Priorities, last updated March 24, 2016, accessed April 5, 2016, http://www.cbpp.org/research/policy-basics-introduction-to -the-supplemental-nutrition-assistance-program-snap.

14. "Tax-Exempt Organizations and Charitable Giving," Senate Finance Committee Staff Tax Reform Options for Discussion, June 13, 2013, http://www.finance.senate.gov /imo/media/doc/06132013%20Tax-Exempt%20Organizations%20and%20Charitable %20Giving.pdf.

15. See "Campaigns, Research & Policy," National Committee for Responsive Philanthropy, https://www.ncrp.org/campaigns-research-policy.

16. Madoff, "A Better Way."

17. Jane Mosaoka and Jeanne Bell Peters, "What We Really Need: Eight Reforms to Make Nonprofits More Accountable and Effective," *Stanford Innovation Review* (Summer 2005), accessed April 5, 2016, http://www.sdgrantmakers.org/conference/SSIR%20 Eight%20Reforms%20Masaoka%20Peters%206-05.pdf.

18. Jeffrey N. Gordon, "The Rise of Independent Directors in the United States, 1950–2005," Social Science Research Network, August 2006, http://papers.ssrn.com /sol3/papers.cfm?abstract_id=928100.

19. Conor O'Cleary, *The Billionaire Who Wasn't: How Chuck Feeney Secretly Made and Gave Away a Fortune* (New York: Public Affairs, 2007), 324.

20. Amy Markham and Susan Wolf Ditkoff, "Learning from the Sunset," *Philanthropy Magazine*, (Fall 2013), http://www.philanthropyroundtable.org/topic/donor_intent /learning_from_the_sunset; for more on Atlantic Philanthropy see "The Long Goodbye: Atlantic Philanthropies Approaching the End," *The NonProfit Times*, July 29, 2014, http://www.thenonprofittimes.com/news-articles/long-goodbye-atlantic -philanthropies-approaching-end.

Chapter 12: The Moment We Are In

1. "Climate Change 2014 Synthesis Report Summary for Policymakers," Intergovernmental Panel on Climate Change, https://www.ipcc.ch/pdf/assessment -report/ar5/syr/AR5_SYR_FINAL_SPM.pdf.
2. Pope Francis, "Encyclical Letter Laudato Si' of the Holy Father Francis On Care for Our Common Home," Vatican, May 24, 2015, accessed May 2, 2016. http:// w2.vatican.va/content/francesco/en/encyclicals/documents/papa-francesco _20150524_enciclica-laudato-si.html.
3. Jeremy Leggett, "Why Coal and Many Oil Investments Are Losing Luster," *Fortune*, February 24, 2014, http://fortune.com/2014/02/24/why-coal-and-many-oil -investments-are-losing-luster.
4. Saez and Zucman, "Wealth Inequality in the United States Since 1913."
5. Chuck Collins and Josh Hoxie, "Billionaire Bonanza: The Forbes 400 and the Rest of Us," Institute for Policy Studies, December 5, 2015, http://www.ips-dc.org/billionaire -bonanza.
6. Ibid.
7. Thomas Piketty, *Capital in the Twenty-First Century* (Cambridge, MA: Belknap, 2014), 351.
8. Over the five years between 2008 and 2012, FedEx paid an effective federal corporate tax rate of 4.2 percent and United Parcel Service paid an effective rate of 27.5 percent. See Robert S. McIntyre, Matthew Gardner, and Richard Phillips, "The Sorry State of Corporate Taxes: What Fortune 500 Firms Pay (or Don't Pay) in the USA and What They Pay Abroad — 2008 to 2012," Citizens for Tax Justice, February 2014, http:// www.ctj.org/corporatetaxdodgers/sorrystateofcorptaxes.pdf.
9. For a history of the social movements that reversed the first Gilded Age after World War I see Sam Pizzigati, *The Rich Don't Always Win: The Forgotten Triumph Over Plutocracy That Created the American Middle Class, 1900–1970* (New York: Seven Stories Press, 2012).
10. For more on this history, see Gates and Collins, *Wealth and Our Commonwealth*.
11. James Gustave Speth, "Getting to the Next System: Guideposts on the Way to a New Political Economy," Next System Project, October 14, 2015, http://thenextsystem .org/gettowhatsnext.

Chapter 13: A Stake in the Common Good

1. From Bloomfield Hills, Michigan, accessed April 4, 2016, http://www.bloomfield hillsmi.net; and The Village Club, http://www.thevillageclub.org.

2. Mike Fredenburg, "The F-35: Throwing Good Money After Bad," *National Review*, July 22, 2015, accessed April 4, 2016, http://www.nationalreview.com/article /421473/f-35-throwing-good-money-after-bad-mike-fredenburg.

Chapter 14: Neighborhood Real Security

1. David M. Herszenhorn, Carl Hulse, and Sheryl Gay Stolberg, "Talks Implode During a Day of Chaos, Failure of Bailout Plan Remains Unresolved," *New York Times*, September 25, 2008, http://www.nytimes.com/2008/09/26/business/26bailout.html ?pagewanted=all&_r=0.
2. The Resilience Circle facilitator's guide and other resources are available at "Resilience Circle Curriculum," Resilience Circles, http://localcircles.org/facilitators-corner/six -session-facilitators-guide.
3. "What Is a Resilience Circle?," Resilience Circles, http://localcircles.org/what-is -a-resilience-circle.
4. See more information at Local Circles, http://localcircles.org.
5. To learn more about the transition town movement see Transition Network, http:// www.transitionnetwork.org; and, in the United States, see Transition United States, http://www.transitionus.org.
6. "Americans Have Fewer Friends Outside the Family, Duke Study Shows," Duke University, June 23, 2006, https://today.duke.edu/2006/06/socialisolation. html; Miller McPherson, Lynn Smith-Lovin, and Matthew E. Brashears, "Social Isolation in America: Changes in Core Discussion Networks Over Two Decades," *American Sociological Review* 71, no. 3 (June 2006): 353–357, doi:10.1177/000312240607100301.
7. Charles Eisenstein, *Sacred Economics: Money, Gift, and Society in the Age of Transition* (Berkeley, CA: Evolver Editions/North Atlantic Books, 2011), chapter 22.

Chapter 15: Community Resilience

1. To learn more about the transition movement, see Transition Network, http://www.transitionnetwork.org; and Transition United States, http://www .transitionus.org.
2. Rob Hopkins, *The Power of Just Doing Stuff: How Local Action Can Change the World* (Cambridge, U.K.: UIT Cambridge Ltd., 2013), 27.
3. Artisans Asylum, https://artisansasylum.com. See Boston Makers, http://www.boston makers.org.
4. The farmers market not only uses SNAP "food stamps" but has a municipally funded coupon called "Bounty Bucks," which makes purchasing fresh produce and other products even more affordable.
5. See Egleston Farmers Market, http://www.eglestonfarmersmarket.org.
6. Jamaica Plain Local First, http://jplocalfirst.org. For information on the multiplier effect, see "The Multiplier Effect of Local Independent Businesses," American Independent Business Alliance, accessed April 7, 2016, http://www.amiba.net /resources/multiplier-effect. There are many studies about the multiplier effect. For an

overview, see "Key Studies: Why Local Matters," Institute for Local Self Reliance, last updated January 8, 2016, https://ilsr.org/key-studies-why-local-matters. The study citied from Salt Lake City is most relevant to our Jamaica Plain neighborhood, which has a vibrant independent business sector. See "Indie Impact Study Series: A National Comparative Survey with the American Booksellers Association," Civic Economics (Summer 2012) http://localfirst.org/images/stories/SLC-Final-Impact-Study-Series .pdf.

7. Charles Eisenstein, "To Build Community, an Economy of Gifts," *YES! Magazine*, December 21, 2001, http://www.yesmagazine.org/happiness/to-build-community -an-economy-of-gifts.

8. Hopkins, *The Power of Just Doing Stuff*, 45.

Chapter 16: Bringing Wealth Home

1. Marjorie Kelly and Sarah McKinley, "7 Paths to Development That Bring Neighborhoods Wealth, Not Gentrification," *YES! Magazine*, November 11, 2015, http://www.yesmagazine.org/new-economy/7-paths-to-development-that-bring -neighborhoods-wealth-not-gentrification-20151111.

2. Kevin G. Hall and Marisa Taylor, "US Scolds Others About Offshores, But Looks Other Way at Home," McClatchy DC, April 5, 2016, http://www.mcclatchydc.com /news/nation-world/national/article70008302.html.

3. See Chuck Collins, "The Panama Papers Expose the Hidden Wealth of the World's Super-Rich," *The Nation*, April 5, 2016, http://www.thenation.com/article/panama -papers-expose-the-hidden-wealth-of-the-worlds-super-rich.

4. "Offshore Shell Games 2015: The Use of Offshore Tax Havens by Fortune 500 Companies," Citizens for Tax Justice, October 5, 2015, http://ctj.org/ctjreports /2015/10/offshore_shell_games_2015.php#.VpEOgBFl3k.

5. Gabriel Zucman, *The Hidden Wealth of Nations: The Scourge of Tax Havens* (Chicago and London: University of Chicago Press, 2015).

6. Author interviews with Renstrom, November 11, 2015, and January 15, 2016.

7. John Schwartz, "Rockefellers, Heirs to an Oil Fortune, Will Divest Charity of Fossil Fuels," *New York Times*, September 21, 2014, http://www.nytimes.com/2014/09/22 /us/heirs-to-an-oil-fortune-join-the-divestment-drive.html.

8. "Archbishop Desmond Tutu on Climate Change," YouTube video, 3:37, posted September 26, 2014, https://www.youtube.com/watch?v=mm7PBHFdYCQ.

9. Brian Merchant, "Mark Ruffalo Wants the *Avengers* to Divest from Fossil Fuels," *Motherboard*, September 17, 2014, http://motherboard.vice.com/read/mark-ruffalo -wants-the-avengers-to-divest-from-fossil-fuels.

10. Blair Fitzgibbon, "Divestment Commitments Pass the $3.4 Trillion Mark at COP21," *Common Dreams*, December 2, 2015 http://www.commondreams.org/newswire/2015 /12/02/divestment-commitments-pass-34-trillion-mark-cop21.

11. Seventeen of these 20-gallon containers would be a ton. See Chris Berdick, "Massachusetts' New Composting Rules: What They Really Mean," *Boston Globe Magazine*, September 25, 2014, https://www.bostonglobe.com/magazine/2014

/09/25/massachusetts-new-composting-rules-what-they-really-mean/SM9KF0Rw7I1
Gq8KZTtx5dL/story.html.

12. "Carbon Beta and Equity Performance: An Empirical Analysis: Moving from
Disclosure to Performance," Innovest Strategic Value Advisers, October 2007, http://
www.kellogg.northwestern.edu/faculty/mazzeo/htm/sp_files/021209/(4)%20
innovest/innovest%20publications/carbon_20final.pdf.

13. "Report on US Sustainable, Responsible and Impact Investing Trends," Forum for
Sustainable and Responsible Investment, http://www.ussif.org/trends.

14. "CDFI Fund Statute," CDFI Coalition, accessed April 8, 2016, http://www.cdfi.org
/about-cdfis/cdfi-fund-statute.

15. "CDFI 20th Anniversary Report," CDFI Coalition, March 5, 2014, http://www.cdfi
.org/cdfi-20th-anniversary-report.

16. For information about the crowd-funding campaign, see "CERO Is Creating Green Jobs
That Pay Off for People, Community & the Planet," Indiegogo, https://www.indiegogo
.com/projects/cero-is-creating-green-jobs-that-pay-off-for-people-community-the
-planet#/funders.

Chapter 17: Openhearted Wealth

1. Dariel Garner interview with author, July 9, August 3, August 14, and August 24–26,
2015; Rivera Sun, *Billionaire Buddha* (El Prado, NM: Rising Sun Press Works, 2015),
afterword; and Occupy Radio interview, March 4, 2015.

2. Tod Leonard, "The Wright Way," *San Diego Union Tribune*, May 30, 2004, http://www
.utsandiego.com/uniontrib/20040530/news_lz1t30nakoma.html; also see Chaco
Mohler, "A Wright Masterpiece Bursts to Life in the Sierra," *Tahoe Quarterly*, (Fall
2001), http://www.hldesignbuild.com/assets/tahoequarterly-2001-inside.pdf.

3. Ibid.

4. Arthur Cornfeld interview with author: first interview April 2, 2015, second interview
December 14, 2015.

5. Committee on Un-American Activities, *Investigation of Communist Activities,
New York Area (Entertainment): Hearings*, 84th Congress, August 18, 1955,
page 2447-2460, https://archive.org/stream/investigationofc19530608unit/
investigationofc19530608unit_djvu.txt; "I Have Sung in Hobo Jungles: Pete Seeger
Refuses to 'Sing' for HUAC," History Matters, accessed April 12, 2016, http://
historymatters.gmu.edu/d/6457.

6. Eisenstein, *Sacred Economics*, 426.

Chapter 18: Wealthy, Come Home

1. Jonathan Rowe, *Our Common Wealth: The Hidden Economy That Makes Everything Else
Work* (San Francisco: Berrett Koehler, 2013), p. 11.

2. Peter Barnes, *Capitalism 3.0: A Guide to Reclaiming the Commons* (San Francisco:
Berrett Koehler, 2006), 4–5.

3. Divest-Invest, http://www.divestinvest.org.

4. Marjorie Kelly, *Owning Our Future: The Emerging Ownership Revolution* (San Francisco: Berrett Koehler, 2012).

5. See more about the new economy movement at New Economy Coalition, http://new economy.net; and Next System Project, http://thenextsystem.org.

6. Learn more at Slow Money, http://www.slowmoney.org.

7. Learn more at Bolder Giving, http://www.boldergiving.org.

8. Learn more at Close the Billionaire Loophole, http://www.closethebillionaire loophole.org.

9. James Carroll, *Constantine's Sword: The Church and the Jews, A History* (Boston/New York: Mariner Books, 2002). There's also a documentary by the same name.

10. See Resource Generation, http://www.resourcegeneration.org.

11. David Horsey, "Nick Hanauer Explodes Myth of Capitalist 'Job Creator'," *Los Angeles Times*, February 17, 2014, http://articles.latimes.com/2014/feb/17/nation/la-na -tt-job-creator-20140216.

12. "Who Pays? A Distributional Analysis of the Tax Systems in All 50 States," Institute for Taxation & Economic Policy, January 2015, 71, http://www.itep.org/pdf/who paysreport.pdf. For information about the campaign to change the Massachusetts convention, see the Raise Up Coalition, http://www.raiseupma.org/constitutional -amendment-campaign.

Chapter 19: All Hands on Deck

1. Adam Hochschild, *Bury the Chains: Prophets and Rebels in the Fight to Free an Empire's Slaves* (New York: Mariner Books, 2006); and Adam Hochschild, *King Leopold's Ghost: A Story of Greed, Terror, and Heroism in Colonial Africa* (New York: Houghton Mifflin, 1999).

2. See Peter Dreier and Chuck Collins, "Traitors to Their Class," *New Labor Forum*, January 2012, http://scholar.oxy.edu/cgi/viewcontent.cgi?article=1545&context =uep_faculty.

3. Landon Thomas Jr., "The Price of Privilege," *New York Times*, January 16, 2015, http:// www.nytimes.com/2015/01/18/style/thomas-s-gilbert-jr-the-price-of-privilege .html?_r=0.

Index

accompaniment, 139–40, 236

adversity insurance, family wealth as, 88, 97

Affluentville, 19–20

African Americans. *See* race privilege/
inequality

Alperovitz, Gar, 129–30, 136–40

anti-Semitism, 217

Atlantic Philanthropies, 125

Barnes, Peter, 209

bartering, gifts/needs, 154–8, 166–8, 178

Billionaireville, 22

Black Lives Matter, 77, 195–6

Bloomfield Hills, Michigan, 10–11, 231–6

Boeing Corporation, 28–31

Boston Impact Initiative, 166, 176, 178–80,
182–3

Buffett, Warren, 1, 24–5, 214

Bush, George W., 44–5, 46

business incubators, 161

Byrnes, Sarah, 159, 164

Cabot, Paul, Jr., 111–12

campaign finance, 91, 135, 218

Canada, 92, 122, 134

cancer-free economy, 163–4

capital. *See also* investments
crowd-sourced (*See* crowd-sourced
businesses)
local, 166, 176, 178–83, 212

capitalism, 4, 138, 177, 226–7

Carnegie, Andrew, 12, 113, 136, 223

CERO waste management company,
175–6, 182–3

change, 14. *See also* policies for change;
social action
local community, change within (*See*
community)

organizing wealthy peers for, 216–17
small groups for, 153–4, 217–18
systemic, need for, 4–6, 129–40

change organizations, donations to, 12,
107, 113–14

charitable foundations, 103–14, 189
assets of, 106–7
educational, 115–18
land trusts, donations to, 109–10, 120
perpetual trusts, 119, 124
reforms, proposed, 123–5, 213
self-interested charity, 107–10, 114–20
trustees, payment of, 111–13, 124
youth enrichment supported by, 98–9

charitable giving, 6, 91, 213–14, 241. *See
also* charitable foundations; gift economy;
wealth, giving away
GDP, percentage of, 122
justice disrupted by, 115–26
needs not met by, 120–3
recipients, 98–100, 107–10, 113–20
subsidies, 118–20
tax deductions, 100, 108–9, 113, 114,
117–20, 123–5
warehousing of funds, 107, 111–13

charitable industrial complex, 6, 103–14

Citizens United v. FEC, 91, 135

civic engagement, 93

class privilege, 5–6, 60–2, 78, 86–100, 239

class wars, 1, 16–19, 22–7, 32, 135, 224,
233. *See also* one percent, attitudes toward

climate crisis. *See* ecological crisis

Coates, Ta-Nehisi, 79, 84–5

college education
cost of, 91–2
financing, 65, 68, 80, 87–9, 95–7, 99, 222
(*See also* GI Bill)
public college enrollment, 98

college education (*continued*)
 segregated, 80
 value of, 94–5
coming home, by wealthy, 3–4, 25–6, 150,
 167–8, 201–3, 207–19, 225–6. *See also*
 empathy
 accompaniment, 139–40
 Bloomfield Hills, Michigan, 231–6
 boundaries for sharing wealth, 139, 201–2
 case studies, 169–84
 elements of, 208–17
 organizing peers for, 216–17
 small groups, forming, 217–18
 transformative pressure, 230
commonwealth, 5, 23, 43–5, 53, 141–50,
 208–11, 234. *See also* community
community, 25–6, 137, 210. *See also*
 commonwealth; localized economy
 bringing wealth home to (*See* coming
  home, by wealthy)
 emergency preparedness, 165
 energy efficiency, 166
 interconnections, 209–10
 leadership, 164–5, 216
 opting in, 141–9
 promoting resilience of, 159–68
 Resilience Circles, 152–8, 217
 small groups, forming, 153–4, 217–18
community development financial
 institutions (CDFIs), 181–2
community foundations, 114
community investment sector, 180–2, 241.
 See also capital, local
consumption, reducing, 212–13
Conyers, John, 85
cooperative ownership, 166, 180–1
Cornfeld, Arthur, 191–3
corporations, 28–31, 227, 230. *See also* fossil
 fuel industry
 bailout of, 136
 charitable giving by, 106, 118
 investments in, 212 (*See also* Divest-
  Invest movement)

power of, 15, 24, 130, 132, 136, 138, 150,
 214, 234
taxation of, 28, 69, 73–4, 134, 190, 215
 (*See also* tax havens)
crowd-sourced businesses, 162, 164, 176,
 182
Curtis Hall Community Center, 141–3,
 146–8

Demere, Charles, 16
democracy, 2–3, 91, 130, 150
 charitable giving, effect of, 114, 119
 concentrated wealth, undermined by,
  105, 135
 opting in/out of, 144, 148, 210
 wealth, democratizing, 138–9, 160, 175,
  214–15
Derber, Charlie, 225
deservedness, 5, 32–3, 70–1, 73. *See
 also* individual actions, wealth
 accumulated by
disconnection
 class/race privilege and, 62
 myth of, 5
 opting out, by wealthy, 144–6
 overcoming, 156–8, 167–8, 200–2, 226,
  229–30
 Richistan/Billionaireville, 21–2
 of working-class youth, 93
Divest-Invest movement, 134, 139, 172–5,
 198–9, 211, 241
divestment, apartheid and, 173, 180

ecological commons, 41, 208–9
ecological crisis, 2, 30–1, 120, 130, 138,
 210, 233, 240. *See also* Divest-Invest
 movement; fossil fuel industry
 averting, 131–4, 140, 159–60, 212–13
 charity and, 108
 energy efficiency, 166
 green businesses, 175–6
economic collapse, 2008, 79, 87, 136, 151–8
economy, localized. *See* localized economy

education, 60, 210–11. *See also* college
    education
    budget cuts, 91–2, 145–6
    charitable donations to, 100, 107, 109,
        115–18, 120
    community, 153–4
    funding, 68, 98–100, 122
    K-12, 93–4, 98, 122, 148–9
    parental involvement, 92–6, 115–18,
        144–5, 148–9
    pre-K, 98, 122, 135, 211
    private, 10–11, 90, 91, 100, 109, 144–5
    segregated, 69
Eisenstein, Charles, 158, 167–8, 203, 207
emergency preparedness, 165
empathy, 4, 12, 26–32, 208, 226–30
employee ownership, 135, 175–6, 182–3,
    233
employment, 60–2, 65, 87–9, 134, 218–19.
    See also internships
energy. *See also* fossil fuel industry
    consumption, reducing, 212–13
    efficiency, 166
    renewable, 166, 172
equal opportunity, 2, 91, 93–4, 97–8, 122,
    135–6, 240. *See also* inequality
Espinoza-Toro, Carlos, 159, 163, 164
estate taxes
    charity, estate reduced by, 119
    farms, effect on, 73–4
    preservation, case for, 17, 37–8, 43–4,
        49–55 (*See also* public investment)
    progressive, case for, 70, 99, 135
    repeal, case for, 37–9, 73–4 (*See
        also* individual actions, wealth
        accumulated by)
Europe, 92, 98, 134
Evans, Jodie, 140
extractive capitalism. *See* capitalism
extreme inequality, 1–3, 13, 233. *See also*
    class wars; wealth, concentration of
    charity and, 120–3
    deservedness and, 30–3

equal opportunity, effect on, 97–8
    movement to reverse, 222–3

fairness, 100, 150. *See also* taxation, fair
Farmers Home Administration, 65
farms, 73–4
fear, current system built on, 25–7, 31
Federal Housing Administration, 65
Feeney, Chuck, 125
financial literacy, value of, 95
financial markets, 211–12
financial transaction taxes, 220, 222
fossil fuel industry, 131–4, 172–5, 198–9,
    211
foundations. *See* charitable foundations
Frank, Robert, 19, 21
Frazer, Edorah, 13
Frieze, Deborah, 175–83, 212

Garner, Darnel, 185–91
Gates, Bill, Sr., 17, 24, 37, 49–55, 145, 208,
    215
General Electric corporation, 190
generational transfers. *See* inherited
    privilege; inherited wealth
generative capitalism. *See* capitalism
George Jr. and Harriet Woodward Trust,
    112–13
GI Bill, 39, 65–8, 70–2, 80
gift economy, 106, 166–8, 178, 199. *See also*
    bartering, gifts/needs
Gilbert, Thomas Strong, Jr., 228
Gladwell, Malcolm, 42–3
government subsidies, 45, 65, 67, 70–5,
    118–20. *See also* greatest subsidized
    generation; public investment
gratitude, 53, 199, 208, 234–5
greatest subsidized generation, xi, 5, 63–76,
    80, 92, 134
guilt, 12, 69, 84, 196, 208, 229, 233

Hanauer, Nick, 218–19
Haymarket People's fund, 12

health care, 10, 74, 89, 98, 122, 134, 166, 211
hereditary aristocracy, 3, 22, 133, 136
Hiatt, Arnold, 219
higher education. *See* college education
Hochschild, Adam, 223
home, invitation to come. *See* coming home, by wealthy
homeownership, 69, 73, 78, 80. *See also* mortgages
Hopkins, Rob, 159, 160

impact investment, 138–9, 168, 180–3, 201, 212. *See also* localized economy
income
    median, US, 19, 91–2
    of one percent, 20–2, 106, 132
income and wealth inequality, x, 25, 65, 129–31, 239. *See also* extreme inequality; inherited privilege
    accelerating, 2, 87–90, 93–4, 130, 132–3
    charity, exacerbated by, 101–10, 114–20
    coming out as wealthy, effect on, 201–2
    deservedness and (*See* deservedness)
    policies for changing (*See* policies for change)
    racial, 69, 78–84, 94, 133
    Richistan, 19–22
    US compared to world, 18–19
income taxes, 68–9, 135
individual effort, wealth accumulated by, 38–9, 60, 81, 92, 97–8. *See also* deservedness
    inherited wealth and, 44–6
    makers and takers, 46–8
    public investments, role of, 39–44, 52–5, 126, 189–90, 208–9
inequality. *See also* extreme inequality; income and wealth inequality; race privilege/inequality
    of opportunity, 86–100
    wealthy people, addressed by, 16, 23–8, 134, 167–8, 193–7 (*See also* wealth, giving away)

inherited privilege, 5–6, 10–12, 60–2, 68–70, 72, 78–82, 86–100, 211
inherited wealth, x, 10–13. *See also* hereditary aristocracy
    giving away, xv–xvi, 12–13, 197–202
    greatest subsidized generation, 5, 68–70, 72
    inherited advantage and, 87, 90, 95–7 (*See also* inherited privilege)
    meritocrats, 44–6
    Richistan, 21–2
Institute for Community Economics, 180–1
International Reparations Summit, 83
internships, 87, 97, 99, 100
Interstate Highway Act, 67
investments, 22, 241. *See also* capital; public investment
    community investment sector, 180–2, 241
    in new economy, 212, 240, 242
    traditional, 211–12

Jamaica Plain New Economy Transition (JP NET), 159–68, 239
jobs. *See* employment

King, Martin Luther, Jr., 78–9

labor unions, 16, 22–4, 138, 220–3
Ladd, Jenny, 197–202, 211
land trusts, 109–10, 120, 138
Lateiner, Abe, 193–7
Latinos. *See* race privilege/inequality
leadership, 164–5, 216, 222
Leblanc, Jacques, 169–72, 215
Leopold, Les, 18, 222
Lloyd, Henry Dearmest, 136
localized economy, 3–4, 6, 26, 138, 167–8, 226. *See also* bartering, gifts/needs; capital, local; coming home, by wealthy; community
    food sector, 161–2
    green businesses, development of, 166, 175–6

main street businesses, 162–3
resilience and, 159–68
toxic exposures, limiting, 163–4

Madoff, Ray, 118–19, 123
makers spaces, 161
Menino, Thomas, 147–8
meritocrats. *See* individual actions, wealth
accumulated by
middle class, 91, 95, 136, 150. *See also*
greatest subsidized generation
military veterans, benefits for, 71–2.
See also GI Bill; greatest subsidized
generation
minimum wage. *See* wages, minimum
mobile home owners, xiii–xv, 180
Morgan, Anne, 223
mortgages, 65, 67, 69–71, 73, 80
museums, donations to, 110
mutual aid, 153–8

Nader, Ralph, 24–5, 223
National Defense Education Act, 68
National Nurses United, 220–2
national service, benefits for, 71–2
needs/gifts, exchange of. *See* bartering,
gifts/needs
networking, 87, 226, 229–30
high-networth people under age 35,
167, 193
Resilience Circles, 153, 156
time exchanges, 166–7
new economy investments, 212, 240, 242.
See also localized economy
New Haven, Connecticut, urban
infrastructure, 121–2

offshore tax havens. *See* tax havens
oligarchy, 3, 91. *See also* power, wealthy
people's
one percent, 3, 20–2. *See also* power,
wealthy people's; wealthy people
in all of us, 226, 227

attitudes toward, 9–10, 13, 15, 18–19,
31–2
income and wealth of, 20–2, 106, 132–3
opportunity, inequality of, 86–100. *See also*
equal opportunity
Oscar Mayer company, 5, 10, 23
Otto Bremer Trust, 112

Patriotic Millionaires, ix, 139, 218–19, 239,
242
Paul and Virginia Cabot Charitable Trust,
111–12
personal narrative explanations. *See*
individual actions, wealth accumulated by
Piketty, Thomas, 2–3, 133
Pillsbury, George, 12, 208
plutocracy, 91
policies for change, 24, 129–40, 241–2. *See*
also localized economy
climate catastrophe (*See* ecological crisis,
averting)
philanthropy, reform of, 123–5, 213
wealth inequality, 16, 134–6, 138–40,
150, 171, 213, 215, 218–19, 222–3 (*See*
also taxation)
populism, regressive and progressive, 15–16
power, wealthy people's, 189–90, 222–3,
230
change campaigns, engagement in,
133–6, 150, 215 (*See also* Patriotic
Millionaires)
philanthropy and, 91, 109, 119
populism, target of, 15
rule-rigging, used for, 23, 91, 130, 216,
234
predatory capitalism. *See* capitalism
privilege, 59–62. *See also* class privilege;
inherited privilege; race privilege/
inequality; wealth
comforts of, 26
of living in affluent society, 226, 227
productivity, 132, 133, 135
progressive taxation. *See* taxation

public education. *See* education
public investment, 67–8. *See also* greatest
  subsidized generation
  budget cuts, 87, 91–2, 98–9, 145–6
  charitable giving and, 120–3
  fair, 150
  individual wealth supported by
    (*See* individual effort, wealth
    accumulated by)
  in infrastructure, 28, 39, 41, 44, 52–4,
    67, 118, 120–2, 125, 133, 189, 214, 219
  wealthy, leverage of, 91, 150

race privilege/inequality, 5, 61–2, 77–85,
  195–7, 226, 240
  business ownership, 176
  capital, access to, 176, 178–9
  homeownership, 69, 78, 80
  income and wealth, 69, 78–84, 94, 133
  post-World War II benefits, access to, xi,
    69–70, 72, 80
  reparations, case for, 79, 82–5
  understanding, 81–2
Rand, Ayn, 41, 47
Reich, Rob, 117–18
relationships, 209–10
Renstrom, Lisa, 172–5, 211
reparations, case for, 79, 82–5
resilience, 159–68, 194, 240, 242
Resilience Circles, 152–8, 217
Resource Generation, 167, 193
resources, 239–42
Responsible Wealth, 16
Richistan, 19–22
Rockefeller, John D., 113, 198
Romney, Mitt, x, 10, 45–7
Roosevelt, Theodore, 223
Rosewood, Florida, pogrom, 83
Rothenberg, Martin, 39–40, 208
rules, rigged. *See* power, wealthy
  people's
rural communities, opportunities in, 89
Ryan, Paul, 47–8

Salam, Reihan, 97–8
Sanders, Bernie, 18, 233–4
Seeger, Peter "Pete," 192–3
Shapiro, Tom, 81–2
Slow Money, 212
small groups, forming, 153–4, 217–18
social action, 153–4, 178, 202, 217–18, 223.
  See also policies for change
social capital, 93, 99, 145–7, 210
social change movements, theory of, 16,
  22–5
social isolation. *See* disconnection
social mobility, 2, 87–9, 92, 97–8, 100, 125,
  136
social ownership, 138
social safety nets, 92, 134
socially responsible investment, 181
society, wealth creation supported by,
  39–44, 52–5, 60, 71. *See also* public
  investment
Speth, Gus, 138
student debt. *See* college education,
  financing
Sun, Rivera, 185, 186
superiority, myth of, 5

tax havens, 28, 169–72, 211, 215, 240
taxation. *See also* estate taxes; tax havens
  charitable giving (*See* charitable giving)
  corporate (*See* corporations)
  fair, 16, 134, 135, 150, 211, 240
  of financial transactions, 220, 222
  home mortgage deduction, 73
  income, 68–9, 135
  makers and takers, 46–8
  progressive, 68–9, 135, 150, 215, 218–19
  of wealthy, 16, 125, 145, 150, 189–90,
    214–16, 223 (*See also* estate taxes)
Thomas, Michael, 228
time exchanges, 166–7
toxic exposures, limiting, 163–4
transition towns, 159–60, 240
Trump, Donald, xi, 45–6, 233

trusts, 10–13, 21–2, 95, 119, 136, 138, 211, 215–16. *See also* charitable foundations
Tulsa race riots, 80
Tutu, Desmond, 173–4

Uchitelle, Louis, 121–2
United for a Fair Economy, 15, 224, 239
usury, 211–12

Veterans Administration, 65, 67, 70–1

wages
minimum, 16, 134, 135, 218, 222, 235
stagnation, 65, 132, 133, 135
wealth
boundaries for sharing, 202
bringing wealth home (*See* coming home, by wealthy)
concentration of, 18, 69, 97, 130, 132–3, 135–6
democratizing (*See* democracy)
expansion program, 69–72, 80
giving away, xv–xvi, 12–13, 29–30, 189–93, 213–14, 241 (*See also* charitable giving)
inequality (*See* income and wealth inequality)
inherited (*See* inherited wealth)
more wealth created by, 11, 21–2

redefinition of, 209–10
tax havens, percent in, 171
true stories of, 193–7, 208–9
wealthy people, 18–22, 224–5.
See also coming home, by wealthy; one percent
acceleration of advantages of, 5, 90, 97–100, 107–10, 117–18 (*See also* privilege)
disconnection from community (*See* disconnection)
donations by (*See* wealth, giving away)
globally, American place in, 19
inequality addressed by (*See* inequality)
organizing peers for change, 216–17
power of (*See* power, wealthy people's)
small groups interested in change, forming, 217–18
taxing of (*See* taxation)
working-class leadership, 216, 222
World War II veterans, benefits for. *See* greatest subsidized generation

Yeskel, Felice, 15–17, 22, 103–5, 194, 223–5, 230
youth enrichment programs, 98–9

Zaleska, Andrée, 159
Zuckerberg, Mark, 10

About the Author

C huck Collins is a researcher, campaigner, storyteller, and writer based at the Institute for Policy Studies. He has written extensively on income inequality in previous books like *99 to 1*, *Wealth and Our Commonwealth*, and *Economic Apartheid in America*, as well as in *The Nation*, *The American Prospect*, and numerous other magazines and news outlets. Collins grew up in the 1 percent as the great-grandson of meatpacker Oscar Mayer, but at age 26 he gave away his inheritance. He has been working to reduce inequality and strengthen communities since 1982 and in the process has cofounded numerous initiatives, including Wealth for the Common Good (now merged with the Patriotic Millionaires), United for a Fair Economy, and Divest-Invest. He is also a leader in the transition movement, and a cofounder of the Jamaica Plain New Economy Transition and the Jamaica Plain Forum, both in the Boston-area community in which he lives.

the politics and practice of sustainable living

CHELSEA GREEN PUBLISHING

Chelsea Green Publishing sees books as tools for effecting cultural change and seeks to empower citizens to participate in reclaiming our global commons and become its impassioned stewards. If you enjoyed *Born on Third Base*, please consider these other great books related to social justice, community resilience, and new economic thinking.

WHAT THEN MUST WE DO?
Straight Talk About the Next American Revolution
GAR ALPEROVITZ
9781603585040
Paperback • $17.95

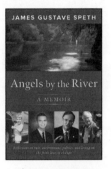

ANGELS BY THE RIVER
A Memoir
JAMES GUSTAVE SPETH
9781603586320
Paperback • $17.95

INQUIRIES INTO THE NATURE OF SLOW MONEY
Investing as if Food, Farms, and Fertility Mattered
WOODY TASCH
9781603582544
Paperback • $15.95

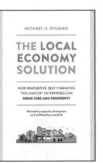

THE LOCAL ECONOMY SOLUTION
How Innovative, Self-Financing "Pollinator" Enterprises Can Grow Jobs and Prosperity
MICHAEL H. SHUMAN
9781603585750
Paperback • $19.95

the politics and practice of sustainable living

CHELSEA GREEN PUBLISHING

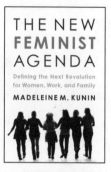